Past Trauma in Late Life

of related interest

Hearing the Voice of People with Dementia
Opportunities and Obstacles
Malcolm Goldsmith
Preface by Mary Marshall
ISBN 1 85302 406 6

Dementia
New Skills for Social Workers
Edited by Alan Chapman and Mary Marshall
ISBN 1 85302 142 3

The Psychology of Ageing
An Introduction 2nd edition
Ian Stuart-Hamilton
ISB 1 85302 233 0

Developing Services for Older People and their Families
Edited by Rosemary Bland
ISBN 1 85302 290 X

Dementia
Challenges and New Directions
Edited by Susan Hunter
ISBN 1 85302 312 4

Reviewing Care Management for Older People
Edited by Judith Phillips and Bridget Penhale
ISBN 1 85302 317 5

Past Trauma in Late Life

European Perspectives on Therapeutic Work
with Older People

*Edited by Linda Hunt, Mary Marshall
and Cherry Rowlings*

Jessica Kingsley Publishers
London and Bristol, Pennsylvania

First published in the United Kingdom in 1997 by
Jessica Kingsley Publishers Ltd
116 Pentonville Road
London N1 9JB, England
and
1900 Frost Road, Suite 101
Bristol, PA 19007, U S A

Library of Congress Cataloging in Publication Data
A CIP catalogue record for this book is available from the Library of Congress

British Library Cataloguing in Publication Data
A CIP catalogue record for this book is available from the British Library

ISBN 1-85302-446-5

Printed and Bound in Great Britain by
Athenaeum Press, Gateshead, Tyne and Wear

Contents

List of Tables

List of Figures

Preface

The rising number of older people within the population in western Europe is often presented as a problem, but in many senses it is in fact a triumph. Across the whole of the European Union area people are living longer, healthier lives and older people (i.e. those over 60) are making significant contributions to the social, political, cultural and economic lives of the families and communities in which they live. Of course, like other age groups within our society, some of them may also have health and social concerns with which they need special help. One of these needs may be for professional help with emotional and social distress – that is, they may be helped by counselling or therapy, by support and encouragement, to come to terms with past, but still troublesome, personal experiences. Within the group with this sort of need is a significant number of older people whose earlier lives included traumatic experience of war, persecution, sexual and family violence, or of human or natural disaster. Little attention has so far been given to this group by the generality of professionals working with older people and, to help put this situation right, a group of experts from five European countries came together to share their knowledge and experience and to make it available to a wider audience.

This book is the result of their willingness to work together, for some in a language (English) other than their own, and to discuss and debate their ideas and approaches to practice. What they shared with each other is now presented to readers who, as general practitioners, nurses, psychologists, social workers and residential and day care staff, are regularly working with older people or are responsible for the management and development of services for older people. We believe this book demonstrates the importance of paying attention to the possibility that some older people in their care are struggling with the consequences of trauma they experienced many years earlier (perhaps half a century ago).

The book also has an optimistic story to tell, despite its focus on the impact on older people of earlier harrowing events. Many of the chapters show us that older people are capable of making changes in their lives and that they are often very well motivated to confront painful issues and work through distressing material and feelings towards a more integrated and peaceful position. In other words they often have strength enough to make the journey from being a victim of what has happened to them to being a survivor who can move on to another phase of life.

Therapeutic work with older people still struggling with the impact of their earlier traumatic experiences of armed combat, imprisonment, incestuous relationships and other frightening events is still in the process of development. Research and practice are at a formative stage, coming to grips with a wide variety of trauma and very individual responses among the older people still burdened by the impact of what they have experienced. For these reasons the book does not attempt to be an academic text, nor is it a practice handbook. Rather it tries to offer a distillation of what is known and some very practical accounts of direct work with older people. The authors have risked making very personal contributions, making use of their own experience and sharing their current thinking about how to help. They have been ready to do this first of all because they recognise that, by sharing their ideas and their experience openly, they assist the more rapid development of effective ways of working with older people; second, they are convinced of the importance of bringing to the attention of all professionals who are concerned about the well-being of older people the significance of 'old' trauma in the current lives of many older people.

This book would not have been possible without the enthusiasm of the contributors to work together to make what they have learnt available to a more general readership. Equally, we want to acknowledge that the project could not have got off the ground at all without the appreciation of staff of the European Commission of the importance of the subject matter and the willingness of Directorate General V of the Commission to assist us with funding for a colloquium meeting at the University of Stirling in 1995. That meeting proved to be a most stimulating and fascinating experience for everyone who participated and laid the foundations for the subsequent work. As Editors we are delighted to have had the opportunity to follow through our original idea and are grateful to the Social Work Services Inspectorate of the Scottish Office for giving staff time and for helping to meet the costs of preparing this text for publication. The views expressed in this book are, of course, those of the writers.

Linda Hunt, Mary Marshall and Cherry Rowlings
Stirling, Scotland, October 1996

CHAPTER 1

The Past in the Present

An Introduction to Trauma (Re-)Emerging in Old Age

Linda Hunt

The capacity of shocking experiences to have a profound impact on behaviour and feelings in ways which are unanticipated and difficult to understand has been widely known at least since soldiers returned from the terrible battles of the First World War with conditions described then by such terms as 'neurasthenia' and 'shell shock'. The poetic and prose writings of some of those who took part (for example, Graves, 1929; Owen, 1920; Remarque, 1929) have made successive generations aware of the horrors of that war, and recent novels such as Pat Barker's *Regeneration* (1991) have brought home the enormity of the trauma suffered by some of the combatants.

Twenty years after the Armistice of 1918, the implementation of Nazi policies and then the Second World War brought persecution, bombing, combat and the destruction of communities to millions of people. Once again there was some understanding that direct experience of these terrible events would, at the time of their occurrence, have psychological and social effects as well as physical consequences. As the century has progressed, fuller and more public discussion of the impact of rape, domestic and street violence, and of child abuse has led to a better understanding of the profound distress suffered by the victims of such attacks. As a result, we now recognise that counselling and/or therapy have to be elements of the services available to help victims regain their equilibrium.

Over the last ten years an increasing realisation has developed of the distressing psychological impact of disasters on those who experience them. The sinking of the *Herald of Free Enterprise* at Zeebrugge in 1987, the fire on the Piper Alpha Platform in the North Sea in 1988 and the death and injury of football fans at Hillsborough in 1989 are among the incidents that have brought the ordeal of those involved to the awareness of helping professionals and to the public at large. These and other incidents, such as the crash of an airliner on Lockerbie in 1988 and the shooting of schoolchildren and a teacher in Dunblane in 1996, have also made plain the severe distress that bystanders and relatives and friends, not present at the actual event, may suffer. The importance of providing therapeutic services to help people overcome the distress experienced in the aftermath of these sorts of event is now well understood (see, for example, Gibson, 1991; Scott and Stradling, 1992). At the same time media attention and autobiographical accounts (see, for example, Keenan, 1992) have increased awareness of the psychological and personal impact of acts of terrorism and oppression, and of the need of help and support for those who have suffered them.

What has been much less well recognised is that the distress resulting from traumatic experience may be persistent, disrupting for decades the lives of those burdened by it. As Primo Levi (1981) wrote more than 30 years after his own experience of persecution:

> ...memory of the offence persists, as though carved in stone, prevailing over all previous or subsequent experiences...Without any deliberate effort memory continues to restore to me events, words, sensations, as if at that time my mind had gone through a period of exalted receptivity, during which not a detail was lost. (pp.10–11)

Recent media attention and biographical accounts relating to the Second World War in the Far East (for example, Lomax, 1995) have also begun to highlight that perpetrators as well as recipients may suffer long term as a result of the horrific events in which they have been involved.

A lifetime of effort may be required by people seeking a way of trying to come to some kind of terms with what has happened to them. Bruno Bettelheim, who as a young man had been incarcerated in Nazi concentration camps for a year, thought that he could understand and explain the psychological impact of this experience a year or two after the events, but in his old age he acknowledged that he was still having to work on their meaning and their consequences (Sutton, 1995).

Even less well understood than the persistence of distress has been the fact that some people successfully cope or suppress the emotional pain for many years, only to find that it returns in later life and in ways that may be very difficult for persons affected and those around them to understand. For example, the fact that 'difficult' behaviour in old age, anxiety and apparent confusion may be consequences of the continuing struggle to come to terms with earlier traumatic experience is not yet widely appreciated. Nor is it well understood that these responses can occur because painful memories have been triggered through reminiscence work or life review. Sometimes even professional practitioners working with elderly people in residential and day care seem to encourage talk about times past as if it were just an enjoyable means of spending time. Reminiscence can be life enhancing, of course, and for some elderly people opportunities for life review are very valuable, but currently too little attention is given to the possibility that times past include traumatic experience with which it has not yet been possible to come to terms.

In fact much of the distress associated with traumatic experience and the effort of trying to deal with its consequences remain hidden or misunderstood, since our society does not readily sanction recognition and discussion of these persistent and painful burdens.

Perhaps because it is indeed the time for life review and for preparation for endings, it is particularly in old age that people have time, motivation and energy to resolve previously unresolved problems, to recognise and accept what has happened and to move forward with more satisfaction and comfort. The contributions to this book collectively illustrate the fact, too seldom recognised, that in old age people demonstrate very significant capacity for personal development and for making changes in their lives. The experience of the authors suggests that, in reality, it may be *only* in old age that some of the so far unresolved issues can be addressed. It is essential, therefore, that the professions working with elderly people give attention to the possibility that earlier traumatic events may still be a major factor in the lives of some older people to whom they are providing services.

Trauma: A Definition

'Trauma' and 'traumatic' are commonly heard words. They are freely used to describe something unpleasant, but this colloquial use does not convey a precise or technical meaning. In this book we are using these two words in a very particular way.

An incident is defined here as traumatic when it 'alters our experience of reality suddenly and against our will' so that 'we see what we were not ready to see, we hear what we were unable to hear and smell what we were unable to describe' (Winn, 1994, p.ix). Such an event is outside the normal range of human experience and would be extremely distressing to anyone who was subjected to it. The experience is one which causes a disjunction between the person's past and the present and future. This disjunction can be so catastrophic that the person involved no longer finds it possible to see meaning in life and may feel there is no point to its continuation. As a consequence of the trauma, innocence is lost and the person's moral and cultural framework and expectations may be thrown into disarray. The experience may even thrust the person into contact with a hidden feeling, present somewhere in most people, that she/he may have no right to be alive.

Trauma can occur in many different situations. By their nature, traumatic events are unexpected and those involved are unprepared for what happens to them. Following his experience of Nazi concentration camps, Bettelheim described traumatic and extreme situations as ones in which 'we are suddenly catapulted into a set of conditions where old adaptive mechanisms and values no longer apply any more and where some of them may even endanger the life they were meant to protect. Then we are, so to say, stripped of our whole defensive system and thrown back to rock bottom.' (Bettelheim, 1979, p.11).

These sorts of situation can be seen to fall into five different types:

1. Subjection to, or subjecting others to, bombing and other forms of attack or torture in war or within repressive political regimes.

2. Acts of terrorism which aim to influence organisations or governments but which are directed against individuals or groups. These include hostage-taking and the explosion of bombs.

3. Personal attacks directed at individuals, such as rape, sexual and other forms of violence within families and on the street.

4. Disasters, such as that at Zeebrugge and at Chernobyl.

5. Natural occurrences, such as the earthquakes in Armenia in 1988 and Kobe in 1995.

The Impact of Traumatic Experience

The disorienting and distressing impact of trauma seems to have been recognised first by Freud (1896). However, it was only following the recognition of combat stress in the First World War and the more systematic study of the experience of combatants in subsequent wars in Europe (for example, Swank, 1949), Vietnam (for example, Alford, Mahone and Fielstein, 1988) and the Middle East (for example, Solomon, 1987), that the damaging impact of traumatic experience began to be more thoroughly described and understood. Recently research and therapy has also been carried out with ordinary citizens caught up in extraordinary events such as natural and other disasters (for example, Raphael, 1986; Spurrell and McFarlane, 1993). It is now possible, therefore, to describe the distress that follows trauma in rather precise detail.

Trauma may result from a single incident or may be the consequence of longer-term experience, for example, of torture, incarceration or repeated acts of incest. The responses are very similar whatever type of trauma has been experienced, although the order in which the different elements appear may vary. Initial shock is often followed by disorganisation and feelings of being overwhelmed by the enormity of what has happened. Later there is likely to be denial and avoidance. These are two understandable defences, which are designed to protect the person from the excruciating pain associated with thinking through and making sense of what has happened.

The general expectation in our society is that the person who has been traumatised will quickly 'pull themselves together', put the experience behind them and avoid any discussion that will cause distress to others. This cultural ambience tends to reinforce the reluctance of the person to examine what has happened and to leave him/her with a secret pain in a world that now feels a much more insecure and unpredictable place than before the traumatising experience. The friends or relatives with whom the person has the most intimate relationships and with whom a sense of security and confidence might be built anew, may now be the very people who are unwilling or unable to reach out to understand the horrible aspects of the traumatic events and the consequences to those who experienced them. To the person who has actually been directly involved in the events, it is her/his friends and relatives who may seem to need protection from awareness, so perhaps prompting her/him to feel guilty about her/his own distress. This leaves the person concerned in a peculiarly isolated position at a time when they would be particularly helped by being able to 'ground' perceptions and feelings through discussion with others whom they trust. Repeatedly telling the story is a critical part of coming to terms with what has happened.

It is common, in the aftermath of traumatic events, for those who were present to be burdened by powerful feelings of guilt. These feelings are often associated with the person holding strongly to a belief that he/she failed to do enough to help the other people who were caught up with him/her in the traumatising experience. After the experience, people may also feel that they brought the situation (and therefore the suffering) upon themselves by their own inadequacy, and that they are not worthy to survive when others did not. These feelings may persist even though it is very clear from the facts that this is not at all an accurate perception of the situation. When a death-threatening traumatic situation is over, the people who survive are likely to be acutely aware of their own vulnerability and mortality and, associated with this, they may have an abiding dreadful sense of doom and fearfulness. Often physical signs of a heightened level of anxiety are persistently present.

The aftermath of traumatic experience is essentially a situation of loss (not necessarily associated with death) and grief which may prompt the expression of anger and aggression about 'what has happened to me' or about the way in which other people react to the events and those who have experienced them. The person may then move into a period of despair and depression before it becomes possible to take any step towards accepting what has happened or to begin developing a new personal integration and the ability to look forward to a future life.

Follow-up studies (for example, Bromet, 1989) have shown that high levels of psychological distress can persist for years after the events took place. Also of major significance is the finding that many people who have suffered trauma are reluctant to speak about, or seek help with, the resulting feelings and distress. For some, the symptoms of distress continue to be severe and meet the criteria for Post-Traumatic Stress Disorder (PTSD) as defined in the *Diagnostic and Statistical Manual* of the American Psychiatric Association (APA, 1994). The criteria for this disorder can be summarised as follows:

1. The person has experienced, witnessed or been confronted by an event(s) that involved actual or threatened death or serious injury, or by a threat to physical integrity *and*, in addition, the person's response to this experience has included intense fear, helplessness or horror.

2. This traumatic experience is regularly re-experienced. The re-experiencing may be in the form of recurrent dreams, or of repeatedly having flashback episodes in which the events seem to be recurring and the person's response to this situation includes all the physical activity that would be appropriate if the events were actually recurring. Alternatively the person may show intense distress at anything that acts as a reminder of an aspect of the traumatic experience.

3. The person persistently avoids stimuli associated with the trauma or demonstrates numbing of general responsiveness to life events.

4. Persistent symptoms of increased arousal. These may be demonstrated in difficulty with getting to sleep or staying asleep. There may also be signs of irritability and anger and difficulty in concentrating. The person may regularly express anxiety about the possibility of dangerous situations arising and show an exaggerated startle response.

5. The symptoms described must have continued for at least a month.

6. The level of distress is of clinical significance or results in impairment in social, occupational or other important areas of functioning.

Follow-up studies of people who have survived disasters suggest that for as many as 40 per cent of those affected, these symptoms persist for periods of two years or more (Hodgkinson and Stewart, 1991). The symptoms may sometimes disappear, only to reappear some considerable time later with equal intensity.

How Many Older People Are Affected?

When we began work on this project, it was suggested to us that while our subject matter was interesting it was not central to the development of services for elderly people or to the professional practice of those in direct contact with elderly people. It seems important, therefore, to address this point at the outset. Is this book about a marginal matter of real concern only to a small group of specialists? We think that the answer to this question is an emphatic 'No'. We believe it is necessary for the generality of professionals working with older people and of those responsible for developing and managing services, to be able to recognise the current significance of earlier trauma and to make available the assistance that will enable older people affected by traumatic events to reach a more comfortable integration of their experience into their life stories.

Just what proportion of older people might still be troubled by earlier traumatic experiences? It is not possible to provide a precise figure, but there are a number of pointers.

The Second World War has been an important factor in the lives of older people throughout Europe. A study carried out in the Netherlands in 1978 (Werk en Advies College) predicted that just over a million Dutch people born before 1945 and still alive in 1995 would be war victims (that is, 15% of the population born before 1945). These estimates were confirmed by another study carried out in 1988 (Centraal Bureau voor de Statistiek, 1990). In these studies victims were defined as people who had been exposed to wartime violence; of course it cannot be assumed that all of them were traumatised by it. There are other special features of this Dutch group which might not be a feature in some other European countries. For example, three-quarters were exposed as civilians. They had been subjected to bombardments, enforced labour and incarceration, or had been living in hiding in an occupied country; 15 per cent were combatants; a further 4 per cent were members of the Resistance movement and 1 per cent are Jewish people who have survived persecution.

A more recent study carried out in the Netherlands (Bramsen, 1995) has tried to estimate the number of people currently experiencing distress and other problems directly attributable to their wartime experience. The initial sample of *circa* 10,600 was intended to be representative of the Dutch population born between 1922 and 1929, and therefore old enough to have been very directly affected by the Second World War and the colonial war in Indonesia. However, the use of postal questionnaires and Bramsen's approach to follow-up are likely to have led to some over-representation among respondents (44% of the 10,600) of people damaged by their wartime experience. Nevertheless her figures are revealing. Ten per cent of respondents were still frequently affected by distressing memories of war and 5 per cent had levels of distress of such intensity that they met the criteria for PTSD at the time of the study (that is, almost 50 years after their war experience). A further 24 per cent frequently took action to avoid situations that might remind them of the war. Only a third of those who were still suffering significant distress as a result of their wartime experience were in contact with any professional help at the time of the study. For most of these, the contact was with their general practitioner. None of the Dutch studies attempted to quantify the effects on the children of parents who are continuously struggling with the impact of their war experience, although it is known that some children (now adults) have been adversely affected.

More recent conflicts (for example, colonial wars in Africa and Asia and the Korean War) had their shocking impact too, and some people have settled in Western Europe following persecution or other traumatic experiences in the countries of their birth. The number of people affected by these events is smaller than the population touched by the Second World War, but their need for help may be even less well understood or available for discussion. The continuous violence in Northern Ireland for over 25 years may be a particular source of trauma and long-term distress for the thousands (whether civilians, paramilitarists or security forces) who have been touched by it, and the future need for service development for the Northern Ireland community in particular is discussed in Chapter 14.

Work carried out in Britain suggests that approximately one in ten people have some experience of sexual abuse as children or young people, (Baker and Duncan, 1985). The prevalence of other forms of physical violence within families has proved very difficult to establish, but estimates of incidence indicate that more than 4500 children are likely to be victims of violence in any one year (Creighton, 1988). Even less clear is the prevalence of continuing stress resulting from violence between spouses and on the streets. It is clear, however, that taking these categories of events together, large numbers of people have experienced sexual or physical violence and it is well known that pressure has been on the victims to remain silent. Since not talking about earlier trauma is associated with subsequent difficulties, it can be anticipated that the proportion still seriously distressed by their shocking experience will be significant.

The indications are, then, that (at a rather conservative estimate) in some European countries at least 10 per cent of the population over 60 years of age may be suffering some continuing difficulty resulting from earlier traumatic experience. This is a significant number of people: for example, in Britain it means 1.19 million people over 60 are likely to be affected. The countries of the European Union have had differential involvement in the wars of the 20th century and in other types of traumatic experience, and consequently the proportions of the elderly population that have been affected by different types of trauma will be variable across Europe as a whole. However, we are discussing phenomena which have been common during the present century and which have touched large numbers of people. Further, precisely because old age is a time for review and resolution as well as a time of loss and vulnerability, it is a period in life in which much change and personal development takes place. The many publications and documentary programmes on television and radio that were prompted by 50th anniversary commemorations of events occurring during the Second World War and by the approach of the millennium also act as triggers which reactivate distressing memories in some older people. It is likely, therefore, that the need of therapeutic services is large, and growing larger, among older people who have been exposed to shocking wartime experience (van der Ploeg, 1990) and to other traumatic events.

In these circumstances we can with justice argue strongly for the importance of giving attention to this topic within the generality of services for older people and for a high level of sensitivity, on the part of all professional practitioners in contact with older clients, to the continuing problems that stem from earlier traumatising experience.

The Journey from Victim to Survivor

The older people who are still burdened by the consequences of earlier trauma, or dominated by the struggle to make sense of what has happened, remain in some ways victims of their experience. If they can review their experience and begin to make links between the past, the present and the future, they can move beyond being victims to take up the more positive role of survivors. To achieve this, they will have to make a painful journey through memory, feelings and intellectual understanding. This journey will enable them to re-examine what has happened, to put it into context and to understand better how and why it has continued to affect their lives. The evidence is that there is the real possibility that making this journey will enable these older people to reach a point in their progress through life from which a more positive orientation can be taken and a less rocky route for its next stage can be mapped.

If therapists and carers (professional and informal) are to be helpful to older people still struggling with the impact of earlier traumas, they will have to be prepared to journey with their clients through some very difficult territory. The journey may feel rather dangerous at times and cause distress and anxiety to both the travellers and their therapist/carer companions. There may be aspects of the past experience that are just too horrific for the person to revisit, and the help of professional practitioners will be needed in the process of finding a satisfactory path around these parts of the terrain so that the horror can be better contained and therefore become less damaging to life now and in the future. Practitioners will be able to accompany, guide and learn from such journeys only if they are also ready to prepare by making their own related journey. Their journey is needed to enable them to bring together what is known about trauma and its consequences with what is known about ageing and dementia, and to learn how to apply this synthesis in their practice.

A Travel Guide

This book is designed to assist professional practitioners in particular with their journey towards achieving the integration of knowledge and practice experience in these areas. It has to be recognised that this is a relatively uncharted journey and that it is not yet possible to provide a map of Ordnance Survey standard or to write the definitive guide. There are different starting points for the journey and there are also different perspectives on some of the terrain. The book contains contributions to the present state of collective knowledge made from three different starting points. The first section offers knowledge and practice experience developed by professionals who specialise in work with people who are suffering the consequences of trauma; Section 2 draws together knowledge and practice examples from among those providing services to people who have suffered as a result of the enormity and horror of the Holocaust; and Section 3 contains contributions from practitioners working in geriatric and psychogeriatric services.

In Part 4, the last two chapters of the book look towards the future in two ways. The chapter by Gibson reviews the potential need for service development in a community of approximately 1.6 million people (in Northern Ireland) which has been subjected to 25 years of more or less continuous violence, but which has not yet considered the extent to which people, when they reach old age, will need help to come to terms with what has been happening.

The last chapter brings together, from all of the contributions, key information and aspects of theory and practice to help formulate an approach to practice that can be adapted and used by professionals working with older people in a wide range of settings. The aim here is to try to set the scene for more sensitive and effective services in the future. As such, it is of relevance to service planners and managers as well as to those working directly with older people. The chapter focuses in particular on initial contact and assessment, because of the extent to which the problems of elderly people still suffering the consequences of earlier trauma so frequently remain unspoken by the older people themselves and unnoticed by those around them. This means that the process of eliciting the continuing difficulties experienced by clients is critical. The final chapter also draws out points from contributors to help to guide continuing contact.

It is clear from this concluding chapter that professional education and training should include opportunities to learn about the long-term effects of traumatic experience and help practitioners of all the professional disciplines working with elderly people to develop sensitivity to the possibility that among the elderly people referred to them are some who are engaged in a continuing struggle with the consequences of an earlier trauma. Being open to this possibility will help practitioners to avoid incorrect assessment and inappropriate responses to behaviour that at first cannot easily be understood.

The contributors to this book come from different cultural backgrounds and different professions. Each of the sections includes several professional perspectives, from the disciplines of clinical psychology, social work, nursing, psychiatry, psychotherapy or psychoanalysis. The perspectives are different, giving emphasis to different aspects of the subject and of approaches to helping clients. There are differences, too, in the style of the contributions, with some authors starting from a research base and others describing and reviewing their practice. The contributions reflect the stage of development that has been reached in addressing the difficulties that result when earlier trauma still intrudes on the lives of older people; they also illustrate very clearly the heterogeneity of older people affected and the necessity for practitioners to develop and apply differentiated, not general (stereotypical) responses. However, as Editors we have been struck by the extent to which the contributions are complementary. Indeed, it was clear from the outset, at the colloquium that was the beginning of this project, that bringing a range of perspectives together would make it possible to develop a better framework for practice and a more effective service to elderly people.

Many of the contributors to this book give emphasis to the rewarding nature of their work with older people who have struggled for half a century or longer with the burdensome consequences of experiences that were shocking and even, in some instances, of unimaginably horrific dimensions. The contributors recognise the positive motivation among those older people to come to terms with their experience and they are providing the kind of support and help that enables them to assist their clients both to achieve a better quality of life in old age and to reach a peaceful ending. This book invites other practitioners, be they specialists in work with people who have had traumatic experiences or providers of services to elderly people, to make a real and effective contribution towards the achievement of these two objectives by other elderly people who are similarly burdened and whose distress has not yet been recognised or understood.

References

Alford, J.D., Mahone, C. and Fielstein, E.M. (1988) 'Cognitive and behavioural sequelae of combat: conceptualisation and implications for treatment.' *Journal of Traumatic Stress 1*, 4, 489–501.

American Psychiatric Association (1994) *Diagnostic and Statistical Manual of Mental Disorders*, fourth edition. Washington DC: APA.

Baker, A. and Duncan, S. (1985) 'Child sexual abuse; a study of prevalence in Great Britain.' *Child Abuse and Neglect 9*, 457–467.

Barker, P. (1991) *Regeneration*. London: Viking.

Bettelheim, B. (1979) *Surviving and Other Essays*. London: Thames and Hudson Ltd.

Bramsen, I. (1995) *The Long Term Adjustment of World War II Survivors in the Netherlands*. Delft: Eburon Press.

Bromet, E.J. (1989) 'The nature and effects of technological failures.' In R. Gist and L. Lubin (eds) *Psychosocial Aspects of Disaster*. New York: Wiley.

Centraal Bureau voor de Statistiek (1990) *Statistical Year Book 1990*. Den Haag: CBS.

Creighton, S.J. (1988) 'The incidence of child abuse and neglect.' *Early Prediction and Prevention of Child Abuse*. In K. Browne, C. Davies and P. Stratton (eds). London: John Wiley and Sons Ltd.

Freud, S. (1896) *The Aetiology of Neuroses*. Volume 3 of the Standard Edition of the Collected Psychological Works, J. Strachey (ed) (1962) London: Hogarth Press.

Gibson, M. (1991) *Order from Chaos; Responding to Traumatic Events*. London: Venture Press.

Graves, R. (1929) *Goodbye to All That*. London: Jonathan Cape.

Hodgkinson, P.E. and Stewart, M. (1991) *Coping with Catastrophe*. London: Routledge.

Keenan, B. (1992) *An Evil Cradling*. London: Vintage.

Levi, P. (1981) *Lilit e Altri Raconti*. First published in English as *Moments of Reprieve*. London: Michael Joseph Ltd.

Lomax, E. (1995) *The Railway Man*. London: Cape.

Owen, W. (1920) *Poems* (ed. S. Sassoon). London: Chatto and Windus.

Raphael, B. (1986) *When Disaster Strikes; How Individuals and Communities Cope with Catastrophe*. New York: Basic Books.

Remarque, E.M. (1929) *Im Westen Nichts Neues*. Published in English as *All Quiet on the Western Front*. London: G.P. Putnam and Sons.

Scott, M.J. and Stradling, S.G. (1992) *Counselling for Post Traumatic Stress*. London: Sage.

Solomon, Z. (1987) 'Combat related Post Traumatic Stress Disorder among Israeli soldiers: a two year follow up.' *Bulletin of the Meninger Clinic 51*, 80–96.

Spurrell, M.T. and McFarlane, A.C. (1993) 'Post Traumatic Stress Disorder and coping after a natural disaster.' *Social Psychiatry and Epidemiology 28*, 194–200.

Sutton, N. (1995) *Bruno Bettelheim; the Other Side of Madness*. London: Gerald Duckworth and Co. Ltd.

Swank, R.L. (1949) 'Combat exhaustion.' *Journal of Nervous and Mental Disorders 109*, 6, 475–508.

Van der Ploeg, H.M. (1990) 'Psychotraumatologie door oorlog en geweld (psychotrauma resulting from war and violence).' Lecture given at the University of Leiden (quoted by I. Bramsen. In *The Long Term Psychological Adjustment of World War II Survivors in the Netherlands*).

Werk en Advies College (1978) *Psychosocial and Medical Care for War Victims.* Den Haag: Staatsuitgeverij.

Winn, L. (1994) *Post Traumatic Stress Disorder and Dramatherapy: Treatment and Risk Reduction.* London: Jessica Kingsley Publishers.

PART ONE

Starting from Trauma

It is clear that the quality of life of older people who are still living with distressing symptoms that are the result of much earlier traumatic experiences is severely damaged. It is also now quite clear that it is possible to work with these older people in ways that can significantly improve their quality of life. The contributors to this section are all experienced professional practitioners who have developed special knowledge and skill in helping people who have suffered one or another type of trauma. They write from their experience and deep understanding of working with trauma, focusing here on helping older people who have sought assistance with coming to terms with experiences that may have taken place as much as 50 years earlier. They take rather different approaches, illustrated by case examples, but together they point out factors critical to success in reducing the damaging effects of earlier trauma.

Schreuder's contribution builds on his extensive experience (as a psychotherapist and psychiatrist) of helping severely traumatised people, to develop a clearer understanding of the factors that determine the extent to which it is possible for a particular person to come to terms with the traumatic experiences of his/her life. From this basis it then becomes possible to assess with greater accuracy when a person is likely to benefit from a psychotherapeutic approach and when it is necessary to pursue a supportive approach which helps the person to mobilise defences against further reflection on the traumatic experiences. Schreuder's clarity of thinking about the types of re-experiencing that intrude on the lives of people 40 or 50 years after the events to which they refer, are of real and practical use to specialist practitioners and professionals working with older people. His chapter offers an understanding that will help practitioners to think through what goals can be appropriately offered to older people still suffering from early trauma.

Robbins has used his clinical experience of working with servicemen from the Second World War to develop a model of treatment which helps to set realistic limits in work that can be frightening for both the helper and the person struggling with aspects of his/her traumatic experience. Robbins makes a point to which we will return (Chapter 15) and to which we attach particular importance, namely that professionals working to help older people with early trauma need to have ready access to support for themselves if they are to bear the pain and distress of helping their clients effectively. Crocq also focuses on the effects of war trauma. He draws on his experience as a psychiatrist in the French army and in a clinic providing a service for victims of trauma, but focuses on his work with a sample of 100 older people whose wartime experience continues to cause them distress. He describes the process by which he has developed his approach to treatment and argues in particular for a proactive, as well as a supportive, style on the part of therapists.

Bergström-Walan's experience is especially of working with people who have sexual experiences of a traumatising nature. Her sensitive account of the process by which she enabled one older woman to come to terms with her childhood experience of sexual abuse and her fear of physical violence from her father shows how, after half a century of distress, it is possible to move on and to achieve an enhanced quality of life.

The development of the person's capacity to move on is very much a focus of attention for all the contributors to this section and, as will emerge more clearly in subsequent sections, the readiness of older people to try to mobilise this capacity in themselves is a significant factor making it possible to achieve a successful outcome to difficult and painful work. It is an impressive capacity in many older people and a humbling reminder of their courage and tenacity.

Linda Hunt

CHAPTER 2

Post-Traumatic Re-experiencing in Old Age
Working Through or Covering Up?

J.N. Schreuder

...I was in the former Dutch-Indies. One of my comrades, in fact my buddy, was severely wounded during an attack by the enemy when we were on a patrol. He had a terrible bullet wound in his belly. I could see his intestines. We had to carry him on an improvised stretcher. It was a ten mile walk through the jungle to a field hospital. I gave him plasma and morphine. As we approached the camp, he shouted: 'Poor mum, poor mum!' and then he died. I can still see his eyes...I often have this nightmare from which I wake up distressed and fearful.

Mr S. told this story during psychotherapy in 1993. The events he described actually happened to him when he was a soldier in the Dutch army in 1947.

Introduction

One of the major, often underestimated, consequences of war trauma, and of many other kinds of trauma too, is the powerful nocturnal re-experiencing which occurs long afterwards. The psychotraumatic events are relived again and again, and the frequency and intensity of this re-experiencing can increase in old age. In our daily practice at Centrum '45 (the Netherlands National Centre for the Treatment of Members of the Resistance and War Victims) with the Dutch victims and veterans of the Second World War and of the colonial war in Indonesia, it is repeatedly demonstrated to us that, even after more than 40 years, intrusive re-experiencing is still present or has returned after years without symptoms. The re-experience may be manifested in a very severe form with recurrent distressing dreams and intrusive terrifying recollections. These may include images, thoughts or perceptions of what was happening. In some cases, the original psychotraumatic event or part of it is actually relived in a dream. These instances of re-experiencing may be referred to as 'nightmares' by those who experience them, although the sufferer may not always be asleep throughout.

Re-experiencing is an intrusive phenomenon; one which produces anxiety in patients and those around them and which is more often than not misunderstood by family and by doctors and other professionals. Yet there is much we can learn from the ways in which post-traumatic recollections and re-experiences manifest themselves. In particular, a close understanding can provide the key to therapy with a particular individual. It is important in the first instance to distinguish nightmares from re-enactments. Two examples are used in this chapter to help clarify the differences. After that the implications of this distinction for therapy will be outlined, using the psychodynamic model as the theoretical frame of reference. First of all, the general meaning of the term 'war trauma' is clarified.

General Context and Individual Perception of Psychotraumatic War Experiences

The general context in which traumatisation occurs reveals similarities between various groups of individuals. The specific situation of the individual and the significance of the traumatic experiences in that person's life together give the psychotrauma an individual character, and for this reason it is necessary to be cautious about making generalisations. Not only is there a fundamental difference between the historic reality of, say, a German concentration camp and a Japanese internment camp, but the experiences and perceptions of two survivors of exactly the same camp also have a strictly personal meaning. It is advisable, therefore, to draw a distinction between the general, often more concrete, characteristics of trauma and their individual perception and significance. The latter are relevant in the discussion and clarification of each individual patient's treatment, while from the former it is possible to draw out a few general characteristics which are fundamental elements of war traumatisation.

First and foremost, in every traumatic experience there was an abrupt disruption of existential continuity. As a consequence, many people lost their sense of security within their emotional environment, within their family and within their work all at the same time. For some of them the feeling of security never returned; they lost their trust in moral values and their belief in the purpose of their existence suffered a severe test. A sense of loss ensued but the possibility of being able to mourn was remote; whether the loss was of a significant other or of existential meaning. Second, there was a severe threat to physical and psychological integrity in combination with prolonged, extreme psychological and physical stress. And third, the individual was absolutely powerless to change the situation. These elements are the core of war traumatisation, and one or more of them will always be present in the re-experiencing of psychotraumatic war events.

Two Cases of Post-Traumatic Re-experiencing

Ms L (55) has recurring nightmares about what she went through during the Second World War. Sometimes her dreams are re-creations of a situation from the war as it actually happened. On other occasions real elements are intertwined with imaginary elements of a more symbolic nature. The following nightmare is an example of the latter case:

> We are put in a queue. I am still a little girl. My mother and two brothers are standing next to me. We have lost our freedom – I can feel it. We are not free to do what we please. Everyone has to get a ticket. Once we have got our tickets we have to queue up again. Suddenly I notice that we have been separated. I am separated from the others. I am standing in a different queue and my mother and brothers are not there any more. I catch a glimpse of them in the distance, moving up in a different queue. I am not allowed to go to them. I am separated from the ones I love. We end up in different camps, they and I. An intense feeling of dread comes over me; I am afraid I will never see them again. I start crying and I wake up crying. I am terrified that I will never again see the ones I love. I cannot find words to express the intensity of the fear.

This is a nightmare dreamt by Ms L, who was sent to a camp with her mother when she was four years old. That was the last time she ever saw her father. As far as Ms L can remember, she was never separated from her mother. However, she was separated from her father, never to see him again. She lost a loved one. This nightmare has real elements, such as confinement and queuing up, mixed with symbolic ones – the loss of her father has been transformed into the loss of the persons she was with in her dream. It is very plausible that, in the dream, her mother has replaced her father. This could be because she has no lasting consistent image of her father in her memory, or because the father image has not yet been admitted to her dream world.

Ms L says that often in her dreams she is in a situation from the war and comes close to death, always waking in the nick of time. Waking saves her life, but the fear of dying remains a constant, almost unbearable, presence.

The second example involves Mr N (61). Mr N says that he wakes from a nightmare several times a week. He does not exactly remember how long this has been going on, but knows that for at least a year he has had the following experience two or three times a week.

He wakes up in fear in the middle of the night and finds himself in situations he experienced as a soldier in Indonesia at the time when that country was still a Dutch colony. Not just one, but four or five situations are re-created regularly in his dreams, one per night. These are exact re-enactments of actual experiences. In one scene, he is driving a jeep when he is caught in an ambush. There are three passengers in the jeep. A soldier who is a particular friend is sitting next to him. When the shooting starts, Mr N leaps out of the jeep and crawls underneath it. He sees his mate and the other two passengers have been shot and killed. There is nothing he can do and he stays under the jeep the rest of that day and through the night. The next day a patrol finds him. When he wakes from the dream in the middle of the night, he finds he is lying on the floor next to his bed, drenched in sweat and terrified. His heart is pounding. His wife is standing over him, speaking to him softly. After a while he stands up, but is still in a state of distress. He goes downstairs and his wife makes him a cup of warm milk. He gradually comes to his senses. His wife tries to take his mind off it by talking about something else. After about half an hour the two of them return to bed. He is scared to go to sleep, but after lying awake for some time, he manages to do so. In the morning the alarm clock wakes him up. He is tired and unrested.

His wife describes it like this:

> In the middle of the night, my husband becomes extremely restless and starts kicking and sometimes thrashing his arms about. He usually gets tangled up in the sheets. He sits up, dives out of bed and lands on the floor next to the bed. By that time, I have tried to no avail to wake him up. Not until I have got out of bed and started talking to him does it dawn on him that it is me. He is petrified, sweating profusely and white as a sheet. I see mortal terror in his eyes. The first thing he says when he sees me is, 'get down, you idiot!'. After a few minutes he gets up and goes downstairs. Only then can I get through to him. I try to calm him down. Once I have made him a cup of warm milk, I ask him what happened. He does not want to talk about it. I change the subject to take his mind off it. I am worried about his heart. I feel his pulse; his heart is beating wildly. After a while it slows to a more regular pace. After half an hour or so we go back to bed. In the morning, he does not always remember what happened the night before. He never wants to talk about it during the day either. This has been a regular occurrence for the past few years. It used to happen only a few times a year; some years it never happened at all. Once in a while he gets out of bed and runs downstairs, yelling at me to find cover. On one occasion he ended up in the cellar.

This example contains several striking aspects.

First of all, the memory is such a clear image, with such a high reality content, that one has the impression that the man is actually reliving the experience. His perception has a hallucinatory intensity, while his actual surroundings are distorted. His behaviour seems to correspond with the situation as if he were experiencing it. He remains in this state for some time, even while his wife is trying to call him back to reality, which she eventually succeeds in doing.

The physical symptoms are also noteworthy. They are, on the one hand, a manifestation of fear: tachycardia, perspiration, high blood-pressure, pupil dilation and reduced blood supply to the skin. On the other hand, there is hyperarousal, causing him to be extremely alert within the bounds of the perceived situation of maximum threat, but to shut out anything extraneous to that. In this case, it is the actual situation that Mr N excludes since it does not fit the situation as he perceives it. Although the nocturnal events still cause the man's wife alarm, she has, in a sense, learned to live with them and has an implicit understanding of what to do.

The case described is not an unusual one; this kind of experience is a regular occurrence for many elderly people living in their own home, in nursing homes and in old people's homes. The phenomenon is often misunderstood and it is not unusual to hear it described as mental confusion.

The examples of Ms L and Mr N illustrate two different phenomena: post-traumatic nightmare in the first case and post-traumatic re-enactment in the second. The term *symbolisation* is used to characterise the post-traumatic nightmare: *replication* more accurately characterises the phenomenon of post-traumatic re-enactment. The word 'replication' is chosen because what is re-experienced is perceived as a replication by the person him or herself. It does not mean that these memories are like photographs, pictures or documents stored in a computer and retrievable unchanged. From research on the processes involved in remembering we know that all memories are conceived as reconstructions and not as replications, but in the case of re-enactments the scenario that is lived through is always the same. Indeed it often remains unchanged over a period of years.

Distinguishing between the two phenomena in this way introduces the possibility of drawing on the findings of neurophysiological research and psychodynamic theory to increase our understanding of what is going on. The distinction makes it clear that we are dealing with different methods of processing the trauma, as well as different pathogeneses. A fascinating article by Laub and Auerhahn entitled 'Knowing and not knowing massive psychic trauma: forms of traumatic memory' (1993) also explores the concept that different forms of post-traumatic memories provide insight into the manner in, and extent to which, patients come to terms with their experiences. Their hypothesis is that there are many levels of remembering about past traumatic experiences. These are described as ranging along a continuum of difference in the degree to which an observing ego is present. The more there is emotional distance from the traumatic experience, the more it is possible to speak of the integration of that experience and the more the person feels she/he is the owner of her/his memories. Laub and Auerhahn link this with what they describe as forms of knowing and not knowing. The post-traumatic nightmare and the post-traumatic re-enactment can also be seen in this way. The former is a form of knowing and reflects emotional integration, whereas the latter is a form of not knowing, reflecting a much lower degree of psychological integration.

The Post-Traumatic Nightmare

Nightmares are described as repeated awakenings from the major sleep period or from naps with detailed recall of extended and extremely frightening dreams, usually involving threats to survival, security or self-esteem (criterion A of the Nightmare Disorder, 307.47; DSM-IV, American Psychiatric Association, 1994). Nightmares occur all night, but particularly in the second part of the night, and they manifest themselves exclusively during Rapid Eye Movement (REM) sleep (Hartmann, 1984). In this form, post-traumatic nightmares occur frequently. In these nightmares, the recollection of the dream content refers to the traumatic experience. Accounts of the dream content of post-traumatic nightmares are consistent with accounts of REM sleep dreams. The scenario corresponds with the traumatic experience, but the people featuring in the events, the scenes and the time sequence of the events are subject to alteration. For instance, people from the sleeper's present may appear in a nightmare that refers to a psychotraumatic experience of long ago. Thus a number of identical and structural similarities can be seen to exist between the dream and the original psychotraumatic event. Ordinary nightmares tend to be repetitive. This is the kind of repetition in which the contents may repeat in a thematic way with symbolic distortions remaining present.

If we regard the nightmare in general as an expression of intrapsychic conflict, it is evident that anxiety plays an important role. Freud's second anxiety theory (1926), which is now generally accepted, assigns to anxiety the central role in intrapsychic conflict. According to this theory, anxiety is produced by the ego when it perceives danger – the signal anxiety. The ego responds on the basis of remembered early traumatic instances of anxiety in which the ego was powerless in the face of internal or external danger, for example, early childhood anxieties precede the ability of the ego function of signal anxiety.

The extreme intensity of the anxiety in the nightmare not only follows from conflicts the child or adult is experiencing at that point in time, but also from associated anxieties referring to an earlier period of development, which are reactivated under the regressive and isolated conditions of sleep (Mack, 1970). Early childhood anxieties are intimately connected with an ego that is still immature and vulnerable. Overwhelmed by anxiety, the ego regresses to a state of infantile helplessness. The defensive ego functions are paralysed, with the result that patterns of primitive, primary-process thinking prevail, characterised by projection, externalisation and displacement. This explains why attempts have been made to link the nightmare with processes in which primary-process thinking prevails, such as in psychosis (Hartmann, 1984).

Although the actually experienced psychotrauma is present in the post-traumatic nightmare, it is not difficult to recognise in these nightmares the symbolic representation of the earliest and most deeply rooted anxieties and conflict centring on existential threats: threat to life, threat of abandonment and death, and – at a rather more advanced level – the threat of narcissistic wounding and loss of identity. It could be said, therefore, that the post-traumatic nightmare is about existential anxieties. The pre-verbal nature makes them difficult and complicated to describe but they are associated with:

- the fear of annihilation with threat to life and destructive aggression
- the fear of disintegration with loss of identity
- the fear of abandonment with loss and abandonment
- the fear of fusion with loss of identity, paranoia, devouring and being drowned.

These are the fears of early childhood but they can be triggered at any age by the experience of a life-threatening situation. In later life, the fears play an equally important role, for in old age, anxieties and conflict centre on the same existential situation and are reactivated at the approach of death.

In post-traumatic nightmares there is a coming together, on the one hand, of these early anxieties and, on the other, of the actually experienced psychotrauma. The latter therefore acquires symbolic meaning – the power of which is greatly increased not just because the elusive anxieties of early ego development have acquired a real basis through the feared event having actually happened, but also because the real psychotraumatic experience was a repetition of the early anxieties of the immature and vulnerable ego.

Post-Traumatic Re-enactment

The clinical manifestation of the post-traumatic nocturnal re-enactment is clearly different from that of the post-traumatic REM nightmare, as is evidenced primarily in the description of the dream content. The processes which result in alteration in the sequence of events in the nightmare are wholly or partially absent, and in the re-enactment incongruities in time, place and persons are also absent. In its most explicit form, the re-enactment is perceived by those involved as an exact replication of whatever happened during the traumatic experience. The people, the scene and the sequence of the events in the dream content and those in the traumatic experience correspond perfectly. Indeed, the reality content is so high that one can speak of a re-enactment. Post-traumatic re-enactments can occur repeatedly with exactly the same content and without distortion. A good description is offered by Póltawska (1967) in an article in which she identifies the phenomenon as paroxysmal hypermnesia. She describes the post-traumatic re-enactments in Jewish children who were in Auschwitz at ages 6 to 12, and who survived their concentration camp experience:

> Paroxysmal hypermnesia entails a sudden and violent coming to the fore of recollections which do not take the shape of thoughts, but of images, scenes, sometimes a sequence of scenes that these people went through. The memory then starts to reproduce the mental impressions felt earlier, such as the entire atmosphere of the scene which they lived through in the past; the noises they then heard; the smells as well as the tactile sensations from those times. These recollections are so realistic that the erstwhile prisoner is under the impression of experiencing all this afresh. This impression is accompanied by vegetative symptoms: a sudden paling in the face, tachycardia, trembling, sweating... The fear is sometimes so intense as to bring about physical activity in the form of jumping up, running away, pacing up and down the room. The fear does not become less intense despite the fact that the reality check of the person enduring this is undamaged. (p.191)

In replicating re-experiencing, the repetition is not symbolic, but closely corresponds with the core facts. The anxiety is felt within the re-experienced situation and, being directly connected to the dangerousness of the situation, can be seen as a case of signal anxiety. The anxiety that occurred in the real psychotraumatic situation formed adequate protection against external threats. This signal anxiety becomes fixated. The essence of this nocturnal mental activity – the replication re-experiencing – is not associated with early anxieties or recent real-life conflicts. If early childhood anxieties are triggered here, this is secondary to the basic signal anxiety. It is possible there may be a connection between the childhood anxiety and the actual triggers for the signal anxiety, but that too would be a secondary response to the real post-trauma with which the person is still living.

Implications for Treatment

It is clear that the differences between post-traumatic nightmares and post-traumatic re-enactments should lead to entirely different psychotherapeutic approaches to the two phenomena. Replicational re-experiencing occurs in isolation, without any connection to a person's continuing experience, though it is part of it, and without the context of a meaningful whole. The situation that is re-experienced has been given no place in the present, representational world other than as an isolated, encapsulated unit of meaning. In other words, the experience has not been processed, and the re-experiencing has no significance, symbolic or otherwise, for anxieties and conflicts in later life. Where replicational re-experiencing is concerned, it will generally not be possible to make a connection, let alone interpret it on an emotional level for the individual concerned.

This is not the case, however, for the nightmare. In nightmares, there is a link with the anxieties of early childhood, which connect in some respects with those of later age. Thus a meaningful context emerges, albeit of a predominantly symbolic nature. Where a symbolic association is present, a connection can be made with a wider meaning in relation to early childhood anxieties and possibly also to current conflicts based on the same anxieties.

Shalev, Galai and Eth (1993) have pointed out that repeated intrusive mental images stand in the way of exploratory psychotherapy, because they infiltrate 'much of the patients' conscious and unconscious mental processes' (p.167). For this reason they use desensitisation to enable patients to have 'a vivid image of the traumatic memory without experiencing psychological arousal and distress' (p.168). In the multi-dimensional treatment protocol of Shalev et al., this is followed up by psychodynamic psychotherapy.

The notion that recurring memories have a disruptive effect on exploratory therapy appears to have found general acceptance. I would, however, like to qualify this on the grounds that it is an over-generalisation. Post-traumatic re-enactments do indeed pose an obstacle, given the isolated position they occupy in the patient's representational world. Post-traumatic re-enactments are more resistant to psychodynamic psychotherapy and often do not show the alterations inherent in a process of integration. This is much less the case, however, for post-traumatic nightmares, which can even constitute a key component of psychodynamic or exploratory psychotherapy. The intensity of the arousal occasioned by nightmares is nowhere near that of re-enactments.

Because of their disturbing character, post-traumatic re-enactments require a different therapeutic strategy. First of all it is necessary to diminish the influence of the re-enactments with a behavioural treatment such as desensitisation or through the use of psychopharmacology. Also, if re-enactments continue to be a feature of the situation, one has to question whether psychodynamic psychotherapy is at all relevant. Since talking about what is experienced during the re-enactments produces hyperarousal and severe distress, it is arguable that covering up is the thing to do, not exploration. However, sometimes post-traumatic re-enactments unexpectedly emerge during psychotherapy.

From a psychodynamic perspective, the meaning of post-traumatic night-mares can be compared with the meaning of normal dreams, as a symbolisation of inner conflict. In this sense the nightmare could be a manifestation of the working through of psychotraumatic experiences in order to integrate them into one's own representational world. Clinical experience shows that a patient's shift towards integration is often accompanied by an alteration in the content of his or her post-traumatic nightmares and that a decrease in the frequency of nightmares is sometimes associated with this change.

The Role of Early Anxieties

The major themes and technical questions in the psychotherapeutic relationship with the traumatised older person are:

- ° basic security damaged by the psychotraumatic experiences
- ° early childhood anxieties with which the conflicts and concerns of later life are intimately related
- ° separation and loss
- ° memory and reconstruction
- ° recent concerns and conflicts.

In a great many psychotraumatic situations, early childhood anxieties are reactivated because the object and themes of that early anxiety are repeated. The object is the aggressor, who does not respect the boundaries of the ego, and the themes are those mentioned above. Under extreme pressure, the ego boundaries are overstepped and the individual is placed against his or her will in a situation where the ego is once again helpless, vulnerable and without boundary. The extreme helplessness of this situation evokes infantile feelings of complete dependence, but at this later stage of life the protective mother is no longer available. The psychotraumatic experience re-creates the state to which the early anxieties pertain. The feared becomes reality in the psychotrau-matic experience, causing severe damage to the basic security which is at the core of psychological development.

The starting point in a therapeutic relationship is the establishment of trust between therapist and patient. This trust can develop if the patient has a sufficient sense of basic security (Erikson, 1950). If this is not present, as in the case of the traumatised patient, trust will take much longer to establish and require much more of the therapist. An additional problem is that the main themes are, as we have seen, intimately connected with early, pre-verbal material. The result is that the early and pre-verbal (that is, non-verbal) elements occupy a prominent position in the therapeutic relationship. In other words, the beginning of therapy is, to a large extent, dominated by damaged basic security, the influence of early existential anxieties and the non-verbal aspects of communication. Because of the preponderance of non-verbal aspects in the beginning phase of therapy and also later on, therapies based on non-verbal techniques, such as psychomotor therapy and creative therapy, are of significant help. In Centrum '45, these therapies are used to help establish trust within the therapeutic environment as a whole.

The psychotherapist must be capable of creating a sufficient sense of basic security through a holding environment, but also be able to establish a therapeutic relationship in the absence of that basic security. Experience in treating disorders such as schizophrenia and borderline schizophrenia can be of help in developing the necessary therapeutic skills, as can experience with elderly depressed and paranoid patients. The psychotherapeutic attitude of empathic listening has great practical value, but does not suffice. Something more than that is required. The practitioner has to achieve an approach which Auerhahn, Laub and Peskin (1993) describe as, 'the presence of a passionate listener' (p.436). In addition to the well-known techniques of supportive structuring in psychotherapy (Dewald, 1994), it is necessary for practitioners not only to display a real interest but also to have factual and historical knowledge of the psychotraumatic situation.

The Reconstruction of Meaning: Possible or Not?

Once the psychotherapist manages to create a relationship of trust and a safe atmosphere, it will be possible to deal more specifically with the meaning of the psychotraumatic experience in the context of a person's life. This is to some degree equivalent to the contextualisation of the early anxieties that are triggered by the psychotraumatic experience. At an early age, the child is not able to realise what is happening in dangerous situations because the nervous system has not yet sufficiently matured. Threat means anxiety. But the cause of the anxiety cannot be identified yet, nor can it be explored. The absence of boundaries and the specific existential themes are characteristic of the early anxieties. On a primitive level, destructive aggression does not mean damage, but rather total destruction. Abandonment means death. The all-or-nothing character is part of this phase of psychological development. A crucial point in this respect is that the psychotraumatic situation displays a comparable all-or-nothing character. The pre-verbal child has no capacity for cognitive distancing and no, or only a limited, inner frame of reference. We could also say that, at this stage, the representational world is shaped exclusively by primitive forces, primal violence is not yet linked to representations of objects and self.

It appears to me that, on a fundamental level, the way in which early childhood anxieties are overcome during healthy psychological development can have a bearing at a later age as well. In the first place, it is essential for the anxieties to be connected to identifiable objects, situations and facts. The actual situation, no matter how grave, rarely has the dynamic strength and limitlessness of the anxieties of early childhood. The threat is, after all, real and not imagined. By reconstructing the situation, it is stripped of its mystery and lack of limits. Two things happen. First, with the protection offered by mystery now destroyed, the object of anxiety becomes more real, with all the attendant consequences. Reconstruction of the facts triggers a range of emotions which are congruent with a more mature ego and which can be worked through more easily: humiliation, object-linked rage, guilt, and so on. are felt and experienced. A torrent of emotions is unleashed.

Second, it becomes possible to speak about the traumatic experience in terms of facts, to name and contextualise those facts, or to face up to the realisation that there simply is no sane or rational context in which to set the facts, for example as is the case with concentration camps. Auerhahn *et al.* (1993) stress that the psychotherapist must explicitly and actively help the patient to construct or reconstruct his or her own story. The importance of this type of participation by the therapist is referred to elsewhere in this book, for example by Crocq (Chapter 4), Robbins (Chapter 5) and Hassan (Chapter 9). It is an extraordinarily difficult and confrontational process which should be taken slowly and carefully. The (re)construction can only be successful if the patient and psychotherapist are prepared and committed to getting to the bottom of whatever actually happened.

But the nature of the re-enactments is that they can occur at any moment, with or without prompting. The patient may become overwhelmed and, in that state, reconstruction is not possible. This poses the main threat to therapy. Here we are confronted with the essential difference between nightmares and re-enactments.

From the outset, re-enactments will be present or can be triggered through therapy. Post-traumatic re-enactments will make it impossible to contextualise the early anxieties, because of the extreme arousal accompanying them. We cannot proceed until the re-enactments have been treated, for instance by means of systematic desensitisation as described by Shalev *et al.* (1993). If this is not, or is only partially, successful, one should ask oneself whether exploratory treatment is possible in this patient's case. Often it is better to aim at examining the meaning of re-experiencing in the current life; to address the difficulties it causes. In this respect talking with the partner, if there is one, can be very helpful. The people in the patient's environment, whether they are family members or professionals caring for the person, are often fearful as well. If these people can become better informed about what is going on, their fear will become less and they will be able to react constructively to the patient's fears and distress. Sometimes the result of this intervention will be of more value than psychotherapeutic exploration of inner meaning. This is especially the case with re-enactments.

As we have seen, where post-traumatic nightmares are concerned, memories of psychotraumatic experiences are closely linked to early childhood anxieties which also have relevance to later stages of life. In the case of replicational re-enactment, on the other hand, an isolated event (or events) is concerned; the anxieties connected with that event are relived and seem not to have any symbolic or other connection with older age. Given the isolated character of post-traumatic re-enactment, it is less responsive to psychotherapy. In such situations, the limits of therapeutic possibilities are being tested. This point is a major theme of Brainin and Teicher (see Chapter 6). They, too, are grappling with the question: how can psychotraumatic experience take on meaning and be manipulated or processed if the experience itself has no meaning and is, in essence, the antithesis of any kind of meaning? Many psychotraumatic situations emerge for the precise reason that the aggressors are themselves victims of their own early anxieties and are left no choice but to act them out. The only *a posteriori* meaning that can be assigned to the life-threatening post-traumatic experiences is survival. Lidz (1946) calls this a key motive for people who become preoccupied with earlier psychotraumatic experiences or unconsciously relive the experience at a later age. In fact, surviving is the same as overcoming early anxieties. In elderly people who are afraid of approaching death, this triumph over death is, the reasoning goes, reactivated. This is an example of the current meaning that re-experiencing can have and which can be explored in psychotherapy.

As other authors in this book also point out, work of this kind places particular demands on the therapist. He or she must be able to create the safety needed by someone who regresses to the level of a small child. The therapist must have a reasonable understanding of the situation in which the psychotraumatic experience occurred and be able to hear the gruesome details of the real psychotraumatising experience. He or she must be capable of bearing the fact that the nature of some psychotraumatic experiences render them non-treatable, as they are bereft of any contextual meaning. Finally, the therapist must be able to bear, recognise and, if necessary, treat the transference evoked in and by the elderly trauma patients who are in therapy.

Summary

Post-traumatic re-experiencing is a key symptom of severe distress resulting from earlier psychotraumatic experiences. It is important to establish whether we are dealing with nightmares or re-enactments. Post-traumatic nightmares are an expression of intrapsychic concerns and conflicts and, in and of themselves, need not impede exploratory psychotherapy. Post-traumatic re-enactments have an isolated position in the representational world of the person and are accompanied by hyperarousal and intense vegetative symptoms, which is why they are considered an impediment to exploratory psychotherapy. They can also be a manifestation of a coping process which was never initiated. Post-traumatic re-enactments first and foremost require symptomatic treatment. Only after that can exploratory psychotherapy be considered.

Reconstruction of the psychotraumatic experience entails regression to the perceptual level of a small child. This regression occurs in post-traumatic nightmares, too. Early childhood anxieties are closely related to the themes and anxieties of later life and before the patient can reach the stage of being able to work maturely through the psychotraumatic experiences, it is necessary to contextualise the early childhood anxieties and restore the patient's damaged sense of basic security. If this is not possible, it will be necessary to resort to treatment which covers up the experience rather than explores the current significance of the post-traumatic complaints.

References

American Psychiatric Association (1994) *DSM-IV*. Washington DC: APA.

Auerhahn, N.C., Laub, D. and Peskin, H. (1993) 'Psychotherapy with Holocaust survivors.' *Psychotherapy 5*, 434–442.

Dewald, P.A. (1994) 'Principles of supportive psychotherapy.' *American Journal of Psychotherapy 48*, 505–518.

Erikson, E. (1950) *Childhood and Society*. New York: Norton, New York.

Freud, S. (1926) *Hemmung, Symptom und Angst*. Ges. Werke XIV, London: Imago Publishing Co., 1948 edition.

Hartmann, E. (1984) *The Nightmare*. New York: Basic Books.

Laub, D. and Auerhahn, N.C. (1993) 'Knowing and not knowing massive psychic trauma: forms of traumatic memory.' *International Journal of Psychoanalysis 74*, 287–302.

Lidz, T. (1946) 'Nightmares and the combat neuroses.' *Psychiatry 9*, 37–49.

Mack, J.E. (1970) *Nightmares and Human Conflict*. Boston: Little, Brown and Company.

Póltawska, W. (1967) 'States of paroxysmal hypermnesia.' *Przeglad Lekarski 1*, 190–218.

Shalev, A.Y., Galai, T. and Eth, S. (1993) 'Levels of trauma: a multidimensional approach to the treatment of PTSD.' *Psychiatry 56*, 166–177.

Further Reading

Lansky, M.R. (1990) 'The screening function of post-traumatic nightmares.' *British Journal of Psychotherapy 6*, 384–400.

CHAPTER 3

Psycho-Sexual Therapy with Elders

Maj-Briht Bergström-Walan

Mr B came to me for therapy. His appearance was that of a very old, broken person and he could hardly begin to speak of his problems. In fact he was only 62 years old but he was burdened by devastating feelings of guilt. He had been born and brought up in a sparsely populated rural area of scattered farms. When he was in his late teens he had been persuaded by an older brother to copulate with a cow. As he was a religious person he regarded this act of sodomy as sinful, and developed severe guilt feelings and anxiety. As an adult he had been unable to develop a significant relationship with any woman because he was convinced that anyone would see from his face what he had done. He worked in an old people's home – a safe environment for him – and isolated himself more and more. When his father lay dying, he had tried to confess what he regarded as his 'sin' as he felt that would free him from his burden, but he could not do it. After a year of psychotherapy (using a combination of psychodynamic approaches and behavioural techniques), he achieved release from the most severe and self-destructive guilt feelings. By that stage he had a noticeably improved level of self-confidence and could even laugh, something he confessed he had not done for many years.

Introduction

Many problems in a relationship have their roots in sexual dysfunctions, which may be of both medical and psychological origin. Some of these sexual problems are the consequence of traumatic experiences in childhood and adolescence, such as sexual abuse within the family or the use of physical punishment. Other sexual dysfunctions, for example premature ejaculation (among men), orgasmic dysfunction (among women) and low sexual desire, generally develop from conflicts within a current relationship. The reasons for this type of dysfunction can be sexual inhibition, stress and unrealistic expectations of oneself or one's partner.

The problems deriving from earlier traumatic life experiences demand longer and deeper individual treatment, including a combination of psychotherapy and sexual therapy. When it comes to current disorders in a relationship, therapy focuses mainly on the emotional and sexual communication between the partners and both individual and couple therapy may be offered. The partners may also benefit from special physical exercises (sensate focus) which they can do together and which make it easier for them to understand and change behaviour that is problematic.

During the 1970s and 1980s, several new psychological treatments were developed, including primal therapy, 'symbolic drama' and psycho-sexual therapy. This last is an approach which is based on the research into human sexual responses and human sexual inadequacy by the pioneers in the field, the sexologists William H. Masters and Virginia E. Johnson (1970). As a result of their work as researchers and therapists, more attention was given to the development of training and therapeutic skills in psycho-sexual therapy. At the same time, the social changes taking place in society, and in the western world in particular, reduced the sexual taboos and made it more acceptable to seek help with sexual problems. The media have been of great help in making information about sexual dysfunctions more readily available and in showing that effective treatment can be provided. The American, Dr Ruth Westheimer, is an example of a skilful and highly professional educator and sexual therapist who has had a huge impact: her television programmes have reached people all over the world. Nevertheless, it is primarily young and middle-aged people who seek the help of psycho-sexual therapists.

Senior citizens more frequently have difficulties in seeking help with their sexual problems (Bergström-Walan and Nielsen, 1990). They grew up in a period in which sexuality was a taboo subject and there was little or no discussion of sexual difficulties within families. Treatment for sexual problems was almost non-existent until the mid 1970s. It is only in the last ten years that a greater openness about sexuality and a willingness to seek treatment for sexual problems have been observed among older people, and especially among older women. During this same period average life expectancy has risen markedly; this change has brought greater emphasis on good physical and mental health throughout life and has increased the need for sexual welfare among elderly people.

The Case of Mary, a Victim of Incest

Mary came to me for psychotherapy. For some time she had suffered from severe distress which she was unable to relate to any present situation or to a traumatic event. One year before coming to see me she had seen my name mentioned in an advertisement about psychotherapy for victims of child abuse. This had prompted her to wonder whether her own fear and distress could be connected with her early childhood experience. Although Mary was 66 when she came to see me she was still a working woman. Just before she contacted me she had a dream in which a voice very clearly said, 'call Maj-Briht!'.

Mary is in her second marriage and has a grown-up son from her first marriage. Both her husbands have had alcohol problems but her son does not. She herself is teetotal.

When she started therapy, Mary had very few memories from her childhood. She had grown up in a small town in the middle of Sweden in a working-class family with two sisters, one younger than she and one older. Her father had an alcohol problem. He was a 'binge' drinker, i.e. from time to time he drank excessively. Both his wife and children were afraid of him when he was drunk and would hide in an attic where he could not reach them.

Mary had had a problem with men for as long as she could remember. She saw men as 'a terrible threat' and she felt that she must take care to protect herself from them. She was also aware of feeling aggressive towards men and had difficulty having sexual intercourse. She was physically disgusted by herself and reluctant to engage in sexual activity. Nevertheless, she had given in to the demands of her husbands because she did not dare to refuse them. She was able to masturbate and to have an orgasm in this way, but was seldom able to obtain one through sexual intercourse. This annoyed her and she was anxious to solve this problem. She wanted to understand her aversion towards men and her inability to enjoy sex with them.

After a week of intensive psychodynamic therapy, Mary recalled several unhappy experiences from her childhood. She had no difficulties in working with me in therapy, and was able to go into a slight trance and in this way to reach a deeper level of awareness. She told me that she trusted me 100 per cent and did not hesitate to relive unpleasant, even terrifying, events.

In one session she relived experiences from the time when she was about eight years old. She was at home at the farm with her father. They were alone. Her father made a sexual approach and asked her to suck his penis. When she showed reluctance, he forced her with threats to do as he told her and she satisfied him. This abusive behaviour was repeated several times by her father. He forbade her to say anything to her mother and sisters. She was afraid that her father would kill her if she disclosed what was going on. Her sisters and mother were also terrified of him. When Mary re-experienced this abuse in therapy she felt disgusted and wanted to vomit, but did not.

Her father worked as a forester and the saw for cutting wood was at the farm. During therapy sessions Mary perceived this saw as a gigantic tool with which her father would kill her if she told anyone about his sexual abuse. She cried and screamed in fear and panic during the therapy. After several weeks, during which this trauma was re-experienced with intense emotion, she gradually calmed down and began to understand the reason for her fear of men and of having sex with them. At this stage she was able to connect her current problems with her childhood sexual abuse. Her fear gradually diminished and more mature and reflective reasoning began to take over.

Before Mary relived the incest in therapy, her attitude towards her father had been extremely ambivalent. She both loved and hated him. Immediately after the re-experiencing of the traumatic events, her hatred was reinforced and she would shout in a childish way, 'I am going to kill you'. Later her attitude towards her father changed. At the present time, for the most part she feels sorry for him and tends to blame her mother for having rejected him sexually. Mary is on the way towards forgiveness of her father: the damage has been done and nothing can change the facts.

In spite of her frightening experiences during therapy, Mary felt relieved by what had happened in the sessions and wanted to continue the therapy. Her aim was to come to terms with any childhood traumas which remained and thereby to heal psychologically.

Mary is artistically gifted. In her youth she had wanted to become an actress and had written plays and acted in them. Her parents never encouraged her in this and she did not have the strength to pursue her interest without support. Instead she chose an administrative job and studied art in her spare time. Mary has always painted and made patchwork. During the course of therapy, she started making drawings and paintings of her rich and vivid dreams. She brought this material into sessions, where it was used as an additional means to gain insight into her problems. She made a beautiful patchwork which was a visualisation of herself at eight years of age and she was able to discuss its meaning in therapy sessions. Her ability to express aspects of her experience in this creative way was of significant help in the process of coming to terms with what had happened and moving on to a new phase of her life.

During therapy, Mary began to understand that she should be encouraging her husband to seek help with his alcohol misuse and the problems it created. She felt she could no longer live with a man whom she feared and with whom she found sexual intercourse an unpleasant experience.

After two years of therapy, Mary is now a happier and more creative person with a closer relationship with her husband. He has now started treatment for his problem drinking.

One might ask why Mary did not seek therapy earlier, since throughout her life she had felt unwell. However, when Mary was in her 30s and 40s (the period of life when people normally are referred for psychotherapy), it was unusual in northern Europe to seek psychological help. At that time, it was embarrassing to be recognised as having a psychological problem without being diagnosed as mentally ill. Today the situation in Sweden and some other parts of Europe has changed radically. Most people in younger and middle-aged groups from all classes of society, are no longer ashamed of seeking help for psychological problems. Among elderly people, the situation has changed less. They often resign themselves to their situation and accept their medical practitioners' prescriptions of tranquillisers instead of seeking help from a psychotherapist. This is an unfortunate situation which we should be seeking to change. Many elderly people have existential problems such as painful feelings of loneliness, difficulties in relationships and fear of separation and death which psychotherapy or counselling would help them to resolve.

Methodological and Theoretical Comments

The therapeutic method I used in Mary's psychotherapy does not differ much from the methods used with other patients with similar profound problems deriving from traumatic childhood events. It is a psychodynamic-oriented psychotherapy combined with theory and techniques from primal therapy and hypnotherapy. The therapy sessions normally last from one-and-a-half to two hours and, at the beginning, these sessions take place every day for eight to ten days, interrupted only by the weekend. This intensity is necessary because engagement in the therapeutic process should not be interrupted by other activities. If the person is in employment, she/he does not go to work during this period so that they can be engaged entirely with themselves and their mental experiences. Following these eight to ten days of intensive therapy, the person will normally consult me once a week for between one and two hours of follow-up therapy. The duration of therapy differs from person to person, but for most people it lasts from one to three years.

Psychodynamic therapy is built on psychoanalytic theory: traumatic but repressed childhood memories are considered the main reason for the person's present psychological problems. By means of various techniques (working with the person's resistance, interpretation of transference, and so on) new opportunities are opened for enabling the patient to become consciously aware of important childhood events. In the safe 'therapeutic room' a person is able to relive and verbalise repressed experiences and the feelings associated with them. These feelings may include pent-up rage, fear and sorrow. When the present problems are connected to the previous events and emotions, the influence of the early trauma on the person's present situation will diminish and psychological problems will disappear.

In recent years, many therapists have started to apply other methods as an adjunct to traditional psychodynamic approaches. This enables the therapeutic goals to be achieved in a faster and more efficient way. Among the newer methods that can be drawn upon are techniques from hypnotherapy (deep relaxation and inductions leading to a light trance and a deeper level of consciousness). Other techniques which I have integrated in my therapy originate from 'symbolic drama' (Leuner, 1982) and 'primal therapy' (Janov, 1970; 1971).

Symbolic Drama

In symbolic drama the person is enabled to reach a state of deep relaxation and then encouraged by the therapist to 'see' and identify him or herself with various scenes which can serve as symbolic expressions of earlier important and unresolved conflicts. Experience shows that at the beginning of therapy, it is less threatening to be confronted with, and to find solutions for, personal conflicts at a symbolic level. Later the insights and experiences from the therapy room can be tested and consolidated in real life.

For example, the therapist using symbolic drama may ask the patient to visualise a house and imagine that he or she enters that house and successively visits the different rooms. Through this 'guided affective imagery' the therapist asks the person to describe in detail what he or she 'sees' and experiences. The person's experiences in the house are understood as symbolic representations of some of his or her personal psychological problems and unconscious conflicts. Through co-operation between the therapist and the person receiving help, different ways to solve these conflicts may be tried out – at first on a symbolic level in an imagined, visualised scene (in this case the house), and later on transferred to the real life of the person concerned. One patient had great difficulty visualising going into the main bedroom in the house. Later it emerged that this woman had been sexually abused by her father in her parents' bedroom. At the beginning of the symbolic drama, she did not even dare to use the keyhole to look into the bedroom in her visualised house. Further on in therapy she was able to use her imagination to 'see' herself walking into the bedroom together with the therapist. At that point she was able to confront herself emotionally with the anxiety, disgust and pain of her childhood abuse. Most people find it is easier to approach the traumatic events from early life in this symbolic way.

Primal Therapy

Primal therapy was among the first to demonstrate the tremendous importance of emotionally reliving original traumas as well as achieving intellectual insights about them.

The function of the therapist in primal therapy is mainly to help a person to reach his or her early feelings of anxiety and despair, that is, the so-called 'primal pains'. The therapist asks the person to recall early traumatic events and experience the feelings related to these events. This sort of therapy demands time, unlimited confidence in the therapist and a quiet and undisturbed environment. The therapeutic effects are achieved when the patient connects the 'primal feelings' (the strong childhood feelings) with his or her present problems, as occurred when Mary connected her aversion to her father with her aversion to her husband's sexual approaches.

Mary had no difficulties in co-operating in this sort of therapy, because of her high level of motivation and, probably, also because of her artistic talents. It is my experience that people with what might be described as an artistic temperament find it easier to reach the pre-conscious level of awareness and to release strong feelings than do people whose orientation is of a more technical and intellectual nature.

Mary was able to develop a high level of trust in her therapist, and here the age of the professional offering help may well be important. Many elderly people feel most at ease with a therapist or counsellor of approximately their own age, and so it was with Mary. She often mentioned how confident she felt with me and my long experience, not only as a human being but also as a therapist. This was an important point for her, and I have come across other older people who have expressed similar feelings.

Concluding Comments

Mary's story confirms that in late life it is not too late to use psychotherapy to help resolve old and still seriously inhibiting and painful problems which stem from traumatic experience in early life. Mary's quality of life has been improved significantly and it is likely that she still has several years of active life ahead of her.

It is particularly important to recognise that older people can be helped to overcome sexual problems which they have endured for many years. In most European countries there are opportunities for medical practitioners, psychologists, social workers and nurses to train in psycho-sexual therapy. It is clear, however, as I said above, that the age and experience of the therapist are significant factors which assist older people who are seeking help with psycho-sexual problems to become fully engaged in the therapeutic process. Given the continuing difficulty older people experience with seeking help with psycho-sexual problems, these are especially important issues. Fortunately there is now a growing number of experienced psychologists and other professionals who specialise in providing services to elderly people, and it should be possible to ensure that a sufficient proportion of these are also skilled psycho-sexual therapists.

Training programmes in psycho-sexual therapy require the study of human sexuality and psychotherapy, and trainees must also undertake supervised practice. In addition it is necessary for trainees to develop awareness of their own attitudes towards different sexual behaviours and to work to be free of any sexual prejudices. So far as older people struggling with the consequences of earlier trauma are concerned, this last point is particularly relevant. The therapist will need to examine his/her attitude to sexuality in old age and must also be able to hear and to work with the consequences of painful and damaging sexual behaviour.

References

Bergström-Walan, M.-B. and Nielsen, H.H. (1990) 'Sexual expression among 60–80 year old men and women: a sample from Stockholm, Sweden.' *The Journal of Sex Research 2*, 289–295.

Janov, A. (1970) *The Primal Scream.* New York: GP Putnam and Sons.

Leuner, H. (1982) *Katathymes Bilderleben, Einfuhrung in die Psychoterapie mit der Tagtraumtechnic.* Stuttgart: Georg Thime (1982 edition).

Masters, W.H. and Johnson, V.E. (1970) *Human Sexual Inadequacy.* Boston: Little, Brown.

Further Reading

Janov, A. (1971) *The Anatomy of Mental Illness: The Scientific Basis of Primal Therapy.* New York: GP Putnam and Sons.

Kaplan, H.S. (1979) *Disorders of Sexual Desire.* New York: Simon and Schuster.

CHAPTER 4

The Emotional Consequences of War 50 Years On

A Psychiatrist's Perspective

Louis Crocq

...In June 1940 I was on the beach at Dunkirk. German planes were constantly overhead, bombing and strafing for several days without a break... I have never seen so many wounded and dead men...so many corpses...and there were so many dead horses too. My companion was killed as he stood near me. He suddenly called my name and then his blood just spurted all over me. There wasn't a thing I could do to save him... This scene has often come back to me in the years since then. I see it all as if I was still there, with all its details, its colours and its atmosphere and I become very distressed. This has happened more frequently since I retired...(recorded in 1994 during psychotherapy with a former French soldier, who was 20 years old in 1940).

Introduction

As a doctor in the French army from 1952 to 1987, I developed a special interest in the treatment of Post-Traumatic Stress Disorder arising from experience of the Second World War and the later conflicts in Indo-China (1945–54) and Algeria (1954–62) (Crocq, 1987). More recently I have provided a service to victims of a wider range of traumatic events, including rape, accidents, terrorism and hostage-taking. Some of the people referred are young, but over the last three years I have treated 100 people aged between 60 and 80 who were continuing to suffer from unresolved psychological trauma resulting from their war experiences. Most (85) of this group are former soldiers whose traumatic experience occurred in combat or during captivity. For half of this number, one particular event was the single cause of their continuing distress. For others there was an accumulation and reinforcement through several battle experiences and imprisonment during the Second World War. A smaller number of the Second World War combatants were also subjected to further shocking events in the later wars in Indo-China and Algeria. Fifteen of the 100 people are civilian victims of war whose traumatic experience was of bombing and strafing, of arrest or deportation, or a consequence of their involvement in the Resistance movement. Some of this last group had also suffered mistreatment and torture. My experience of trying to help people to deal with the psychiatric illnesses resulting from wartime trauma has led me to conclude that a specially adapted approach to treatment is required if their distress is to be relieved. This chapter summarises the main features presented by the 100 older people referred to me and describes the approach I have taken to the treatment of this group.

The Patients

Among the older people who have come to see me it is very striking that the emotions they felt, perhaps 50 years ago following their traumatic experience of war, have retained their destructive force and can reappear following a second trauma and even after a minor event in their lives. The clinical symptoms that follow from these old traumas are extremely damaging, persistent and distressing for the person experiencing them and for her/his family.

Some of the older people who come to see me come as a result of a recent event, such as an accident, a disaster or drunken violence. In their thoughts and in their conversation there are many recollections of old trauma or painful events experienced during the Second World War which they had seemed to have forgotten, but which had now returned in force, intermingled with the recollections of recent disturbing events. Others begin to re-experience such memories as a result of a current event which seems to have the potential to be life-threatening.

For example, a 67-year-old man, until now well adjusted in his family life, professional life, and to his recent retirement, was interviewed by a psychologist at a cardiology clinic as part of the routine preparation for a common surgical procedure. Suddenly the man developed intense psychological and physical anxiety accompanied by tearfulness and severe tremor. He began to describe his vivid memories of his wartime experience. In 1944, when he was 16 years old and living in occupied France, he pushed a German officer under a train in the Paris metro. At that time he was a member of the Resistance and this led to his involvement in combat on several occasions. Later he was captured by the Germans and sentenced to death. During a riot in the prison in which he was held, he escaped (although several of his friends were killed) and continued his Resistance activities. In retaliation the German authorities killed his brother and deported his mother, who was never to return. After the liberation of France he joined the French army and fought in Germany until the war ended. He stayed on in the army and served for two years in Indo-China, followed by two further years of service in Algeria. He was actively involved in combat during these periods and saw many people, including friends, combatants of opposing forces and civilians, wounded and killed. After the end of the war in Algeria he left the army and had a civilian job until he retired at the age of 65.

It was the newly awakened awareness of death, prompted by the prospect of surgery to deal with his heart condition, that triggered the sudden upsurge of these old traumatic memories. This all came together in a total experience of extreme fear. However, when I talked to this man about his life over the last 50 years, I discovered that throughout these years there had been periods when he was bothered by distressing memories and when he suffered nightmares about his wartime experiences. He had also experienced other psychological symptoms of trauma intermittently during the intervening years. I saw this man twice before his surgery and once after. I believe he continues to suffer some distress as a result of his earlier traumatic experiences, but he has not come back for further help. Perhaps he prefers to rely on his own resources, as he did before the development of his cardiac problem.

Among the older people referred for help are some who have experienced unexpectedly distressing memories of painful wartime events following participation in ceremonies celebrating the 50th anniversary of the Normandy landings and the fighting during the liberation of France. The ceremonies commemorating the people who were deported to concentration camps and labour camps during the Second World War have acted as the trigger for the return of old, distressing memories for others. Television, radio and newspaper reporting of present day wars and of other violent events have had a similar impact on some older people. The realism of the television images (with each channel seeking to outbid the others in sensationalism) and the details provided, bring memories flooding back, and with the memories comes identification with the victims.

The common feature for all these older people, whether former combatants, civilian war victims or survivors of deportation, is the nature of the vivid and distressing memories which intrude on their lives unexpectedly and repeatedly, against their will. Most of them say that they thought these memories had been forgotten and that they are surprised to find them firmly entrenched in their minds with such continuing power to hurt. These intrusive recollections do not generally lead to spectacular abreaction, with crying, tremor and agitation, but rather to painful and abnormally high levels of psychological and physical anxiety; to obsessive thought processes about shocking wartime events, about the paltry results of the great sacrifices made and about society's ingratitude; and to bitter and depressed withdrawal.

The hundred people I have seen include some whose problems have emerged following the recent French law (20 January 1992) which established that victims of war neurosis could be eligible for compensation. My experience of working with them is similar to that described by Brainin and Teicher (Chapter 6) in relation to concentration camp survivors in Austria. For claimants the process of having to gather together the necessary administrative and medical papers and to search out witness statements, has revived painful memories of wartime which they had thought were forgotten. The people concerned are surprised at the intensity of the images that now intrude on their awareness with an extraordinary precision and clarity ('like a film that unrolls') and are astonished to find their sleep is once again disturbed by nightmares that first occurred many years ago. All the memories that recur are painful and recall is accompanied by obvious signs of distress and anxiety and by a defensive body posture. When, in the course of preparing a case for compensation, these people come to a psychiatrist for assessment, they often display spontaneous abreaction and a release of emotion which is painful to experience, but beneficial because of the relief that can follow.

Sometimes the person concerned appears to have maintained an emotional withdrawal from family members and from the external world. However, during a psychiatric consultation it emerges that this is a facade and that profound suffering underlies it, as is illustrated by the following example.

A woman who had already received compensation for wartime injuries to the chest and legs is now seeking compensation for war neurosis, in the terms of the law introduced in 1992. The circumstances in which she received her wartime injuries were dramatic. In 1944, when she was eight years old, her father was arrested by the German occupying forces (he was killed in 1945). Immediately after this event, her mother decided to send her away from Paris to a rural area in the middle of France, so that she would be safe and away from the bombing. She went to a small village with her sister, her aunt and her grandmother. Some time later the German SS entered the village and rounded up the whole population of 100 people in one room. In that room the villagers were shot with automatic weapons; the bodies of the dead and wounded were then drenched with petrol and set on fire. The woman told me how she was shot in the chest and legs, but managed to escape from the room through a small window, with the help of a little boy. These two children were the only villagers to survive the ordeal. She still remembers her sister being killed as she stood next to her in the room and her dying grandmother trying to protect and help her.

After the war was over, the woman's mother, who felt very guilty about the consequences of the decision to send her daughter out of Paris, rejected her emotionally and sent her to a boarding school. While there, she felt deeply the loss of the love of her parents. She finished her studies, found a job and married, but the marriage was not a happy one and her husband left her. However, it seemed as if she had managed to overcome all the vicissitudes of her life, although she had always been sad, quiet and reserved and had often been distressed by memories and nightmares of the traumatic events of her child-hood. Then, in order to prepare her evidence to support an application for compensation, she had to recall the events of her wartime experiences in some considerable detail. For her this has become another period of profound suffering and of more anxiety. When she was interviewed for her psychiatric assessment, she expressed no emotion in her voice. Her speech was monotonous and distant, as if the events she was relating did not concern her, but the expression on her face was tragic and tears ran silently down her cheeks.

Clinical Features of the Group

The majority of this group of 100 older people first presented with significant symptoms some considerable time after the original traumatic event(s) and before the emergence of the neurosis. Thus there was generally an intervening period of 'incubation', 'meditation', 'rumination' or 'contemplation'. The length of this period varied, with return to a secure place and the creation of a new system of psychological defences being critical factors. This 'latency' period between the traumatic event and the emergence of diagnosable illness may last for weeks, months or even for years.

The symptoms experienced by the group were those of traumatic neurosis: repetitive symptoms, such as intrusive memories, nightmares, flashback episodes and shock, associated with a triple blocking of the personality. This showed itself in:

- ∘ blocking of the capacity for filtering and assessing stimuli and events, resulting in increased arousal, avoidance of stimuli and resistance to falling asleep

- ∘ blocking of the capacity for participation, leading to demotivation, diminished interest in the external world and a sense of a foreshortened future

- ∘ blocking of the capacity for love, leading to an insatiable need for affection and a restricted ability to express affection to others.

Some people also presented non-specific symptoms such as high levels of anxiety, physical, psychological and sexual debility, psychosomatic stress diseases (gastric ulcers, asthma, hypertension, spasmodic colitis), disorders such as anorexia, problems associated with alcohol and drug misuse, and antisocial behaviour. The symptoms can be severe or mild, temporary or long-lasting and more or less incapacitating in personal, family, professional and social life.

For some people the symptoms have been intense, permanent and all-consuming, and have resulted in a true traumatic neurosis which has required long-term psychiatric treatment. But in other instances the symptoms have been mild and occasional, and could be treated satisfactorily with episodic symptomatic medication. For some people, even at the first onset and after only brief evolution, the symptoms were very mild and the psychological and social impact was almost non-existent. In these cases the people affected do not consider themselves to be ill and think of their memories and the blocking off of aspects of their personalities as normal after the wartime events they have endured.

However they experience them, the repetition of the symptoms of these psychotraumatic syndromes of war (of which only some are sufficiently intense and long-lasting to be called war neuroses) has become less frequent and less intense over time, although the clarity, realism and level of distress in certain types of re-experience of earlier events are remarkable after so many years. It is also apparent that over time the changes in personality become more entrenched.

The Causes of Trauma

An event becomes traumatising if it overwhelms the psychological defences of the individual. Thus the same event can be traumatising for one but not for another person and may be traumatising today, but not yesterday or tomorrow. So the concept of trauma is relative to the pathological predisposition of the person, to any other vulnerability (for example, exhaustion, lack of sleep or isolation from friends and family), and to the personal meaning of the event for the individual (for example, seeing a dead child may be of more significance for a man who is a father than for a man who has no child).

However, some aspects of war events, such as the violence of the bombing, the spread of destruction, and the number of dead and wounded, are traumatising for everyone. For the individual the surprise, the unpreparedness, the unexpected vision of death, the fear of being killed or wounded, the guilt over not having protected family or friends, the guilt at having killed civilians, the suffering when injured or tortured, and the collapse of moral certainty – all, in varying combinations, are causes of stress and trauma. Concern over moral dilemmas, such as a general commitment to pacifism as opposed to the case arguing the necessity of fighting in a particular war, and the internal 'fight or flight' conflict (Bion, 1961) also increase the potential of events or situations to be traumatic.

In all cases of war trauma there is evidence of deeper psychological processes which explain the onset of symptoms and which must be taken into account in treatment. One of these processes is the collapse of the individual's sense of self-worth. This collapse has three elements. It occurs first when the individual suddenly discovers the nearness and reality of death; in other words the person experiences the destruction of the narcissistic certainty of personal invulnerability and immortality. Second, the person experiences the failure of the environment to provide protection and third, the person's belief in the goodness and peaceful nature of humanity is cruelly shattered. What is more, at the same time as he/she is deprived of all the aspects of life that had seemed certain until then, the person finds themselves without help from elsewhere and face to face with extreme danger. The breakdown of self-worth and self-confidence and a sense of helplessness together explain the person's withdrawal of affection. The person monopolises love for him/herself and has a need for love that is insatiable. I believe that one aim of any psychotherapeutic treatment offered should be to give back to the individual affective autonomy (that is, the capacity to love others objectively and not simply because they are a source of love for him/herself).

It should be noted, however, that the mechanisms of neurosis arising from trauma are not explicable solely in terms of the Freudian perspective on psychoanalytic theory. Kardiner (1941) has pertinently written that in trauma it is the 'effective' rather than the 'affective' ego which is damaged in its capacity to adjust to the world. Psychotherapy should aim to restore to the individual his or her adaptive capacities and thus the 'effective ego'.

A further process at work in war trauma is the invasion into present life of the total experience of the earlier traumatic situation. This occurs in a way which takes no account of past, present or future, or indeed of the passage of time. The total power of the past situation persists into the present and is projected into the future, becoming a real constraint on the freedom of the individual. In psychotherapy it becomes possible for the person to free him/herself from the domination of the continual presence of the trauma that occurred in the past.

There is debate about the relationship of old trauma to the recent situation which seems to be functioning as the precipitating event for the present breakdown. For older people the question arises as to what the silent power of these past events is, in comparison with the 'retrospective power' of the recent event. Some theorists advance the idea of 'latent neurosis' to explain why the person has not been able to externalise the past problem before now. They also suggest that this concept can help to explain why it is that the impact of the second and recent event acts as a trigger to facilitate externalisation. In my view this is not a satisfactory hypothesis, given that many people show no symptoms over a long period and/or demonstrate a good level of adjustment in their lives.

I prefer to argue that the second event is truly traumatising and reorganises the present life of the person concerned so that it becomes consumed by the trauma; the future becomes ruled by the trauma and so, too, does the past, because only past events with the same meaning as the recent trauma are remembered, resurrected and given significance. I believe that in the phenomenon that Freud called '*aprés coup*' (Freud, 1895) we should see not a closed event which remains dormant until awakened by a second event that acts simply as a trigger, but an open event whose meaning is in suspense or abeyance. It is because the meaning of an event is never closed or completely resolved that therapeutic work is possible. My thinking does, of course, bear some similarity to that of Schreuder (see Chapter 2) and to the idea of 'diachronic trauma' developed by de Levita (Chapter 7). However, de Levita develops his hypothesis in a way which gives more emphasis to the traumatising capacity of the earlier event, suggesting that the recent events may not actually be traumatic in themselves.

In my experience, any other factors that are of significance for older people who develop problems as a result of war trauma are of a general, situational nature, such as beginning retirement and the consequent loss of status from work, the departure of grown-up children and the death of a spouse. All of these events occur at a time when, as a result of ageing, the person may have lost some of his/her previous ability to seek new experiences and consequently has turned in on him/herself and on the past. Changes in the brain may also be significant, as the loss of neurones brings about a reduction in mental capacity and in emotional control. For older people in these situations psychotherapy over several sessions can enable them to achieve acceptance of what they have lost and help them with the management of emotion.

Treatment

My approach to treatment has been to develop a form of abreactive psychotherapy. The aim is not only to create a re-experiencing of the traumatic event with an emotional intensity sufficient to bring about catharsis, but also to enable the person to gain control of the event, for the first time, in their own words. My approach therefore has some similarity with that of Robbins (see Chapter 5) in his work with former combatants of the British forces, but also with Bergström-Walan's work with people who have suffered earlier sexual trauma (see Chapter 3).

In the 1950s, when I began to see combatants who were suffering the consequences of their traumatic war experiences in Indo-China and Algeria, I used pentathol to facilitate initial abreaction of sufficient intensity to obtain a cathartic reaction. This approach had been developed earlier, during the Second World War, by psychiatrists working in Britain, the United States and France (see, for example, Alexander and French, 1946; Sargant, 1944; Suttar, Stern and Susini, 1947). After 1959, a combination of phenobarbital and dextramphetamine was developed as an alternative. The abreaction achieved using these substances had a similar intensity and had the advantage that the person would later remember the sessions and the interactions with the therapist with great clarity. Over time I found that the simple act of providing a comfortable place in which to lie down and encouraging the person to think back and just talk within the intimacy of the doctor–patient relationship was sufficient to bring about an intensive abreactive process. This is the method which I have been using with the 100 older people I have seen in recent years.

Abreaction alone is not sufficient to achieve substantial or lasting improvement. It must be used to facilitate psychotherapy in which the traumatic events are objectified, the drama is reduced and the events are placed within the normal sequence of a lifetime of good and bad memories. In order to be released from the domination of the traumatic events, the person must be able to talk freely to a therapist. I think it is important that this talk does not have a structure imposed by the therapist. It will be simultaneously informative to the therapist and revelational to the person concerned if the story unfolds spontaneously. Following the emotional abreaction, this free-flowing approach allows the person access to his or her unconscious, and lays the foundation for the later development of insight. The real purpose of facilitating verbalisation of the traumatic experiences through the process of abreactive psychotherapy is the achievement of this insight. Among the older people I have seen, treatment has continued for between 3 and 12 sessions. Each session lasts for about an hour and treatment takes place on a weekly or bi-weekly basis.

In my view, the role of the therapist is not just the passive one of witness or confidant who simply listens to what the person says. The traditional 'benevolent neutrality' of psychoanalysis is not appropriate. Older people still suffering the effects of their wartime experiences 50 years later need help and compassion, not impassivity. The therapist has to try to respond to the precise circumstances of each individual and to the emotional significance of those circumstances. It is also important that the therapist focuses on the decoding of the discourse of the person seeking help, and thus identifies the significant relationships between the events that the person describes and is able to help the person to recognise and understand these links. I believe the therapist has to act as a guide in the dynamic process of abreaction and verbalisation, moving the person from a passive preoccupation with the re-experiencing of the trauma through to the point where he/she is free from this domination and able to see a different and unencumbered future. To achieve these aims the therapist has to intervene actively, to counsel, encourage and eventually dissuade or disapprove. In these situations, therefore, the therapist has to serve as a reservoir of knowledge and experience and also as the trustee of the person's confidence.

Conclusion

In work with older people it is important to recognise the capacity of the emotions associated with traumatic experience of war to retain their destructive force and to persist or reappear unchanged 50 years later. The collapse of self-worth and a sense of helplessness experienced during the wartime event(s) seem to be the causes of later pathology, while recent emotional trauma, neurophysiological ageing and retirement can serve as precipitating factors.

Even when treatment begins very late and in old age, abreactive psychotherapy is able to bring release from traumatic anxiety and to enable the person to find the authentic insight and language required if traumatic experience is to be satisfactorily incorporated into the normal sequence of memories.

References

Alexander, F. and French, T. (1946) *Psychoanalytic Therapy.* New York: Ronald Press.

Bion, W. (1961) *Experiences in Groups.* London: Tavistock Publications.

Crocq, L. (1987) 'Trauma and personality in the causation of war neuroses.' In K. Belenky (ed) *Contemporary Studies in Combat Psychiatry.* New York: Greenwood Press.

Freud, S. (1895) *Studen uber Hysterie.* Vienna: Deuticke.

Kardiner, A. (1941) *The Traumatic Neurosis of War.* Washington: National Research Council.

Sargant, W. (1944) *An Introduction to Physical Methods of Treatment in Psychiatry.* Edinburgh: Livingstone.

Suttar, J., Stern, H. and Susini, R. (1947) 'Psychonévroses de guerre: etude d'une centaine des cas personnels.' *Annales Medico-Psychologiques 105,* 496–525.

CHAPTER 5

Understanding and Treating the Long-Term Consequences of War Trauma

Ian Robbins

George was 19 when he took part in the Normandy landings. Shortly after D Day the tank in which he was travelling was hit by artillery fire and caught fire. He escaped, although the rest of the tank's crew were killed. He was very shocked and disoriented and was unable to function. He was evacuated to a casualty clearing station where he was diagnosed as being shell shocked. Within a few days he was further evacuated to the UK. Throughout the intervening years George has had frequent admissions to hospital where the diagnoses have usually been anxiety and depression. He has been treated with tricyclic antidepressants, monoamine oxidase inhibitors (MAOIs) and ECT. At no point in the process were his war experiences even elicited. This lack of recognition of the causal role of war trauma in mental health problems may well have accounted for, at least in part, the lack of success of conventional psychiatric treatments. In 1994 he was still troubled by intrusive thoughts and images, frequent nightmares and high arousal which made him avoid reminders of the war. Exposure to anything which acted as a reminder intensified the problems. Even 50 years on he would meet the criteria for a diagnosis of Post-Traumatic Stress Disorder. Given the importance of the stressor criterion in the process of diagnosis, it is unlikely that this would be recognised unless traumatic events from the past are specifically asked about. The experience of this man demonstrates the importance of a long time scale in history-taking and the recognition of the importance of war trauma in the development of psychological problems in later life.

Introduction

I first developed an interest in treatment of the very long-term effects of war trauma when I returned from the Gulf War during which I had been a member of a forward Field Psychiatric Team. During that war, while acute breakdown was relatively uncommon but readily identifiable, many individuals were showing marked distress and yet were able to continue carrying out their role. This experience intensified an existing interest in war trauma. Coinciding with my clinical practice at the time as a specialist psychologist working with mental health problems of older adults, it brought about an increasing realisation that for a significant number of clients the Second World War was still a very fresh and acutely painful experience. I started to receive referrals of clients from military colleagues, for treatment of problems relating to wartime experiences which in many cases had occurred more than 50 years previously. Since moving to my current post, I have been taking increasing numbers of referrals of Second World War veterans, as well as veterans of more recent conflicts. I also offer advice and supervision to other professionals working with traumatised clients.

While the harmful impact of the experience of war has been recognised for some time, research into the area of combat stress reactions has focused primarily on the acute effects of war. Indeed the experience of the Vietnam War was instrumental in bringing about the creation of the diagnostic category of Post-Traumatic Stress Disorder (PTSD). The continuing impact of the Vietnam War has caused the short-term focus to become gradually stretched over time, but relatively few studies of the long-term impact of war exist. Within the European context, Orner (1992) has detailed the large number of wars in which Europeans have been involved, either at home or overseas. He suggests that there are likely to be large numbers of people Europe-wide affected by warfare, with the Second World War having had the widest impact. Further evidence for the extent of Second World War-related psychological distress is discussed in the research section of this chapter.

Few accounts exist of the mechanisms involved in the maintenance of psychological problems in response to war trauma over many years or of its treatment. In order to develop a coherent treatment approach I have had to integrate diverse areas of literature.

The mechanisms by which the impact of trauma may be sustained over very long periods have been discussed by Danieli (1985) and Krystal (1988) in the context of Holocaust survivors. They suggested that extreme and destructive experiences prevent emotional healing not simply by affecting the past but by contaminating the present. It is clear that extreme traumas may continue to cause problems across the life span, although for most the problems dissipate with time (Elder, 1974). There is also the possibility that symptoms may reappear if circumstances once again come to replicate or symbolise the distant trauma. For example, the loss of status and structure associated with retirement or the vulnerability associated with illness or increasing frailty may be linked to the recurrence of nightmares (Elder and Clipp, 1988).

Background to the Development of a Treatment Model

In my attempt to understand both the mechanisms involved in the maintenance of psychological problems arising from war trauma of many years ago and how such problems might be treated, I became aware of the paucity of literature relating to war trauma. I have therefore had to integrate a wide-ranging literature on trauma and its treatment with the nascent literature on combat stress. Over the next few pages, I summarise the main texts which have influenced my approach; I then go on to describe the treatment model I have developed and I discuss the personal and professional issues I have had to face in my work with war veterans.

Butler (1963) has suggested that, as part of a process of coming to terms with our experiences, we engage in life review, a phenomenon which he sees as universal in later life. This allows for the development of some sort of symbolic integrity, a process which may be fragmented by the experience of severe trauma. Lifton (1988) maintains that part of the task of healing is a requirement for some degree of conceptual integration of the traumatic experiences. This involves a sense of connection of events between past and present, a sense of symbolic integrity and a perception of being able to move on and develop in the post-trauma period. This has much in common with Erikson's (1982) concept of personal integration as an integral part of normal ageing.

✶A further issue is the role of cognitive factors as intervening variables between traumatic events and psychopathology. Horowitz (1986) has suggested that for recovery to take place traumatic experiences must be processed. However, avoidance strategies may prevent this from happening. McFarlane (1992), who looked at the impact of a natural disaster, found that intrusion was a strong determinant of later mental health problems. He saw the intrusive recollections as mediating between the disaster and later psychopathology. Intensity of the intrusive memories was as strong a predictor of disturbances of mood and arousal as exposure to the trauma itself. A similar finding was reported by Creamer, Burgess and Pattison (1992).✶

The treatment principles for acute war trauma were developed following the First World War (Salmon, 1919) and reiterated in the 1922 Shell Shock Committee. These principles are of early treatment close to the front line with an expectation of a return to duty, and they continue to demonstrate their effectiveness in recent conflicts such as the Israeli involvement in Lebanon (Solomon and Benbenishty, 1986) or the Gulf War (Gillham and Robbins, 1993). There is abundant evidence to demonstrate that if these treatment principles are ignored, the likelihood of long-term problems is increased. In the Second World War, forward treatment did not become established until after the American landings in North Africa in 1943, and for the British forces it was only with the Normandy landings in 1944 that forward treatment became well established.

For most of the Second World War, therefore, those showing signs of combat stress reactions were likely to have been treated by evacuation from the battle area – a response which we now know to be linked to poorer long-term outcome than that with front line treatment. In addition, during that war, attention was focused on those presenting with dramatic psychiatric symptoms. Noy (1987) suggests that there are other presentations of combat stress reactions which include physical illness or disciplinary problems; these, too, act as routes out of the battlefield but not as recognised combat stress phenomena. They are rarely monitored and the lack of recognition of a possible link with combat stress can result in inappropriate treatment and ignorance about the extent of distress among combat troops. Noy further suggests that there is evidence from the Second World War that points to a link between the intensity of the battle and the way in which distress is presented. This underlines the importance of proper recognition so as to promote proper treatment. Lack of recognition at the time may be one of the mechanisms involved in the genesis of later psychological problems in relation to war.

Treatments for Trauma

Chung (1993) has suggested that one of the primary requirements of a treatment programme is the integration of one's understanding of the meaning of a trauma with current symptomatology and life events. Krell (1985) has described a process of using tape recordings of disclosure of traumatic experiences in sessions to help some child survivors of the Holocaust to integrate their experiences into a whole. There was evidence that those who were unable to relate their stories continued to bear a considerable psychological burden. This point has also been made by Egendorf, Ramez and Farley (1981). This process of integration is more than simply abreaction. Integration requires confrontation of the experience, in itself a painful process which requires reprocessing of the emotions associated with it, allowing reconstruction of a continuous narrative life story. This process of reconstruction has to continue until the client can withstand the experience.

An example of this process has been described by Mollica (1987) who discusses the central role of the 'trauma story' in the treatment of PTSD. He suggests that once the patient is willing to tell the trauma story, it opens up the possibility of changing previous interpretations of events. Previous feelings of helplessness and hopelessness can be reduced and a new, less rigid and fixed story may be constructed, allowing the possibility of connecting survivorship in the present with having overcome the events of the past. Bleich, Garb and Kottler (1986) have discussed the recounting of events as a corrective experience. They point to its dramatic nature, with the possibility that the process may be extremely distressing. Patients may feel that they are about to be overwhelmed by the experience but as they begin to talk they realise that they can undergo the experience without falling apart.

Several authors, such as Cienfuegos and Monelli (1983) and Agger and Jensen (1990), discuss the role of testimony in the treatment of torture survivors. In addition to recounting the trauma story, their method allows for the channelling of rage and anger into some form of charge or indictment. As a consequence of this, they feel that their clients develop a better understanding of what has happened to them through integration of fragmentary experiences into their life history. They also suggest that because the experience of suffering has been symbolised in a different form, in this case a written statement whose importance was recognised by the therapist, the need to express the suffering through somatisation disappears.

Ochberg (1995) has outlined a number of components of post-traumatic therapy. This usually starts with an educational component which includes sharing books and articles, review of current knowledge, teaching about psychophysiology in order to understand the stress response, discussion of responsibilities under civil and criminal law, and an introduction to the fundamentals of holistic health. The promotion of holistic health is achieved via a programme of positive health activities such as that described by Merwin and Smith-Kurtz (1988). This includes paying attention to the promotion of exercise, good nutrition, humour and a sense of spirituality. He then addresses the need for improved social integration which may encompass family or group therapy, as well as exposure to self-help and community support groups. He also suggests that individual therapies may be employed, including grief counselling, fear extinction programmes, use of medication for particular symptom control, telling of the trauma story, role play and hypnotherapy.

At the heart of most approaches to the treatment of trauma is the disclosure of the traumatic experiences. Indeed Ochberg (1995) suggests that treatment is never complete if the client has not disclosed the details of the trauma. He suggests that people who suffer 'victimisation' or PTSD are still captured by their trauma histories and that they are unable to recollect without fear of overwhelming emotions. They also recollect when they are unprepared to do so. The purpose of recounting the trauma in therapy is to return to the terror and thereby to eliminate its power to terrorise. If disclosure is neglected, the potential of overwhelming emotion to interfere with the course of therapy is very high. The use of a staged model makes retaining a sense of direction possible and allows working through of the issues, rather than simply confirming their ability to overwhelm and damage. Ochberg emphasises the importance of the presence of the therapist which transforms this process from merely being cathartic to a partnership in survival.

There have been several other developments in recent years with regard to the treatment of trauma, many of which have grown out of the experience of Vietnam War veterans. Figley (1988) has suggested a role for family therapy in the treatment of trauma which includes an assessment phase and four distinct treatment phases. In the assessment phase a number of characteristics are examined which McCubbin and Figley (1983) suggest distinguish functional and dysfunctional families. These include clear recognition of the stressor as opposed to denial, the family accepting ownership of the problem rather than just being the 'victims', searching for a solution as opposed to apportioning blame, the presence of tolerance, commitment and affection within the family, and open communication.

The four treatment stages are:

1. Building commitment to therapeutic objectives wherein the clinician and family agree that treatment is desirable and each family member describes the impact of the trauma on themselves.

2. This is followed by a stage of framing the problem where the individual stories are viewed as a means of examining the impact on the family as a whole.

3. This is followed by a stage of reframing the problem. Figley (1988 p.102) suggests that, 'the therapist must help the family to reframe the various members and insights to make them compatible in the process of constructing their healing theory'.

4. The final stage of creating a healing theory is about the development of a shared consensus about events of the past and optimism about the future capacity to cope as a family. This requires an appraisal that is shared by the whole family, that accounts for their individual reactions and which contributes to a sense of family cohesion.

Figley's work was initially carried out within the context of war-related trauma. It is not uncontentious. Reservations about the value of family therapy have been voiced by clinicians working with diverse traumas (Herman, 1988; Stark and Flitcraft, 1988), who have suggested that sometimes the family is too damaged and divided to be able to be healed or that individual treatment remains the approach of choice.

Hammarberg and Silver (1994) looked at the impact of a 90 day inpatient treatment programme for 39 Vietnam veterans. They compared them with a previously treated PTSD group and with a non-PTSD group. Their treatment programme consisted of group therapy, relaxation training, patient education sessions, dreamwork group sessions and a peer group wherein members of the therapy group met to work on tasks without therapist supervision. Individual therapy was also available once or twice a week. While the treatment programme results initially suggested that substantial gains had been made by almost half the group, at one year follow-up they had returned to their original baselines.

Vaughan and Tarrier (1992) have described the use of image habituation training for treating PTSD which is of relatively short duration. They initially asked subjects to record verbal descriptions of the traumatic events on audiotape. This then led to self-directed exposure where the subjects visualised the event while listening to the tape. Of ten consecutive patients, six showed considerable improvement, two showed moderate improvement and the remaining two showed minimal improvement. Treatment gains were maintained at six month follow-up.

Another strand has been the development of critical incident stress debriefing (Dyregrov, 1989). This again has disclosure of events at its heart and has been used in the past in terms of prevention of PTSD in those exposed to acute trauma. Debriefing, through its fairly structured approach, may offer a useful model for the treatment of the more enduring aspects of trauma.

The Present Treatment Model

My present approach to treatment of the long-term effects of trauma, which was informed by the literature on helping Holocaust survivors and treating the results of more recent traumas, was inductively developed in the course of working with Second World War veterans. The need for a model of working became apparent early in the process. The extent of the distress and the nature of some of the traumatic memories have the power to be overwhelming for the therapist. It is possible to feel helpless in the face of such intensity of emotion. A simple model was needed to enable me to cope with the level of emotion expressed by clients and with my own responses to the stories told. Without a framework within which to work it is difficult to keep a clear direction in working through some of the experiences. In retrospect this emerged as a very important factor. There were times when I felt stuck, and by referring back to the model it was possible to begin to see a way forward. The model helped me to focus attention on the issues involved in the treatment and to resist any compulsion to try to 'solve' all of the clients difficulties. The model has as an overall aim the reduction of PTSD symptoms, especially intrusion, and the development of symbolic integration of the trauma experience into the overall life experience. It is based on principles embodied in work such as debriefing methods and constructing a trauma story, as well as cognitive behavioural approaches. To some extent the work that focuses specifically on trauma determines *what* to do, while the cognitive behavioural literature informs *how* to do it.

Prior to treatment an assessment is made of the nature of the problems and the extent to which war experience has been a salient factor in the development of current problems. Discussion of the nature and role of treatment and the emotional 'costs' which it will entail ensues. Full information is given before treatment outset, to enable the client to make informed treatment choices and to retain a sense of control.

Treatment consists of four phases:

1. *Disclosure of events.* This is the beginning of the construction of the trauma story and is carried out in great detail in two stages. Initially an overall picture of what happened is gathered by going through the events. This is followed by a more detailed review of events, which clarifies any confusion and identifies dysfunctional cognitions, such as irrational self-blame, and the emotions associated with them.

2. *Exploration of cognitions and emotions associated with events.* This is initially carried out following a process of negotiation to identify specific issues for the individual, referred to as themes, for ease of working. The link between past events and current thoughts and feelings and their impact on behaviour is established.

3. *Behavioural change.* Behaviours arising from the cognitions and emotions and the coping mechanisms used are examined, and the potential for change in these areas is explored and implemented. This can involve anything from opening up communication with close relatives to anxiety management methods. Issues surrounding regaining control are central to this phase.

4. *Termination.* This phase is only partly about the end of treatment. It also involves the client assuming responsibility for planning for the future. Issues in ending treatment, including the sense of loss which this brings, are explored and issues around future contact and follow-up are examined.

Treatment is carried out on average over approximately 15 sessions, with follow-up at negotiated intervals.

Two Case Studies

Two examples of how the treatment model is implemented now follow, together with a summary of the results of treating 11 Second World War veterans.

Mr A is a 74-year-old married man with four daughters. Three years prior to treatment he had been forced to retire as a consequence of the recession.

Before his retirement he had a successful career as a self-employed chartered surveyor. In December 1941, while an NCO in the Royal Artillery, Mr A was sent to the beleaguered island of Singapore. In February 1942 the island fell and he was taken prisoner by the Japanese and imprisoned in Changi jail. The jail was grossly overcrowded, it had poor sanitation and was rife with disease. During his captivity he suffered from dysentery, beriberi, malaria, hepatitis and diphtheria and lost 53 per cent of his body weight. He also had his jaw broken by a guard with the butt of a rifle and needed surgery while in the camp. This was carried out in primitive conditions and resulted in septicaemia and osteomyelitis. He was liberated in 1945 and returned to the UK.

He presented for psychological help because he was plagued for many years by intrusive thoughts and images of life in the prison camp. He described the intrusive thoughts and images as being qualitatively unlike memories in that they were present most of the time and he was experiencing them rather than recollecting them. The experiences in the camp had been compounded by the treatment which he and other Far East prisoners of war had received from the British government. He thought that the fall of Singapore had been an embarrassment for the government and that consequently that aspect of history was being conveniently forgotten. The anger which this engendered contributed to nihilistic feelings which found their expression in thoughts of self-harm. He had experienced a high level of psychological problems throughout the post-war period which had intensified since his retirement.

In approaching treatment the main motivation for Mr A was a desperation to be able to live his life more fully; to do more than merely exist, tolerating the intrusive experiences. At the same time he was worried about his ability to cope with sharing the damaging experiences with a therapist without disintegration and about the potential of his experiences to damage the therapist.

The second example is of Mr B, a 74-year-old man who was an infantry NCO during World War II participating in many of the heaviest battles in Italy and north-west Europe. During the course of this he witnessed the death of many of his friends, had several 'near miss' experiences and was involved in hand-to-hand combat. In the course of this he killed a number of enemy soldiers including some who had surrendered. He remembers feeling nothing for them at all as he killed them. He also watched the sexual assault of a German woman civilian, although he himself did not actively take part.

On return to the UK he returned to a job in sales, did not settle and tried several jobs before becoming a local government officer. He married and had a daughter but his wife died seven years prior to treatment. He has been troubled by nightmares since the war but these became more vivid again recently. He also has had problems with mood swings and depression since his late 30s. Since retirement and his wife's death he has been very distressed by intrusive thoughts and images. He referred himself to me following a BBC Radio programme in which I was discussing the long-term impact of war trauma and its treatment. When he had heard the programme he had been extremely tearful and upset and felt that he had to do something about his distress, which he recognised had been present for many years. He had previously been treated with tricyclic antidepressants on several occasions with varying degrees of success but no one had ever addressed his war experiences.

An outline of the treatment schedule for both men is contained in Table 5.1.

Table 5.1: Outline of treatment for Mr A and Mr B

Session	Mr A	Session	Mr B
1	**Assessment**	1	**Assessment**
2	**Disclosure of events**	2	**Disclosure of events**
3		3	
4		4	
5	**Cognitions and emotions**	5	
6	(A) Guilt	6	**Cognitions and emotions**
7	(B) Degradation and shame	7	
8	(C) Anger	8	(A) Survivor guilt
9	(D) Nihilism	9	(B) Shame and embarrassment
	(E) Helplessness		(C) Sexual guilt
10	**Behaviour change**	10	(D) Anger
11	(A) Relationship with wife	11	(E) Nihilism
12	(B) Talking with other FEPOW	12	
13	(C) Improving self-worth	13	**Behaviour change**
	(D) Taking positive action (control)		
14	**Termination**	14	(A) Talking with other veterans
15	(A) Future plans	15	(B) Reduction in alcohol intake
	(B) Follow-up arrangements and saying goodbye		(C) Exposure to TV war films
16		16	**Termination**

FEPOW: Far East Prisoner of War

Treatment for Mr A, which was carried out over a four month period, was based on the current debriefing model and focused on emotional processing of the prison camp experiences and understanding the post-war adaptation problems. On conclusion of the treatment he described the main benefit in terms of a change in the level of intrusion. The intrusive experiences were no longer present for much of the time. When they were present they were more like 'ordinary' memories and he responded differently. At six and nine month follow-ups, he was still reporting improvement, along with a reduction in the nihilism. He had also stopped thinking about harming himself. At more recent contact by telephone for the 50th anniversary of VJ day, he confirmed that the treatment gains have remained.

Initially Mr B's response to the sessions was fairly poor, partly because of the extent of his alcohol use which had not been apparent until rather late in the treatment, but which was numbing his ability to respond emotionally. The extent of the alcohol use had been denied during the assessment interview when all clients were routinely asked about alcohol and other substance use. At six month follow-up, however, he reported considerable reduction in levels of intrusion, sleep disturbance and mood. He was also drinking considerably less. Mr B continued to maintain his improvement and died peacefully two months later. His daughter made contact to express her gratitude for the change in her father and the sense of his having been more at peace at the time of his death.

Both Mr A and Mr B were extremely damaged by their war experiences. While the effects were always present, an enforced retirement in the case of Mr A and retirement and the death of his wife in the case of Mr B had exacerbated their symptoms. The nihilism which the intrusive experiences engendered had the potential to result in suicide. Intervention which focused on the emotional processing of intrusive experience brought about significant improvements which were maintained at follow-up.

Treatment Cohort

The treatment approach has been extended to include 11 clients (see Table 5.2). All were assessed as suitable for the programme in interviews carried out using a modified version of the Watson *et al.* (1991) PTSD interview. In addition all clients were assessed using the Goldberg (1986) GHQ28 and the Horowitz *et al.* (1979) Impact of Events Scale. All clients were positive on all measures (that is, scored above established cut-off points). One person dropped out of treatment, but the rest experienced considerable reduction in symptoms, although in the case of Mr B, as we saw, it was not immediately apparent. Since treatment, four of the clients seen have died of natural causes. It may well be that this is not surprising given the age of the client population being treated. An alternative suggestion may be that resolution of the trauma allows for a peaceful death. This was an unexpected factor in the treatment programme.

Development of a Treatment Service

Caplan (1970) has suggested that consultation needs to be organised on several levels, ranging from the client-centred through to the organisational level. Similarly, development of a treatment service can be addressed on more than one level. The first, direct client treatment, has already been addressed. Training and supervision of other therapists and dissemination to a wider audience are

Table 5.2: The treatment cohort

Age	Service	Number of sessions	Problem	Outcome
73	Army	15	FEPOW	Reduction of symptoms
84	Army	16	FEPOW	Intrusion reduced, symptoms lowered
75	Navy	16	Russian convoys; sunk twice	Successful resolution
78	RAF	12	FEPOW	Reduction of nightmares
72	RAF	8	Shot down/burns	Intrusion reduced, dream reduction
77	Navy	15	Depth charges/sunk	Death dreams markedly reduced. Other symptoms reduced
81	Army	16	Convoys, multiple bombing	Successful reduction of symptoms
79	Marines	14	Hand-to-hand combat, loss of friends	Reduction of symptoms
83	RAF	3	FEPOW	Dropped out, could not face treatment
74	Army	16	Hand-to-hand combat, multiple losses	Poor initial response. Subsequent reduction of symptoms
72	Army	14	Hand-to-hand combat, multiple losses	Symptom reduction

FEPOW: Far East Prisoner of War

equally important. If all effort is addressed at the individual client level even the most conscientious of therapists can only help a limited number of clients. By addressing all three levels it is possible to influence the treatment of a much larger group of clients. When dealing with a very neglected area this is important.

In conjunction with another psychologist colleague who wished to develop a service for Second World War veterans, a process of training and supervision was commenced. This took place through an initial stage of didactic teaching followed by presentation of case studies and case-related material. This was supplemented by the use of audiotaped therapy sessions and videotaped interviews with treated war veterans talking about their experiences before and during treatment and the consequent effects upon their lives. The audio tapes and video tapes were made with the express permission of the clients involved, who were aware of their purpose.

Supervision was provided on a regular two weekly basis and, as part of the process, audio taped therapy sessions were examined. An important part of the process of supervision was the need for the therapist to debrief following the exploration of traumatic material with the client. The importance of this has been addressed by Talbot, Manton and Dunn (1993) who looked at the needs of psychologists involved in crisis debriefing after a hostage-taking incident. The use of supervision is an essential part of being able to work with severe trauma over a prolonged period without adverse consequences for the therapist.

Supervision has continued on a regular basis and has become a two-way process. Danieli (1980) has addressed the importance of looking at counter-transference issues when working with war victims, in this case Holocaust survivors. She describes feelings of guilt about causing pain to those who have already suffered, repugnance at the horrible things which may be heard and shame about the ways in which people are able to act towards each other. These feelings can then engender feelings of superiority or inferiority on the part of the therapist in relation to clients. Similar issues have been addressed by Lavelle (1987) in relation to refugees, when therapist feelings of helplessness in dealing with overwhelming trauma may turn into antipathy towards the client.

Tiedemann (1987) points to the importance of monitoring one's own emotions as a way of preventing counter-transference issues from impeding therapy. The need for therapists to accept their feelings without guilt has been addressed by Danieli (1985). She suggests that if this is not possible, denial of their existence is the likely outcome, with adverse consequences for the therapeutic process. There is widespread recognition that however much therapists may attempt to monitor their own emotional reactions, the process of analysing these reactions in the course of supervision with colleagues is an essential part of therapy, especially when working with very traumatic experiences.

Issues Arising During Therapy

The Need for Reintegration

The traumatic memories experienced by the clients were perceived as qualitatively different from ordinary memories. They were distinguished by the fact that they do not change over time but instead return in primary format each time and do not fade with the passing of time. These qualities of memories have been discussed by Horowitz (1986) in the context of diverse, severe traumas, and their very difference makes the integration of the traumatic experience into the context of an overall life story more difficult. There was also considerable difficulty in knowing how to convey the intensity of the experience to others. Most of the clients had been unable to talk with their immediate family about their war experience. On the few occasions they did attempt it, the result was usually in terms of platitudes rather than real discussion. Danieli (1985) has observed similar problems in Holocaust survivors being able to talk about their experiences with their families.

The treatment model involved the development and elaboration of a trauma story which incorporated aspects of giving testimony. Indeed, as a consequence of commencing treatment a number of veterans have considered contributing their testimonies to national archives. The process of developing a shared understanding of the traumatic events and a language which allowed communication to others was a major part of the integration process. This inevitably leads to an initial increase in levels of anxiety. Krystal (1988) has pointed to the importance of therapy in increasing clients' tolerance for their own emotions. As a consequence of this, experiencing unpleasant emotions no longer leads to increasingly negative thoughts and a sense of being overwhelmed. Instead the client can reflect on the emotions and start to integrate them.

The Heterogeneity of Trauma

War traumas are not homogeneous. It is important to recognise this heterogeneity both in terms of the original experience and subsequent adaptation. This point has been made (see Hassan, Chapter 9, as an example) with regard to Holocaust survivors, but unlike the experience of the Holocaust many ex-servicemen perceived their experiences of wartime as very positive. This led to a perception of extremes and for many it was the best of times and the worst of times.

The fact that the war contained some of their best experiences as well as the worst, led to the feeling among those who had been traumatised that thinking about one brought to mind the other and gave a sense that the memories of trauma were contaminating their memories of the past as well as their present existence, making every reminiscence in the present extremely upsetting.

The Damaging Nature of the Experience

Any attempt at integration of the trauma into an overall life story necessitates confrontation of the damaging nature of the experience. All but one of the clients spoke of having held themselves together, partly through refusing to talk about their experiences at all. There was a general reluctance to approach treatment because of a belief that if they started talking about their experiences, they would fall apart completely and be unable to regain control.

The fear of disintegration was partly fuelled by the feeling that the memories were so damaging that not only would talking about them damage the client but that it would also affect the therapist. Throughout the treatment process concern was expressed about the therapist having to listen to the things being talked about. The memories were perceived as having a corrosive quality which could eat through attempts to block them out, and it was this feeling which had eventually driven clients to seek help.

There was often a sense of being overwhelmed by intense anger associated with events of the past and in particular with the behaviour of the enemy. For many, however, the anger has become attached to the way in which the government has responded, both to their needs and to the countries with which they were previously at war. Williams (1988) has discussed the way in which soldiers' anger may be displaced from the enemy on to governments. In many cases the feelings of worthlessness which have occurred with increasing age and frailty have evoked feelings similar to those brought about by the war experience itself.

A sense of guilt about survival and the things done in the course of survival is a significant part of the damaging memories. There is also intense guilt about the gratuitous killing and other action which in the heat of battle seemed normal or was exciting, but which in retrospect was seen to be immoral or criminal. This has previously been observed by Elder and Clipp (1988) in work with Second World War veterans and by Danieli (1988) with Holocaust survivors.

This perception of memories as damaging can be mirrored in the reactions of the therapist. It is extremely distressing to watch elderly men still being acutely tortured by events which occurred over half a century ago and there is a risk that, rather than confront the distress, therapists may engage in a conspiracy of silence with their clients. Danieli (1988) has described this phenomenon in the context of Holocaust survivors and has pointed to the importance of an understanding of counter-transference issues. A similar problem of therapist and client entering into a conspiracy of silence appears to exist with the very long-term impact of traumatic war experiences. The intensity of emotional distress expressed can take therapists by surprise, given expectations which may exist because of the clients' age and the length of time since the trauma. Their reaction to this may fuel the fear on the part of clients that further exploration of the memories may result in disintegration. It is important that these fears of the client and therapist are addressed. Consequently, therapists need an awareness of transference and counter-transference issues, irrespective of their underlying therapeutic orientation. Again, the importance of debriefing and good supervision for therapists cannot be overemphasised.

The Impact of Ageing

The impact of ageing and loss of status often led clients to a sense of helplessness. This was reinforced by increasing infirmity and, for many who had been prisoners of war, had reawakened emotions associated with their captivity experience. This phenomenon has been observed by Elder and Clipp (1988) among Second World War veterans. Ehrlich (1988) has also pointed to the power that current losses, such as loss of career and status (upon retirement) and loss of abilities with increasing infirmity, have had to reinvoke a sense of helplessness previously experienced during the war. Ehrlich has pointed to a need to integrate survivor issues with those associated with ageing.

Requirements in Therapists

Very distant, extreme traumas may present problems for therapists. There is a need for experienced therapists, with multiple skills in areas such as cognitive behaviour therapy, anxiety management, working with older adults and so on, who are happy to incorporate treatment methods into the model as client need dictates. As part of this, therapists need to be able to set limited and achievable goals for their therapy and should not try to address every problem that exists. While experience of being in the armed services is useful it is not essential. However, it is essential to have knowledge of the period of history and the events in which clients have been involved. Ehrlich (1988), in the context of treatment of Holocaust survivors, also points to the need for therapists to invest time in developing knowledge of the era and the specifics of the clients' experience; as part of this the therapist has to be willing to learn from clients.

A number of clients stated that the age of the therapist was important. Those who had previous contact with mental health professionals had found the prospect of trying to explain their experiences to someone in their early 20s too daunting. All agreed that having someone closer to middle age was helpful. A number of clients raised the issue of therapist gender and stated that they felt that they would not have been able to undergo treatment with a female therapist. However, a female psychologist colleague working with the British army has had the same reservations expressed by war veterans with regard to male therapists. Making it possible for the client to have choice in terms of therapist gender would seem to be more important than gender *per se*.

Selection of Clients for Treatment with this Model

Several criteria have emerged as potentially useful in determining who can be appropriately helped with this treatment model. These include:

- ° Veterans of the Second World War presenting with psychological problems, in whom Second World War trauma figured prominently.

- ° The psychological distress is evidenced by repeated intrusive recollections of wartime events, avoidance of war-related stimuli or intensification of symptoms when exposed to reminders of the war.

- There is an active choice to engage in treatment once clients are informed of the options.

- There is no evidence of significant organic impairment. While those with organic impairment need help it is unlikely that this approach to treatment will benefit them.

- There is no evidence of heavy alcohol or minor tranquilliser use. This is likely to result in emotional blunting and poor response to treatment.

- There is no evidence of major psychosis.

This list of criteria for client selection for treatment includes a number of factors which would be seen as predisposing to good therapy outcome more generally. Using a set of criteria such as this does not imply that those who fall outside it do not need help. While those who do not meet the criteria may still need help, this treatment approach may not be the most appropriate for them.

Towards Therapeutic Optimism

Working with older adults with problems relating to very distant trauma, as well as being important in its own right, has been a very rich source of inspiration for examining the impact and treatment requirements of war veterans from more recent wars. There has been a general therapeutic nihilism about therapy with older adults dating back to the work of Freud (1905). Being able to observe treatment successes has dispelled many of the myths surrounding the treatment of trauma in general, and of carrying out psychological therapy with older adults in particular. Given the good response of clients to the treatment model and the general professional lack of awareness of both the extent of problems related to Second World War experiences and the potential response to treatment interventions, it is important that these issues receive discussion in a wider context.

Discussion

The model of treatment described is still at an early stage of definition and description but even so has begun to demonstrate its utility. At the heart of the model is the development of a coherent 'trauma story'. By giving testimony to the events which they have experienced, the veterans in this study have been able to integrate their traumatic experiences into the context of the rest of their lives. The majority of those treated with this approach have shown a considerable reduction in symptoms and have felt themselves to have been helped. All of those who have experienced benefits from the treatment have discussed the qualitative changes in their memories.

The veterans distinguish between the 'normal memories' and the 'traumatic memories' in terms of the intensity and their ability to continue to damage. The damaging nature of the earlier experiences and the belief in their ability to continue to damage are central both to the need for treatment and the reluctance to seek it. The intrusiveness and the unchanging quality of the memories which are experienced as distressing are what defines them. The role of psychological factors such as intrusion and avoidance is important. Intrusive experiences of the war (1939–45) were strongly related to current psychopathology and levels of distress. Many of the veterans had also been practising active avoidance of war-related stimuli. This is in keeping with the work of McFarlane (1992) and Creamer *et al.* (1992), who have pointed to the role of intrusion and avoidance in the development of psychopathology. Their work was carried out relatively soon after traumatic incidents. What is interesting is the relatively enduring nature of intrusive memories. Schreuder's distinction between re-experiencing and re-enactment may well help to provide a framework for extending the work of Creamer *et al.* and McFarlane into looking at the very long-term consequences of trauma and the lack of resolution of traumatic experiences (see Chapter 2).

It is important to attempt to understand the active components of therapy packages, and this treatment approach certainly warrants further investigation using more controlled studies. Given the nature of the population in terms of current age and reluctance to seek help or to accept treatment, it is likely that traditional random allocation studies will not be an appropriate method of evaluation. This is certainly the case with Holocaust survivors, where descriptive studies of treatment exist but more controlled studies are absent for identical reasons. The long time scale of the problems prior to treatment and the extent and relative speed of the changes which have occurred for clients would suggest that the approach described here is an effective form of treatment. It may be useful to look at complementing the present descriptive study with process measures such as those described by Stiles *et al.* (1994) or Agnew *et al.* (1994). In many ways the reticence of Second World War veterans to seek help is very similar to Holocaust survivors (Danieli, 1988; Ehrlich, 1988), and it has been suggested by Zarit (1980) that when the offer of therapy to those elderly survivors is associated with other help such as physical treatments, pensions, housing, and so on they are more likely to avail themselves of the opportunity. Elsewhere in this book (see Chapter 8 and Chapter 9 for examples), we have accounts of the importance of informal settings providing the gateway to treatment.

It was apparent in this study that the experience of war continued to distress the clients who were taking part and that this distress had become an increasing problem since retirement. This is in keeping with work on life review such as that of Butler (1963), who assumes that the need to review our lives is a universal phenomenon. All of us, as we age, need to go over our past to try to integrate events so as to make sense of the experience.

The treatment approach has focused on the intrusive memories, attempting to put them into a context of the overall trauma story and life history. Many of the features identified by Ehrlich (1988) in carrying out treatment with Holocaust survivors are pertinent to this population as well. Current losses such as loss of career and of status (upon retirement) and loss of abilities with increasing infirmity have had the power to reinvoke the sense of helplessness previously experienced during the war. Ehrlich points to a need to integrate survivor issues with those associated with ageing. The work with this population of war veterans would bear this out. There is also a need to accept the individuality of each survivor's response as well as the common ground. Again this echoes the work of Danieli (1981) who pointed to the heterogeneity of survivors and disputed the validity of a survivor syndrome as described by Niederland (1968).

This need for integration of traumatic experiences into the overall life story is a central theme for the treatment model. For most of the participants, their war experience had the effect of fragmenting their lives into pre- and post-trauma experience. In addition, there was the problem that the war experience contained both exciting and enjoyable memories as well as very distressing and traumatic ones. It proved impossible for many clients to access the good memories without being troubled by the distressing ones at the same time. As a consequence much of this period was fragmented, with the war being isolated from the context of the rest of their lives. For many there had been no discussion with their families of their war experiences. The phrase 'conspiracy of silence' has been used by Barocas and Barocas (1979) and Krystal and Niederland (1968) to describe this phenomenon between Holocaust survivors and their families. For many of the clients, the process of therapy brought about discussion with their wives and children about their war experience for the first time in 50 years. This was possible because they were no longer frightened by the potential for loss of control and disintegration.

Being able to be sensitive to the individual's needs and at the same time being able to accept overwhelming levels of anger and distress are almost irreconcilable for many therapists, who become antipathetic to their clients as a way of defending against the emotional intensity. It has been suggested by Danieli (1980) that in defending against this intensity, therapists develop a protective shell of defences. Having a mental model of the treatment process is essential for coping with the intensity of emotion without the need for a protective shell. It provides a point of reference when the intensity of the treatment process makes a sense of direction difficult. Once embarked on the process of treatment it is possible to feel lost in a morass of distress and horrific events. Even 50 years on, merely listening to the events is sufficient to re-create a sense of horror.

A basic assumption of the treatment approach is that the client has to feel in control, even though treatment is being moved forward by the therapist. To achieve this, therapist and client have to construct a negotiated shared reality both of the events of the past and the treatment in the present. This requires a non-judgemental acceptance of the events and their consequences. This may include being able to accept the participation of the client in acts which may now be perceived as immoral or criminal. Similar observations have been made by Ehrlich (1988) with regard to treatment of trauma which are seen as pertinent irrespective of underlying theoretical orientation.

There has been a therapeutic pessimism about psychotherapy with older adults which is matched by a pessimism about treating PTSD when there has been a long period between trauma and presentation for treatment. This may be part of what Danieli (1985) has also referred to as a 'conspiracy of silence' between psychotherapists and clients in the context of treating Holocaust survivors. She asserts that traditional training does not prepare people for working with massive trauma, nor does it alert them to the possibilities which therapy offers for understanding reactions to severe trauma.

This treatment model, although still in the early stages of development and description, offers the possibility of therapeutic intervention for men whose trauma may have occurred more than 50 years previously. As a treatment approach it offers a clear focus, enabling therapists to work with severe distress. Working in this way is useful not only in informing on the nature of war trauma, but, as it offers a potential approach to the treatment of other reactions to diverse trauma, it may also serve as a model of working with distressed people in later life who may be engaged in the process of reviewing their lives.

There is a need for further use and development of this approach to treatment as well as more controlled evaluation of its effectiveness. Logically a treatment model has to go through this stage of evolution before being subject to evaluation. This in no way implies that there should be an absence of theoretical underpinning. Rather it assumes that further developments in theory with regard to psychological therapy may be informed by practice. Without this possibility of a developmental stage of utilising practice it is doubtful if many of the current approaches to treatment could have achieved their current level of utility and popularity.

References

Agger, I. and Jensen, S.B. (1990) 'Testimony as ritual and evidence in psychotherapy for political refugees.' *Journal of Traumatic Stress 3*, 115–130.

Agnew, R., Harper, H., Shapiro, D.A. and Barkham, M. (1994) 'Resolving a challenge to the therapeutic relationship: a single case study.' *British Journal of Medical Psychology 67*, 155–170.

Barocas, H.A. and Barocas, C.B. (1979) 'Wounds of the fathers: the next generation of Holocaust victims.' *International Review of Psychoanalysis 6*, 331–340.

Bleich, A., Garb, R. and Kottler, M. (1986) 'Treatment of prolonged combat reaction.' *British Journal of Psychiatry 148*, 493–496.

Butler, R. (1963) 'The life review: an interpretation of reminiscence in the aged.' *Psychiatry 26*, 65–76.

Caplan, G. (1970) *The Theory and Practice of Mental Health Consultation.* London: Tavistock.

Chung, M.C. (1993) 'Understanding post-traumatic stress. A biographical account.' *British Psychological Society. Psychotherapy Section Newsletter 14*, 21–29.

Cienfuegos, A.J. and Monelli, C. (1983) 'The testimony of repression as a therapeutic instrument.' *American Journal of Orthopsychiatry 53*, 43–51.

Creamer, M., Burgess, P. and Pattison, P. (1992) 'Reaction to trauma: a cognitive processing model.' *Journal of Abnormal Psychology 101*, 3, 452–459.

Danieli, Y. (1980) 'Counter-transference in the treatment and study of Nazi Holocaust survivors and their children.' *Victimology 5*, 355–367.

Danieli, Y. (1981) *Therapists difficulties in treating survivors of the Nazi Holocaust and their children.* Doctoral dissertation, New York University, University Microfilms International, 949, 904.

Danieli, Y. (1985) 'The treatment and prevention of long term effects and inter-generational transmission of victimization.' In C.R. Figley (ed) *Trauma and its Wake.* New York: Brunner-Mazel.

Danieli, Y. (1988) 'Confronting the unimaginable. Psychotherapists' reactions to victims of the Nazi Holocaust.' In J. Wilson, Z. Harel and B. Kahana (eds) *Human Adaptation to Severe Stress: From the Holocaust to Vietnam.* New York: Plenum.

Dyregrov, A. (1989) 'Caring for helpers in disaster situations: psychological debriefing.' *Disaster Management 2*, 25–30.

Egendorf, A., Ramez, A. and Farley, J. (1981) 'Dealing with the war: a review based on the individual lives of Vietnam veterans.' In A. Egendorf, A. Ramez and J. Farley (eds) *Legacies of Vietnam.* Washington: US Govt Printing Office.

Ehrlich, P. (1988) 'Treatment issues in the psychotherapy of Holocaust survivors.' In J. Wilson, Z. Harel and B. Kahana (eds) *Human Adaptation to Severe Stress: From the Holocaust to Vietnam.* New York: Plenum.

Elder, G.H. (1974) *Children of the Great Depression.* Chicago: University of Chicago.

Elder, G.H. and Clipp, E.C. (1988) 'Combat experience, comradeship and psychological health.' In J. Wilson, Z. Harel and B. Kahana (eds) *Human Adaptation to Severe Stress: From the Holocaust to Vietnam.* New York: Plenum.

Erikson, E. (1982) *The Life Cycle Completed.* New York: Norton.

Figley, C.R. (1988) 'Post-traumatic family therapy.' In E.M. Ochberg (ed) *Post Traumatic Therapy and the Victims of Violence.* New York: Brunner-Mazel.

Freud, S. (1905) *On Psychotherapy.* London: Hogarth.

Gillham, A.B. and Robbins, I. (1993) 'Brief therapy in a Battleshock Recovery Unit: three case studies.' *Journal of the Royal Army Medical Corps 139,* 58–60.

Goldberg, D.B. (1986) *Manual of the General Health Questionnaire.* Windsor: National Foundation for Education Research.

Hammarberg, M. and Silver, S.M. (1994) 'Outcome of treatment for post-traumatic stress disorder in a primary care unit serving Vietnam veterans.' *Journal of Traumatic Stress 7,* 2, 195–216.

Herman, J.L. (1988) 'Father daughter incest.' In F.M. Ochberg (ed) *Post Traumatic Therapy and the Victims of Violence.* New York: Brunner-Mazel.

Horowitz, M.J. (1986) 'Stress response syndromes: a review of post-traumatic and adjustment disorders.' *Hospital and Community Psychiatry 37,* 241–249.

Horowitz, M.J., Wilner, N. and Alvarez, W. (1979) 'Impact of event scale: a measure of subjective distress.' *Psychosomatic Medicine 41,* 3, 209–218.

Krell, R. (1985) 'Therapeutic value of documenting child survivors.' *Journal of American Academy of Child Psychiatry 24,* 4, 397–400.

Krystal, H. (1988) *Integration and Healing.* Hillside, New Jersey: Analytic Press/Erlbaum.

Krystal, H. and Niederland, W.G. (1968) 'Clinical observations on the survivor syndrome.' In H. Krystal (ed) *Massive Psychic Trauma.* New York: International University Press.

Lavelle, J. (1987) Contribution to a panel on The countertransference of torture and trauma. Third meeting of the Society for Traumatic Studies, October, Baltimore.

Lifton, R.J. (1988) 'Understanding the traumatised self. Imagery, symbolisation and transformation.' In J. Wilson, Z. Harel and B. Kahana (eds) *Human Adaptation to Severe Stress: From the Holocaust to Vietnam.* New York: Plenum.

McCubbin, H. and Figley, C.R. (1983) *Stress and the Family.* New York: Brunner-Mazel.

McFarlane, A.C. (1992) 'Avoidance and intrusion in post-traumatic stress disorder.' *Journal of Nervous and Mental Diseases 180,* 7, 439–445.

Merwin, M. and Smith-Kurtz, B. (1988) 'Healing the whole person.' In F.M. Ochberg (ed) *Post Traumatic Therapy and the Victims of Violence.* New York: Brunner-Mazel.

Mollica, R.M. (1987) 'The trauma story: the psychiatric care of refugee survivors of violence and torture.' In F.M. Ochberg (ed) *Post Traumatic Therapy and the Victims of Violence.* New York: Brunner-Mazel.

Niederland, W.G. (1968) 'An interpretation of the psychological stresses and defences in concentration camp life and the late after effects.' In H. Krystal (ed) *Massive Psychic Trauma.* New York: International University Press.

Noy, S. (1987) 'Battle intensity and length of stay on the battlefield as determinants of the type of evacuation.' *Military Medicine 152,* 601–607.

Ochberg, F.M. (1995) 'Post traumatic therapy.' In G.S. Everly and J.M. Lating (eds) *Psychotraumatology.* New York: Plenum.

Orner, R.J. (1992) 'Post-Traumatic Stress Disorders and European war veterans.' *British Journal of Psychology 33*, 387–403.

Salmon, T.W. (1919) 'The war neuroses and their lesson.' *New York State Journal of Medicine 59*, 993–994.

Solomon, Z. and Benbenishty, R. (1986) 'The role of proximity, immediacy and expectancy in frontline treatment of combat stress reaction among Israelis in the Lebanon war.' *American Journal of Psychiatry 143*, 613–7.

Stark, E. and Flitcraft, A. (1988) 'Personal power and institutional victimisation.' In F.M. Ochberg (ed) *Post Traumatic Therapy and the Victims of Violence*. New York: Brunner-Mazel.

Stiles, W.B., Reynolds, S., Hardy, G.E., Rees, A., Barkham, M. and Shapiro, D.A. (1994) 'Evaluation and description of psychotherapy sessions by clients using the Session Evaluation Questionnaire and the Session Impacts Scale.' *Journal of Counselling Psychology 41*, 175–185.

Talbot, A., Manton, M. and Dunn, P.J. (1993) 'Debriefing the debriefers.' *Journal of Traumatic Stress 5*, 1, 45–64.

Tiedemann, J. (1987) Contribution to a panel on The countertransference of torture and trauma. Third meeting of the Society for Traumatic Studies, October, Baltimore.

Vaughan, K. and Tarrier, N. (1992) 'The use of image habituation training with post-traumatic stress disorders.' *British Journal of Psychiatry 161*, 658–664.

Watson, C.G., Juba, M.P., Manifold, V., Kucala, T. and Anderson, P.E.D. (1991) 'The PTSD interview: rationale, description and reliability and concurrent validity of a DSMIII based technique.' *Journal of Clinical Psychology 47*, 2, 179–187.

Williams, T. (1988) 'The diagnosis of survivor guilt.' In J. Wilson, Z. Harel and B. Kahana (eds) *Human Adaptation to Severe Stress: From the Holocaust to Vietnam*. New York: Plenum.

Zarit, S. (1980) *Ageing and Mental Disorders*. New York: Free Press.

Further Reading

Figley, C.R. (1978) *Stress Disorders Amongst Vietnam Veterans: Theory, Research and Treatment*. New York: Brunner-Mazel.

Kuch, K. and Cox, B.J. (1992) 'Symptoms of PTSD in 124 survivors of the Holocaust.' *American Journal of Psychiatry 149*, 3, 337–340.

Robbins, I. (1984) The consequences of being a prisoner of war fifty years on. Paper presented at the British Psychological Society London Conference.

Robbins, I. and Bender, M.P. (1984) Conceptualisation and treatment of war trauma. Paper presented at the British Psychological Society London Conference.

PART TWO

Starting from the Holocaust

The four chapters in this section specifically focus on the survivors of the Holocaust in their old age. The authors work in different settings. Two of them work in day centres offering therapy as one of a number of services. One specialises in trauma at any age but has a special interest in Holocaust survivors, being one himself. One chapter is written by two psychoanalysts who find the usual understandings of psychoanalysis inadequate for the task of working with Holocaust survivors. Two of the writers are survivors. Three of the authors are Jewish, which provides two of them with the opportunity to share cultural traditions with the people with whom they work. The non-Jewish therapists reflect on their special difficulties.

I mention these characteristics of the authors because of the extent to which working with the survivors of the Holocaust presents a particular personal challenge which cannot be ignored and which the authors usefully address, and because the settings in which therapy takes place have a particular importance, as will become clear. We are privileged to have authors who have been willing to be candid about their own anxieties and learning, as well as their successes.

Numerous themes emerge in these chapters, many of them common to more than one contribution. All the authors address the impact of old age, some more pessimistically than others. They see the more painful experiences of old age causing what Fried refers to as retraumatising. Brainin and Teicher have a very pessimistic view of old age as a time of loneliness, illness and approaching death which reawakens all sorts of awful memories and fears. They draw particular attention to the diminishing of sex drive which reawakens fears of past losses. They point out that ageing in the camps meant death. Attention is drawn by all the authors to two ways in which reawakening of past trauma occurs. One relates to any negative aspect of older age, such as children leaving home, and the other to very specific events which relate directly to camp experience, such as the vulnerability of illness, and the death of other people. De Levita takes the view that survivor triumph enables people to cope as younger adults. They are able to sustain a fine balance between guilt and loss, and triumph. The latter is no longer possible in old age and this can be combined with terrible memories of other people's deaths.

Two of the authors draw attention to the special issue of older people in hospital or institutional care which reawakens old fears. This must in part be the re-experiencing of helplessness and loss of control, but more specifically the processes of admission, having one's possessions taken away and so on must reawaken old memories of concentration camp imprisonment.

This process of retraumatisation, while undoubtedly very painful, seems to open the door to accepting some help. In both the day centres where members have the opportunity of getting to know the therapist in what Fried calls the, 'here and now, wait and see' sense, the therapist is available when the survivor wants help or feels able to ask for it. Hassan sees old age as a time to reflect and re-experience: a 'second opportunity' to address unfinished business. De Levita suggests that this can enable survivors to achieve a peaceful death. He feels that a calm death is a good outcome.

One of the contributions that therapists with survivors bring to this field of the re-emergence of past trauma in old age, relates to the issue of whether the impact of past traumas is quiescent over the life span and re-emerges from nowhere, or whether it is there all the time but to a lesser extent. Clearly the extent of the trauma of the Holocaust is of a different order from most other traumas experienced, a point very forcibly made by Brainin and Teicher, who talk about a permanent frame of reference of persecution and mass murder. The authors suggest that many survivors have coped well with their lives, having jobs and families. They seem to agree that however well the survivor apparently coped they have been haunted by nightmares. It is in older age, as Fried says, that the memories become particularly debilitating. De Levita propounds the concept of diachronic trauma, by which he means that new stages and events in life give new meaning to past events. Young people from the Holocaust having children, for example, will identify with parents they saw giving up children. This implies that events at any stage of life have the potential to give new meaning to past trauma. Many stressful events occur in late life and can have this effect.

A very useful observation about the limits of therapy is made by this set of authors. De Levita draws from his work with children to point out that therapy cannot replace the normal infrastructure of people's lives. Survivors lost everything: their families, financial security, communities and sometimes even their culture. Therapy works to achieve a better resolution of the parts that exist, it does not substitute for what does not exist. Thus, as Brainin and Teicher point out, people may need to be assisted to obtain some financial security. They are very interesting about the issue of compensation, which is given for pathology but not for the experiences people suffered: an inverse incentive to achieving some degree of internal peace and a failure to apportion blame appropriately.

The day centres clearly have a role, to a degree, in filling the gaps in the lives of elderly survivors. Fried says that some survivors often stated that the centre was their second home; some even stated that it was their real home. Hassan talks about the importance of groups which can celebrate festivals together and the importance of other people to 'play' with. Fried suggests too that the centres provide a range of ways for people to open up communication about their memories, such as through art. To some extent the centres are able to provide substitute families and continuity. Fried suggests that she is seen by some of the members as the 'mother'. Clearly the centres are also there to offer an opportunity for mutual support and self-help. Their 'open door' style also leaves control entirely in the hands of the survivor: members can participate as much or as little as they want. One of Fried's case studies is of a woman who only wanted to attend for the Sabbath.

What do the authors say about the therapy itself? De Levita makes the observation that older people are willing to put a lot of work into therapy which can make it more rewarding. Brianin and Teicher reflect on the inadequacy of psychoanalysis and of the concepts usually used with survivors such as 'survivor guilt', 'identification with the aggressor' and 'regression'. They draw attention to the temptation of therapists to offer consolation which can have the effect of avoiding the awfulness of the experience. Perhaps they have been too ambitious in trying to achieve some resolution with their patients whereas Fried is more sanguine. She believes that traumas cannot be healed, but that people can be helped to live with them. She believes it takes courage and acceptance. Her aim is to make the past less overwhelming. Hassan emphasises the need to see the strength of the survivor, which she says is best seen within an equal relationship in which the survivor is, in part, a teacher guiding the therapist. Here we come back again to the issue of the survivor needing to be in control, in this instance in control of the therapy. Fried suggests that an outcome of therapy can be a willingness to consider some degree of reconciliation, as the traumatic past and losses become somewhat less overwhelming.

The issue of self-help needs some reflection. Is it true that, 'survivors feel understood only by each other' as Fried says? Hassan suggests that the ego is strengthened through self-help, which can make the painful journey towards some degree of resolution possible. She emphasises that everyone's individual experience of the camps is different. Both she and Hassan mention that there were some positive experiences in the camps, even if it was only mutual support, which can be built on.

As I said at the start, what distinguishes these chapters is the honesty of the contributors about their personal journeys to be better able to help survivors. Brainin and Teicher are very open about the anxieties, aggressive fantasies and grief experienced by the therapist. As they say: the therapist, in trying to understand a world where death reigned, becomes only too well aware of personal and professional limitations. They provide a painfully honest reflection on the threat imposed to self-esteem by the unacceptable thought, 'thank God I am not a Jew'. Hassan talks in terms of a journey which the therapist needs to undertake in preparation for entering the survivor's world of extreme trauma. The therapist has to get past the theoretical, practical and organisational constraints. Like others she sees the importance of seeing the people with whom she is working as survivors, not victims. Clearly the therapist needs to have support for himself or herself in this difficult journey.

Two remaining linked issues are addressed by these contributors. One is the importance of testimony. As Hassan says, 'if we forget or if we are forgotten, it is as though we never existed – to remember and to be remembered are perhaps the two most important elements to growing old'. The urgency of recording testimony is a crucial piece of work undertaken in the centres. Fried herself has written two books about her experiences. As Hassan points out, dementia is a nightmare in this context.

The second is the impact of the trauma of the Holocaust on the next generation. Fried describes work undertaken in her centre to achieve a greater understanding between the generations, in part by one generation sharing some of their experiences of the Holocaust with the other. In explaining the distress experienced by some of the second generation, Hassan says that they may bear the burden of unfinished business and may need help. Once again this help should be given in a way that does not pathologise people, but recognises their strengths and contributions. De Levita suggests that trauma is carried on to the next generation as children re-experience the anxieties of their parents, like the Mrs C he refers to who relived the guilt of her father.

Many of the themes raised by these authors, with their lengthy experience of working with older people who have experienced very extreme trauma, are very useful to people working with any older people with past trauma. They include the need to see those they are helping as survivors not victims, the importance of self-help, the issue of control by the recipient of help, and the need for therapists to receive support if they are to journey alongside the survivor without giving in to the temptation to fall back on inappropriate explanations or consolation which negate the extent of the trauma.

Mary Marshall

CHAPTER 6

Time Heals No Wounds
Psychoanalytical Considerations of the Consequences of Persecution[1]

Elisabeth Brainin and Samy Teicher

The scientific examination of the consequences of persecution and detention in a concentration camp must needs be biased. Persecution, industrially organised mass murder and genocide left their imprint on the victims, who escaped their fate only by chance. The few survivors of the Nazi terror were saved only because the Nazi regime was defeated in battle. Murder and destruction were normal, everything else was the exception. The way of life of the survivors that had existed before mass destruction, their life connections, their relationships and their moral and cultural attitudes were completely destroyed. Krystal (1968) and Niederland (1965, 1980) describe the consequences of persecution as 'Survival Syndrome'. Other authors speak of the 'Concentration Camp Syndrome' (Baeyer, Häfner and Kisker 1964). With a multitude of very different symptoms, all descriptions have in common the impairment of vital emotions (sensations), of the 'élan vital' of the survivors. It seems as if the frame of reference of feelings, relationships and value associations had shifted. The likelihood of persecution and of mass murder remains the frame of reference forever.

When former persecutees go for treatment many years after the war, it is mostly because they are experiencing problems caused by a new period in life. The children born after the liberation are now mostly grown-up and often have their own families. For survivors, age, separation, seclusion and physical illness are new threats to only apparent stability. For a long time, the real dangers of everyday life could be denied. Physical illness, which is more a result of ageing

---

1   This work is based on an article written together with Vera Ligeti.

than of persecution, calls up old fears, just as it does for all older people. Fears of destruction, which were real fears during persecution, reappear, the extent depending how far ego-strength is reduced or fails for physical reasons. Arousal and vigilance, life-saving during persecution, lead to an often insufferable burden after liberation. In the camp, relaxing vigilance and surrendering instinct-control was a real danger and remained with accompanying fears afterwards. Sleep disturbances resulted from this, due in part to the fear of nightmares, which the world of persecution caused to develop again and again.

Fears of dependency and loneliness in old age create violent tensions, expressed in depressive states, ideas of suicide and psychosomatic complaints. Feelings of helplessness cause anger or despair again. Regression as a result of ageing takes place on several levels. Lessening of sexual drives leads to a regression to pregenital means of satisfaction.

Even in full physical health, ageing leads to a changed view of yourself. The end of reproductive functions in the normal ageing process, which is accompanied by castration anxieties (just think of the importance of the loss of teeth), poses a threat to former inmates, if additionally it reawakens fears of death from the time of imprisonment. In the camp, signs of age meant assured death. White hair, wrinkles, missing teeth, and so on. could be a death sentence. Any illnesses of old age are experienced as being left helpless.

Loneliness in old age, with its accompanying fears of death, leads to a resurfacing of the desire for protective parents. With the fear of death, the camp feeling of having been left alone by absolutely everyone again becomes prominent.

The following short vignette from the practice of one of the authors shows the importance of socially secure circumstances for old people, especially for those who underwent severe trauma, as a basis for all further psychotherapeutic work:

> Mr Y came to seek psychiatric help at the age of 72. He was full of anxieties. His sleep was disturbed, he had nightmares about his concentration camp experiences in Buchenwald during his youth. When Hitler occupied Austria Mr Y was not allowed to continue his studies. He was Catholic, but under the Nazi racist laws he counted as a Jew. He had also joined a students' resistance group. He was captured by the Gestapo and detained in Buchenwald, where he was liberated in 1945. His professional abilities were destroyed forever through an injury to his hands, as he had wanted to be a musician. Nevertheless he could cope with reality and built up a new life after the war. He had a family and became a lucky grandfather.
>
> After a coronary illness he became more and more anxious, which led to his seeking help. In the initial interview, it became clear that his coronary

heart disease not only evoked old anxieties aroused by his imprisonment, but was a real threat to his existence. His pension was very low and he had to continue working to afford a higher standard of living. His heart disease prevented him from continuing to work. With this present threat, all the old anxieties from the past came to the surface. He felt helpless, especially since his financial existence was in danger. I managed to convince him of the necessity to apply for a higher pension, a so-called *Opferrente* (a pension for Nazi-victims), thereby gaining more security in reality. On this basis I was able to help him further to gain more inner security. He slept better and returned to his normal level of nightmares and anxieties, which he had had since the war. This undoubtedly helped him also to live better with his coronary disease.

The aim of treatment of such patients is the reduction of anxiety and the recovery of a positive view of oneself. The feeling of being 'at home' in one's body and mind is in contrast to a pathological, negative view of oneself which may be expressed as worry about one's body, as a depressive state, as self-accusation, devaluation or self-rejection. The difficulty this presents to the therapist is that these negative feelings stem from the memory of real, horrible events and do not represent a 'rejection of empathy' (Grubrich-Simitis, 1979) with these patients. By engaging with the reality of the memories of these patients, the therapist experiences anxieties and aggressive fantasies of his or her own, of such strength that the grief that follows cannot properly be processed and overcome. This failure can be a significant blow to personal and professional self-esteem, for in trying fully to perceive the inferno of persecution, the world in which death reigned, the therapist learns about the limitations of professional help and sometimes, too, of human beings.

When psychoanalysts are working with survivors seeking compensation, the need to create a scientific case for the purpose of the claim involves also dealing with what happened to people as a result of their persecution and concentration camp experiences. It is necessary to balance the requirements for a scientific argument for the authorities with the experience of treating former persecutees and their children. The conditions for compensation and assistance are not the experience of the suffering and the horror, but the presence in the claimant of a pathology which can be traced back to those earlier experiences. The end result is that pathology has to be diagnosed in the victims. They have to have problems in their adjustment or coping mechanisms rather than the pathology being recognised as lying solely and exclusively in the reality that made the claimants victims.

In a judgement for compensation for a woman who was not quite five years old when liberated from the camp and who, miraculously, had survived several ghettos and extermination camps, it was claimed that camp imprisonment could not have had any harmful effect on her because, being a child, she could not experience it consciously at all. Any financial assistance for psychotherapy was denied her and the costs of medical treatment were not compensated, on the grounds that the Federal Republic of Germany could not be expected to pay for daily tranquillisers. In this way, the victims are stigmatised as 'pension neurotics', who are only trying to get something out of the Federal Republic. Yet the truth is that for people who underwent severe trauma, there is a dual need, for psychotherapeutic help *and* compensation from the state. Compensation leads to a greater social and financial security, essential, as we saw for Mr Y, not just for its help towards physical survival but also for the psychological benefit that accompanied this improvement in material circumstances. Importantly, though, compensation also represents public recognition of being a victim, indeed of the trauma itself. This has an additional special significance in countries such as Austria, where forgetting the past is not the exception but the rule.

Testing Concepts Against Reality

In psychoanalytical research of the consequences of persecution, a group of concepts that was never questioned gained vogue. As psychoanalysts, this group needs to be of interest to us. To gain a better understanding of the special pathology of former deportees, we need to examine three concepts in particular:

1. survival guilt.

2. identification with the aggressor.

3. regression.

Survival Guilt

Where, in this context, reference is made to 'survival', survival guilt is an immediate follow-on. This concept has been used in all publications around this theme, irrespective of the period of publication. Most survivors present this 'survival guilt' consciously in psychiatric or psychoanalytical first interviews as a problem and a burden. As psychoanalysts, this should make us wonder what unconscious reasons hide behind this consciously enunciated term. Survival guilt is used to explain depressive states, sleep disturbances, nightmares, and so on. During interviews and treatments it is presented to us with the questions: 'Why did I survive and not the others? Why was I spared and not my brother, my sister, my parents or children, who were so much better than I?'.

If we understand the Survival Syndrome as a severe traumatic 'neurosis', we may try to apply the psychoanalytic concept of trauma and restitution. Primo Levi spoke of the psychoanalysts' 'professional lust', with which they throw themselves at the bewildered helplessness of the former inmates (Levi, 1990). We think that this is due to the helplessness of the analysts, who, with the techniques and means available, are unable to explain this inferno of the *universe concentrationnaire*.

Classical psychoanalytical theory assumes that the less a person is prepared to face a traumatic situation, the more intensive will be the consequences, particularly where the trauma is experienced by an exhausted ego which has already had much to bear (Fenichel, 1983). This is always true for concentration camp inmates. The inferno to which they were subjected was inconceivable. These were industrialised murder factories, designed simply to murder hundreds of thousands as quickly as possible. The transport of the inmates to the death camps was in itself an incomparable physical and mental burden, which many were unable to survive. This was often preceded by a lengthy period of humiliation, deprivation of rights and of terror. Everything was intended to rob these people of their humanity, dignity and integrity. As Levi (1990) said, before the victim died, he had to be humiliated and made worth less, so that the murderer would feel less guilty.

A severe trauma, or rather a multitude of traumata, upsets the sense of self of a person, the feeling of being oneself, the security of bodily and psychic functions. In the repetition of the trauma in fantasy, taking place *inter alia* in dreams, the subconscious attempt to rebuild a sense of self is demonstrated. These dreams are experienced repeatedly. The dreamer must be convinced of his or her own survival. For reconstruction of the personality after each trauma the unconscious triumph of survival of the self is of greatest importance. It is no triumph, on the other hand, to have survived one's own family and millions of victims. This expresses latent conflicts between the ego and super-ego. The ego-endeavours embody the desire to live, while on the other hand the super-ego, one's own moral responsibility, condemns the idea of 'if somebody has to go, it shouldn't be me!' (Levi, 1990). The feelings for the person who has died are irrelevant to the conflict. The conflict is an expression of the camp realities, which were that it was either me or the other one. Primo Levi talks of altered moral scales in the inferno. The most important rule on site was: 'First of all, think of yourself!' (Levi, 1990). The conflict between the wish to stay alive and the suffering of others, where help was hypothetical at best, aggravates the traumatic situation. It results in an insult to the whole self through, for instance, not having fulfilled one's own moral values and having submitted to the strength of the survival wish. This expresses itself in feelings of shame. The super-ego condemns the wish to live and this causes feelings of guilt. The survivors believe that their own survival in a world of death and destruction was only possible at the expense of others' murder or starvation:

A patient remembers how he arrived at the camp with his father and younger brother. Father and brother were torn from his side and sent to the gas chambers. He, 14 years old at the time, survived. Today he suffers obsessional thoughts, causing him to experience this situation over and over again. In his imagination he tries to find solutions which would have prevented his father's and brother's death and he reproaches himself for not having walked between them. If he had done so, they would have been saved also or he would have gone to his death with them. He experiences his own survival as a direct consequence of his wish to live and as a direct consequence of his father's and brother's death. His natural human wish to live conflicts with his thought: 'Had I been killed, they would have survived'.

Control of aggressive impulses is a most important pillar of all cultures and civilisations. For people of the Jewish culture, the primitive social Darwinism of the camp world threatens our confidence in the accepted societal standards in which the death wish is forbidden. For the patient and the analyst the perception of these wishes means the infringement of a taboo, and this is painful to both. Neither of them can bear the choice 'either I or the other must die'. For a non-Jewish analyst, a particular and continuous threat to his or her self-image is the unspeakable thought: 'Thank God I am not a Jew and therefore would not be subjected to all this'.

Survival does not, cannot lead to triumph. Survival was due to a series of coincidences. During camp imprisonment and often after liberation, the unconscious thought: 'Luckily, I'm alive' has been replaced by the conscious task to bear witness to all these horrors, to lift up one's voice for the murdered, 'for the silent ones and the cause of all those forsaken' (Solomon, Proverbs 31.8). This task helped to find the wholeness of one's own person again, without which survival, even after liberation, would not have been possible. This task gave being alive new sense.

Filip Müller (1979), in his moving account of the 'Sonderkommando' at Auschwitz, reports on exactly this problem. In moments of absolute despair, in which only the wish not to die oneself prevailed over the fear of death, there were his comrades, other inmates condemned to death, who reminded him of his task to bear witness of these crimes before the world. This helped him to find his sense of self again and this, together with good luck, kept him alive.

The thought: 'Luckily, it is not my turn' is one that conflicts with all ideas of yourself as a good person as well as with the demands of the super-ego. In a world of destruction, this was the most human and, at the same time, the most forbidden thought. Feelings of shame and of guilt lie close together and are determined by conflicts with the ego-ideal and super-ego. The ego-ideal arises from the wish to be true to one's ideal self, whereas the super-ego means more the actual conscious morality.

Humiliations, degradations, dehumanisation, translation to animal, even vermin, status, abandonment to destruction: all gave rise to feelings of shame. Thoughts such as: 'So many, more valuable than I, had to die and I am alive' express self-rejection, that could co-exist very well with the feelings described above. This self-rejection, described by Amery (1966), is doubtlessly linked with feelings of shame. But it also belongs to the feelings falsely described as identification with the aggressor, and it is to this concept that we now proceed.

Identification with the Aggressor

Anna Freud (1936) describes this defence mechanism as a developmental precursor of the super-ego (defence mechanisms protect the ego, for example the whole person, against anxiety from all sources, inner or outer). Identification with the aggressor consists of subconscious identification with severe parental demands of children, threatening punishment. Only after overcoming the Oedipal complex, with the internalisation of super-ego and good parental images which do not go hand-in-hand with fears and wishes of draconian punishment, does this defence mechanism lose importance.

Until this Oedipal phase (between the age of three and five or six years) has been reached, any kind of danger and fear is experienced as reality. Loss of love objects turns into deadly threats. A revival of this defence mechanism may occur in a traumatic situation, where a continuous, real threat to life, which surpasses all other kinds of fear ever experienced, exists.

The camp inmates found themselves in a reality which overthrew all standards. In most publications, identification with the aggressor is described as one with SS men, Nazis, Capos, the Gestapo and so on, which was expressed, *inter alia*, by aggressive acts against fellow inmates. Even Bettelheim (1964), the psychoanalyst, used this concept. To us this seems questionable, in particular with prisoners from extermination camps. For a normal prisoner, identification with the SS would doubtless have meant an impaired reality-testing and would have led to punishment, if not to certain death. The prisoners who rose in the prison hierarchy were often criminals who behaved aggressively, immorally and without solidarity towards their fellow prisoners. As such they behaved like the SS. But this behaviour had nothing to do with Anna Freud's concept of identification with the aggressor.

If we speak of identification with the aggressor in connection with persecution, this is in relation to a revival of infantile fears of punishment and rejection, which we see in many traumatised people. This trauma is often experienced unconsciously as 'just' punishment for 'outrages' or forbidden wishes and fantasies, since there is a revival of earlier identification patterns with archaic, severe parental images. In the concentration camps, left alone by all the world, in mortal fear and despair, they felt abandoned by comforting parent figures. Humiliation and abasement, mortal fear and despair then seem unconsciously a just punishment for earlier 'sins' or for the wish for survival that was continuously present in the camps, where it was connected with the thought: 'Let's hope they will not take me'.

Identification with the aggressor is therefore the identification with punishing parental images. It is expressed in feelings of guilt and fears of punishment for forbidden wishes and thoughts. It had no connection with an identification with an aggressor such as the SS, the Nazis, and so on. Identification with that form of aggressor would have meant the surrender of all one's own moral standards.

Hoppe (1964) categorised a form of the pathology of former concentration camp inmates as chronic, reactive aggression. We believe that this aggression is not connected with any identification with the aggressor. It is, rather, the result of a traumatic diffusion of instincts. All libidinal endeavours were massively suppressed by the aggression and destruction in the camps. A great part of the pathology of former inmates probably takes the form of aggression. Aggressive impulses can be viewed as disability, caused by the Nazis. The unconscious, murderous aspect of all aggression is probably more present and less repressed in people who survived the extermination camps, than in others to whom that extent of human destruction is unimaginable. These people know that every kind of aggression and destruction is really possible.

A particularly strong ego-control is required to prevent the internalisation of extinguished instincts enforced by the camp reality which produced permanent vigilance, tension and stress. To allow the acceptance of chance as an explanation for survival, all ego-functions connected with reality-testing had to be particularly extended, lucid and alert. A continuous internal struggle was carried on between super-ego and the wish for immediate instinct gratification which meant, in the camp, first and foremost to eat. This raises the question of whether it can be rightly said that camp inmates regressed.

Regression

All publications dealing with imprisonment in concentration camps refer to massive regression, which is claimed to have begun immediately after arrest (for example, Bettelheim, 1964; Grubrich-Simitis, 1979; Hoppe, 1964). No further distinction is made as to whether regression took place on the instinct or the ego level. All former inmates reported that arrival in the camp caused an enormous shock. All of them had been completely unprepared for what they experienced there. In extermination camps they were also often unable to comprehend what was going on for a period of time. This is most likely comparable with the depersonalisation experience in a Gestapo prison, described by Jacobson (1949). Grubrich-Simitis (1979) describes this process as an activation of the ego, an arming of it to assist adjustment. Later she describes this ego-function as regression, but we regard this as a contradiction. Adjustment to a psychotic cosmos, determined by reality-testing, subject to continuously changing, never predictable, but always life-threatening conditions, cannot be a regression. With all the coincidences that determined survival there was a need for an unbelievable ability to retain ego-functions and reality-testing in the face of continuous stress due to threats, hunger, cold and mortal fear. There was a need to protect oneself against all internal emotional turmoil and to be able to recognise external dangers in time. All wishes for passivity and submission had to be suppressed, because they might cause death. Mr R remembers how:

> He was 16 years old and accompanied his father on one of those terrible death marches during January 1945, when an extermination camp was evacuated to the West. His father only wanted to have some rest. Mr R himself could no longer drag him along and so he had to look on and see how his father sat down and could not get up anymore. This meant death.

In order not to surrender passively to the Nazis' deception, the fraud and the lies used to engender hope in people had to be uncovered. All deceptions by the SS, the Gestapo and the Nazi bureaucracy had to be seen as the manoeuvres they were. 'Arbeit macht frei' (work makes you free) was the slogan over concentration camp gates; showers which were gas chambers in reality; the aged and sick who were transported on trucks for preservation – all were deceptions which led to death. They exerted a seductive attraction. If, after a terrible transport and a horrifying arrival at Auschwitz, the aged and sick were told they would be transported on trucks to the camp, this seemed a promise that there would be rest. If you believed that to survive you only needed to work hard, this raised certain hopes. If you had had no water for days, the prospect of a shower was like a hope of life.

The murderers used such deceptive manoeuvres quite intentionally and for specific populations. The people who were transported to the extermination camps from the ghettos in Poland did not expect any 'human' treatment. They were driven out of the railway trucks by force with shots, dogs and whips into the gas chambers. Only for those who came from Western Europe, after inhuman transport, was such deception used, so as to allow the murder to be realised in a more 'orderly' manner.

As a prisoner you had to be alert to all deceptive manoeuvres. This is the opposite of regression on the ego level. On the super-ego level, the prisoner's own morality had to be opposed to lies and death, to serve as a defence against feelings of defacement.

If we try to distinguish between regression of the ego or the instincts we can see that, in the camps, it was primarily a reduction of instincts caused by the experiences, alongside a continuous struggle between the ego and the super-ego for control. In a state of continuous physical exhaustion, reduced to the most primitive biological demands, it is no longer possible to speak of regression of the instincts. Polish physicians, former concentration camp prisoners themselves, described this as hunger disease. It started with a slow down of all bodily functions, proceeded with obsessive thoughts of eating and the collection of nourishment and, as a last stage before death from hunger, to the status of a 'Muselmann' (a person removed from this world). The Muselmann was the symbol of a constant threat to life due to the desire for food. In the camp jargon a person was described as a Muselmann when he or she had reached a state of total physical exhaustion and final psychic prostration (Ryn and Klodzinski, 1983). Any activity that he or she was still able to carry on, was subservient to hunger. The ego-functions were subordinated to the need to eat. The Muselmann was the symbol of a desperate struggle against hunger, with an almost complete loss of the control of instincts and the abandonment of all super-ego demands. This status could only lead to death. It was an expression of mental death. It led finally to a state of apathy, often linked to hallucinations, in which people died unnoticed. The dividing line between life and death had already been crossed before (Ryn and Klodzinski, 1983).

Concepts such as pleasure and gratification are designations not created for the inferno, but for life. This demonstrates clearly how few things can be explained by our analytical vocabulary. The experience described here by Mr X illustrates this:

> In his camp, he had to use a tin bowl and a tin spoon to eat the watery lunch soup which he had to share with a completely strange man. He found this extremely disgusting, not only because the soup stank horribly (it had been cooked with rotten turnips) but also because his partner's nose ran all the time and everything dripped into the 'soup'. He had to force himself to eat, otherwise he could not have survived the severe physical strain. Any 'oral satisfaction' was impossible. Eating was a result of an ego-function in connection with reality testing: 'I have to force myself to eat, otherwise I shall die'.

The average survival time of a prisoner in Auschwitz-Birkenau who had not been consigned to the gas chamber on arrival at the camp, amounted to between three and six months. All those who survived this inferno longer were able to obtain additional food, clothing and sometimes even medication. Where this was impossible, as happened in most cases, death was certain, from selection for the gas chamber, disease or hunger.

Under these conditions, the sense of self was subject to an important change. Survival energies had to be shifted to other structures, such as ego-functions and super-ego. Instinct gratification was impossible. Where the super-ego was able to function positively, self-esteem was possible. Mr X again provides an example:

> A fellow prisoner stole a tin of sardines for him and let him have it, with the order to eat it alone. He shared it with his friends. Everyone had just a tiny piece, there could be no instinct gratification, but everyone was happy. He was the happiest of all, because he was able to share and produce a human atmosphere of solidarity with his friends, which was necessary for survival. It was the moral triumph over the enemy which strengthened him, not instinct gratification. He himself felt strengthened and immediately less alone because of the care of another. Affection by another enabled a person to re-establish his self-esteem for a short period.

To be able to retain the control of instinctive wishes under conditions of terrible threats and privation, ego-functions and super-ego had to function more strongly than other personality structures. This demanded being able to adapt to the continuously wilful changing conditions of camp life and to bear the stress of dammed-up instincts. This continuous tension, linked with fear of death, made up the 'stress' which these people often had to endure for long periods.

Grubrich-Simitis (1979), as well as other authors, describes the Muselmann stage as a state of loss of self, as a reflex existence. Reports by former inmates about others who had succumbed to this state or who had themselves suffered this state, but not to its end, demonstrate clearly how all psychic functions were subordinated to a single purpose. The only aim was to obtain nourishment, irrespective of the price, even at the expense of death. Everything was directed to this aim. At first sight this state seems to describe a victory of the pleasure principle over death, but in reality it was the total opposite. Reality-testing only existed as far as the obtaining of nourishment was concerned and no longer functioned otherwise. Moral considerations no longer played any role.

The Focus on Survival

Former prisoners complained of the feeling of a loss of time in the camp. In the incalculable, wilful, but rigidly bureaucratically organised, world of death, they were only able to perceive a small section of camp life. They existed in a microcosm that extended a feeling of unreality and denial and destroyed the feeling for time and chronological processes. Mr X remembers that:

In the camp there were installations and events which I never saw. When I marched out with my group in the morning, I saw nothing, except the backs of those marching before me and those beside me. We were like animals in a herd, with blinkers on, and we trotted, sharply driven on, to our work site.

During camp imprisonment Mr X was able to keep all his senses at peak attention, allowing him to recognise dangers quickly and to react. He also needed to organise his energies most effectively and not to waste surplus energy, in order to allow him to survive the day. Awareness was limited to what was most needed. During his life after liberation, he suffered from this everlasting tension. Relaxation was nearly impossible for him. French reports (Heftler, 1979) on former concentration camp inmates describe the frequent alcohol and tranquilliser abuse carried out by ex-inmates in order to relax.

There were key positions in the prisoner hierarchy which permitted knowledge of all significant camp events, almost all the inmates, new transports and about changes in the SS hierarchy. These positions, for example those in the 'Sonderkommando' (special group), were the more dangerous, because to a certain extent the occupants became an accessory and a witness and this could lead to death. Members of the Sonderkommando in Auschwitz, witnesses to daily murder, were sent to the gas chambers regularly. Too much knowledge meant certain death and prisoners who survived learnt when not to see and when not to hear.

The Aftermath

After the war the prisoners returned from a world of death to 'normality', to a life no longer determined by destruction and mass murder.

At first they entertained the hope of finding an unchanged world, but they found that they were no longer the same. All their attitudes had shifted and the world was no longer the same either. Only after liberation were they able to appreciate the extent of the destruction of their world, their families, their villages and towns. That awareness itself was a new trauma. Where they were able to establish new families or partly to re-establish their old ones, the dead had no place. Those who had come back from the camps initially wanted to report, to bear witness and to save the dead from oblivion. Instead they came to find that nobody wanted to hear of these horrors. They did not find any willing listeners and felt outsiders all the more, on their own with their memories of the inferno.

Children were born and for a short while the narcissistic structure was re-established. The survivors were a triumph over destruction, but this apparent return to normality did not last very long. It was accompanied by massive fears and conflicts that expressed themselves often in the above-mentioned conscious feelings of guilt, depressive feelings, aggressive tensions and nightmares. To be a concentration camp survivor led to a feeling of invulnerability in 'normal' life. What worse could happen?

The activating of the ego and the upkeep of ego-control, which was so essential in the camp, was retained after liberation and became an intolerable load. Survivors lived with a feeling that the 'normality' could turn into a horrific inferno at any time. Every loss of control was accompanied by fear. Death, 'the Master from Germany', seemed still to rule the life of the survivors. Identity was altered. Compulsive behaviour and rigid controls, which were enforced in the camp from 'outside', were afterwards experienced as internal control. This served primarily for the control of unconscious aggression. The retention of this internal control extended the feeling of intolerable tension, which impaired the enjoyment of life. Rage and the death wish often led to suicide. We know of the suicides of Jean Amery, Primo Levi, Tadeusz Borowski and Paul Celan. We know very little of the reasons for these suicides and there has been a good deal of speculation. The fear of being helplessly subjected to death produces the fantasy of being able to control and determine it. Bruno Bettelheim chose suicide so as not to have to wait for death helplessly.

Many authors report hypermnesias. These assaulting memories act like sudden discharges of emotion that disturb the relationship to reality in the manner of hallucinations. Their appearance has an aggressive character, like the world from which they surface. They cause bewilderment, the feeling of living in another world in which all relationships are abnormal. By increasing fear they seem to interrupt the perception of the present. These memories are similar to sudden discharges of aggression, overwhelming the ego and therefore causing trauma again. They differ from ordinary memories, which are always present and can be called up at will, because suddenly, unpredictably and uncontrollably, they are flooded with hitherto repressed emotion. In the camp, the repression of emotion was of enormous importance. The acknowledgement, internally and externally, of fear, aggression and sadness served to weaken the ego-functions and to blur perceptions. As in depersonalisation there was a withdrawal of object cathexis, to avoid being overwhelmed by the emotions. Only in a protected situation, such as in a dream, were emotions possible. It is our assumption that the withdrawn cathectic energy had passed to the perception of the external world, in which the ego quasi tried to gain hold, which had in turn a life-retaining function.

In the years after liberation, many former camp inmates felt invulnerable to 'normal' threats, such as illness. They had survived the camps, now nothing worse could happen to them. Death was only imaginable as a result of force, by murder. It is interesting to note how much this idea was perpetuated even in the next generation. Children experienced parents who had survived all the horrors as invulnerable, almost immortal. As the parents aged, they had to face the fact that they were just as subject to ageing, death and disease as anyone else. The son of two survivors of Auschwitz, who became psychotic after his mother's death, told his therapist in an interview which took place years after the mother's death, that he was sure that his mother had survived beyond death. This fantasy was also the content of his delusional ideas. He spent his time carrying on calculations about the 'survival' after death.

At the age of 20, Jorge Semprun was arrested by the Nazis and imprisoned in Buchenwald camp. In his newest book (1994) *L'Ecriture ou la Vie*, he describes his experience of liberation and how his life after the end of imprisonment developed. He was unable to escape from his memories and the smell of the crematoria, although he was able to distance death by writing: 'Death was an experience, the memory of which fades' (p.257). Then he describes his feelings when he heard of Primo Levi's suicide. Levi was five years older than he. 'Death was again in his future, on future's horizon,' he wrote (p.257). The experience of death and the experience of the camp were one and the same thing. As he grew older, so the anxieties, the feelings of being threatened and of despair, returned. Fear of death is a real anxiety in old age, just as it was in the camp. The old trauma resurfaces as former prisoners experience threats to their psychological equilibrium.

Working with Victims

The psychotherapist who works with former concentration camp inmates has to cope with his or her own anxieties. The three concepts already discussed can serve to protect the analyst. The most human reactions, like the thought: 'Let's hope I don't get caught' or, retrospectively: 'Luckily, it wasn't me who got caught' are in opposition to the analyst's moral principles. In the '*univers concentrationnaire*', this wish implied the death of another, since the Nazis were committed to killing numbers and who made up the numbers was of no account. For the patients it is extremely painful to confront the strength of their own wishes for survival. This process is linked with strong feelings of guilt. By confronting patients with their powerful survival wishes, the analyst seems to cause the patient fresh suffering. This role of pursuer or protagonist is a feature of many treatments; it happens in many transference constellations which are common to almost all patients. But in working with former prisoners, taking on this role constitutes an assault on the therapist's self-image, involving a struggle with feelings of guilt and retaliation anxieties. It is not enough to regard these patients as victims, deserving of our sympathy. The task of analysis is not just about protection and consolation; it is based on the search for truth and knowledge. The analyst must therefore grasp the enormity of the ongoing struggle of former prisoners against almost overwhelming grief, rage and anxiety, and it is this which causes the impact upon self-image.

The understandable wish of the therapist to spare our patients' feelings and to console and comfort them is often linked with our own rescue and reparation fantasies. Analyst and patients are hindered in perceiving unimaginable grief. Our only hopes are time and repression, but these are only able to heal the wounds of the perpetrators. Victims are unable to forget, even if they wish to do so.

The uncovering of repressed conflict between the wish for survival and the super-ego is painful, but can lead to an unburdening. It is the way to find a rebuilding of self-esteem which may be expressed in the wish to bear witness, to speak for the dead.

The question must be asked: why did reactions of grief not arise in the camps? Grief is caused by a withdrawal of the emotional connection to a lost object. As we have noted, such a process inevitably took place in an extermination camp. It did not take place slowly and individually, but abruptly, in a shocking and massive way. A great deal of emotional energy and ego flexibility was required to retain one's sense of self. Instinct had to be controlled under the most difficult conditions and reality-testing had to be sharpened. This needed to be achieved against all previous experiences, ideas and fantasies. When had people ever been gassed in death factories? Internal instinct pressures, hunger, external dangers and death had to be coped with by ego and super-ego. For grief reactions to occur additional strength, which was not available, would have been needed. The state of continuous physical exhaustion reduced all reactions to a minimum that was life-saving. After liberation all energies had to be directed to the making of new relationships and the control of anxiety and aggression. Again there was no additional strength available for grief reactions.

The defences used during the period of persecution could become a hindrance in the treatment of former camp prisoners. Where the ego threatens to collapse under the attack of emotion, depersonalisation and emotional denial will be necessary, even in the protection of the treatment room.

Grief was a luxury, that one could afford only under relatively secure conditions. During the period of imprisonment, it could not find its ritualised framework. Afterwards nothing was as it had been before. Mass murder does not leave memorials behind. Everything was destroyed. No photos and no graveyards remain. There are memorials to destruction that demonstrate the dimensions of mass murder, but no memory of individuals. But grief needs the security of memory, so as to allow the proper withdrawal of relationships from lost objects. In a grave and through burial the object is retained and preserved.

Mass burial, a lake of ashes, gas chambers and mountains of shoes, combs, spectacles, suitcases, false teeth – all these were left. But the dimensions of an industrially organised mass murder remain inconceivable.

Only one thing is sure: that no beloved dead can be remembered in such locations of horror as they would be in a grave. What is left is only memory, without any real resolution. So as not to lose the dead entirely, the memory must be retained under all circumstances. Thus destruction will always remain conscious:

> Ms A, who survived as a small girl, hidden in Poland, lost not only her parents, but also her beloved grandfather. She remembers him, but no longer knows what he was called. Of her family, no one survived from whom she could ask his name and there is no place where she could mourn for him. She does not even know where he was murdered. This namelessness is an expression of the unimaginable extent of the destruction which destroys every fantasy of undoing it.

Does there exist any consolation for this extent of destruction? Is it not human to remain speechless?

Our attempts at explanation must remain limited. A collective experience, a collective trauma is heard and felt by us as analysts through the account of the individual. Memories describe a world of destruction, of horror and of fear that was never imaginable before. It is questionable whether the individual processing of the trauma can take place with the uniformity of the killing of millions. With our scientific theories, we fail to comprehend a world that was created to exterminate all human life, all human feeling.

In treatment, analysts should take care, because of their own need for compensation and hopes for undoing, not to use the same defences as the victims. In the treatment of former persecutees, there is a need to comfort and an injury to our self-esteem because of our inability to do so, which may turn into hindrances. With the children of the persecutees, it is the fear of vengeance, of the wish for retribution and of the sexual and aggressive fantasies which the analyst has to reject in order to cope with heightened levels of emotion (Brainin, Ligeti and Teicher, 1993). For the analyst, the individuality of the patient, which the latter wants to be understood, must always remain in the foreground. Where the patient is primarily a victim, persecutee or descendant of a victim, the analyst can too easily place him or her in a category. But to do this is little different from the denial of individuality and the lack of differentiation of bureaucratic mass murder.

The reality of these people was so pathological that it can scarcely be understood and comprehended. Our psychoanalytical vocabulary is not adequate. The psychoanalytical theory of trauma was developed before Auschwitz and must be reappraised in the light of this experience. In achieving this, idealisation and mythology can only hinder us. In countries such as Austria and Germany, the former persecutees and their children form a subculture without any real societal recognition. Their cultural reference framework is not only different from that of the majority, it is in contradiction to it. To be able to do justice to these people in their individuality, we analysts and everybody else who is working with former concentration camp inmates must comprehend this other world and what it meant and what it did.

References

Amery, J. (1966) 'Ressentiment.' In *Jenseits von Schuld und Sühne*. München: Klett-Cotta Verlag.

Baeyer, W.V., Häfner, H. and Kisker, K.P. (1964) *Psychiatrie der Verfolgten*. Berlin, Göttingen, Heidelberg: Springer Verlag.

Bettelheim, B. (1964) *Aufstand gegen die Masse. Die Chance des Individuums in der modernen Gesellschaft*. München: Kindler Verlag, 1980. (The Informed Heart, Autonomy in a Mass Age. The Free Press of Glencoe).

Brainin, E., Ligeti, V. and Teicher, S. (1993) *Von Gedanken zur Tat. Zur Psychoanalyse des Antisemitismus*. Frankfurt am Main: Brandse und Apsel Verlag.

Fenichel, O. (1983) *Psychoanalytische Neurosenlehre*, Bd.I, Ffm, Berlin, Wien: Ullstein Verlag.

Freud, A. (1936) *Das Ich und die Abwehrmechanismen*. Wien: Internationaler Psychoanalytischer Verlag.

Grubrich-Simitis, I. (1979) 'Extremtraumatisierung als kumulatives Trauma.' In *Psyche 33*, 991–1023.

Heftler, N. (1979) *Etude sur l'Etat actuiel, Psycho-sociologique, des Enfants nes apres le Retour de Deportation de leurs Parents*. Paris: Centre de Recherche et d'Etude des Dysfunctions de l'Adaptation (CREDA).

Hoppe, K.D. (1964) 'Verfolgung und Gewissen.' In *Psyche 18*, 305–313.

Jacobson, E. (1949) 'Observations on the psychological effect of imprisonment on female political prisoners.' In K.R. Eissler (ed) *Searchlights on Delinquency*. New York: International Universities Press.

Krystal, H. (ed) (1968) *Massive Psychic Trauma*. New York: International Universities Press.

Levi, P. (1986) *Die Untergegangenen und die Geretteten*. München: Hanser (1990 edition). English version (1988), *The Drowned and the Saved*. London: Michael Joseph.

Müller, F. (1979) *Sonderbehandlung. Drei Jahre in den Krematorien und Gaskammern von Auschwitz*. München: Verlag Steinhausen.

Niederland, W.G. (1965) 'Psychische Spätschäden nach politischer Verfolgung.' In *Psyche 18*, 888–895.

Niederland, W.G. (1980) *Folgen der Verfolgung*. Frankfurt: Suhrkamp.

Ryn, Z. and St. Klodzinski (1983) 'An den Grenzen zwischen Leben und Tod. Eine Studie über die Erscheinung des "Muselmanns" im Konzentrationslager.' In *Die Auschwitz-Hefte* (1987), Hrsg. vom Hamburger Institut für Sozialforschung. Weinheim.

Semprun, J. (1994) *L'Ecriture ou la Vie*. Paris: Editions Gallimard.

Further Reading

Brainin, E. (1986) 'Le syndrome des camps de concentration et ses consequences sur la generation suivante.' In R. Thalmann (ed) *Femmes et Fascismes.* Paris: Editions Tierce.

Cohen, E.A. (1953) *Human Behaviour in the Concentration Camp.* London: Free Association Books.

De Wind, E. (1968) 'Begegnung mit dem Tod.' *Psyche 22*, 423–441.

Eissler, K.R. (1963) 'Die Ermordung von wie vielen seiner Kinder muß ein Mensch symptomfrei ertragen können, um eine normale Konstitution zu haben?' In *Psyche 17*, 241–291.

Eissler, K.R. (1967) 'Pervertierte Psychiatrie?' In *Psyche 21*, 553–575.

Freud, S. (1915) *Zeitgemässes über Krieg und Tod.* GW X. 323–355.

Freud, S. (1917) *Trauer und Melancholie.* GW X. 427–446.

Freud, S. (1919) *Einleitung zur Psychoanalyse der Kriegsneurosen.* GW XII. 321–324.

Freud, S. (1920) *Jenseits des Lustprinzips.* GW XIII. 1–69.

Freud, S. (1933) *Warum Krieg?* GW XVI. 11–27.

Hoppe, K.D. (1965) 'Psychotherapie bei Konzentrationslageropfern.' In *Psyche 19*, 290–319.

Langbein, H. (1972) *Menschen in Auschwitz.* Wien: Europa Verlag.

Teicher, S. (1979) *Die Beurteilung jüdischer KZ-Verfolgter und ihrer Kinder in Hinblick auf ihre spätere Integration.* Diplomarbeit Hamburg.

CHAPTER 7

Late Onset of Symptoms in Holocaust Survivors

David J. de Levita

Mrs Q, 77 years old, consulted me because of a severe depression. She was sleeping badly, felt depressed and kept seeing before her eyes a constant film of events that had taken place during the war. She was a stout lady, very determined and controlled, in whom one could straightaway recognise the head nurse of a hospital ward. As a young nurse she was involved in one of the grimmest pages in Dutch history during the war: the deportation of the inmates of a Jewish psychiatric hospital. She decided at the time not to abandon her patients, and accompanied them, along with her sister who was also a nurse. She was to go subsequently to three German concentration camps, which she survived. Her parents and sisters had survived as well, but now they were all dead. She had no relatives left. She had worked as a nurse after the war, but in 1970 was dismissed from her job due to back trouble. In 1982 she had married, a marriage that lasted ten years. She divorced because she could not live without complete independence.

Talking of the connection between her depression and her war trauma she said: 'It's not because of what has happened to me, it's because of what has happened'.

The Late Onset of Trauma Symptoms

It is well known that the symptoms of trauma may start shortly after the traumatic event has taken place, but that their onset may also be delayed for many years after. This certainly is true for Holocaust survivors. The phenomenon has been extensively studied in Israel, where many survivors went after the war. Assael and Givon (1984, p.35) state: '...often the "breakdown" is acute and progressive after a "successful" career, "stable" economic status and good integration in society'. In the present chapter, some comments on the mechanisms underlying the late onset of symptoms in the elderly will be made. The concept of 'diachronic trauma' will, for that purpose, be developed and introduced with reference to the parents of mentally handicapped children.

The Concept of Diachronic Trauma

Counsellors involved with parents of mentally handicapped children are well aware that the sorrow phenomenon occurring in such cases is not limited to the shock experienced on the first discovery. When mental retardation is visible from the start, the shock will coincide with the child's birth. If not, the retardation becomes apparent when the child fails a significant developmental phase, expected by the parents. One meets with complex mixtures of knowing and not knowing; in fact, many parents feel from the very beginning that something is wrong with their child but have been eased into forgetfulness by doctors or relatives. A counsellor can successfully discuss with the parents their anger provoked by the disappointing child and other such feelings, but must avoid demanding from the parents that by receiving counselling they should overcome their grief and thus be cured. As long as the handicapped child lives, there is no cure for their grief. The child's handicap will in the course of time constantly assume new shapes. When other children start walking, their child does not; when other children go to school, their child cannot, and this goes on and on. The parents are up against a long sequence of disappointments.

From my personal clinical experience as a counsellor of this particular group of parents, I remember as one of their striking reactions that they accepted certain inabilities in their child, arising from the mental handicap, but sometimes did not accept new manifestations of this same handicap. One couple, for instance, was reconciled to the slow, defective speech and general mental retardation of their child, but actually believed all along that these phenomena would disappear before it would be time to go to elementary school. They had not at all considered the eventuality of sending their child to a special school. The old belief that the sorrow of having a handicapped child is a chronic sorrow (Olshansky, 1962) takes on a new significance when we realise that the chronicity is built upon a series of identifications, all of them traumatic. A suitable terminology for such a series of traumatic identifications seems to me to be 'diachronic trauma'. Parents of non-handicapped babies may experience a feeling of self-esteem or a certain sense of value that involves fantasies such as taking their child out for a walk and attracting the attention and admiration of passers-by. Such fantasies are important for maintaining a sound feeling of identity. They are strictly personal and of a very complex nature. They emerge from a cultural as well as religious inheritance and have their roots in early childhood memories, such as rivalry with one's own siblings.

Parents of handicapped babies have to go without these forms of narcissistic gratification. They suffer the inabilities of their children and develop feelings of shame and guilt. They can become seriously frustrated and traumatised. The same phenomenon is repeated when the child becomes a toddler, and goes on throughout the various phases of development. The onset of puberty and adolescence in the handicapped child proves to be a particularly traumatic episode, causing acute problems to the parents. This is due to the fact that they compare their situation with parents of non-handicapped adolescents (the role those parents play and the contact they have with their children, the satisfaction of seeing them develop into successful human beings having their place in society, etc.) whereas their own child's puberty is not a success. Adolescence is bound to be a failure because young people with a mental handicap often lack the required social abilities to establish normal contact with their peers and thus they remain dependent on their parents. At each stage of parenting a handicapped child, the parents feel new gaps in their own self-esteem and are traumatised anew.

It is by no means a novel idea that new identifications emerging from someone's life history developing into a new identity may cause traumas. The idea goes back to Freud in his development of the concept of 'Nachträglichkeit'. In its simplest form this is the phenomenon that a very young child who has been a victim of sexual assault does not at the time understand what has happened. Only later, when he/she becomes aware of the meaning of sexuality, is there an understanding of its significance. The memory then becomes traumatic; it is, so to speak, a 'retrospective trauma'. The translation of the term Nachträglichkeit into English has aroused much controversy. The Standard Edition of Freud's works was translated into English and edited by the Stracheys, with the aim of establishing a consistent form of words in English which would cover most of Freud's terminology and become the accepted English name for the theoretical concepts. They took Freud's 1895 explanation of Nachträglichkeit as (p.356), '...a memory which becomes a trauma only after the event' and represented it as, 'has only become a trauma by deferred action' (Thomä and Cheshire, 1991). The use of 'deferred action' has been criticised by some later authors as a departure from Freud's words. Thomä and Cheshire (1991), in their discussion on this subject, make the point that the translater may understand what the author initially meant better than the author and this can be evident in translation. Our present view is that a very young child can be severely traumatised by an event, although at the time he or she is only dimly aware of the event's significance. When eventually words are found to describe what has happened, the outrage and anger are much stronger than was the case in the unformed reactions of the child at the time. Diachronic trauma, thus viewed, is not a new trauma, but a traumatic reaction from an earlier date which at long last finds words to express itself – words which can convey the impact of something not previously experienced in this way.

To give another example, it has been described how a woman giving birth to a child may feel persecuted by the conflict of now identifying with her own mother, who neglected her as a baby (Halberstadt-Freud, 1993, p.408):

> When Mrs X is referred for analysis, she is 37 years old and has a 4-month-old boy. She looks very worried and run down. To her great dismay, her whole life changed after the birth of her unplanned baby. It turns out that she never wanted children. Although she and her partner have lived together for over 20 years (they never married), she seldom gave motherhood a thought. She realizes only now that her mother always warned her and advised her against becoming a mother, telling her how unpleasant and depressing the experience had been. She was the first child of an unhappy, depressed mother who felt overburdened by having to look after her baby and her dying stepmother simultaneously.
>
> Mrs X delayed pregnancy as long as she could, but at the moment of becoming a mother, identified with her own mother who had experienced her birth as a misfortune. An unbearable conflict took place between the fear that she was going to hate her baby, as her mother had done, and her illusions about the baby which, in her fantasies, was going to love her, complete and repair her in every respect. This resulted in a severe postpartum depression.

This example of a trauma by identification seemed appropriate as an introduction to the concept of diachronic trauma as it can be observed to operate in the life of Holocaust survivors. Many of these were young when the persecutions started and still had a whole life before them at the time of liberation. I will focus here on a particular group – young married couples who, optimistic with their regained freedom, decided to have children. These children, as adults, have sometimes been referred for treatment and found to suffer severe psychopathology. We can now deduce that their parents' decision to have a child at that specific moment led to a traumatic situation. At the time of liberation, the general mood was of cheerfulness; the enemy was beaten and the idea of having children in itself carried a symbolic meaning of the victorious thought that the Jewish people had not been completely exterminated. Those who remained set out to repair the inflicted losses. One can, however, hardly call this a joyful thought and we can understand, I think, that this group, by becoming parents, could not escape identifying with the large number of parents who had been helpless to protect their children in the war, had had to separate from them and never saw them again. The new parents, together with the joy of having a child, had to carry the burden of immense pain for which they now had words and feelings, originating from their own recent experiences as parents. An example:

> Mrs C came to consult me for the first time in 1989. She was a Jewish lady, then 40 years of age, and suffered from a severe depression, which she herself related to the war experiences of her parents. She had suicidal fantasies, an obsessional propensity for cleaning and terrible nightmares. She was an over-concerned mother of two young sons whom she never let out of her sight.

> Mrs C's parents had both survived the Nazi persecution by hiding in a non-Jewish family. Her father had lost nearly his whole family, only a paternal aunt surviving. On her mother's side, a few more members were saved.

> Her father had lost the chain of textile shops he had established by hard work before the war. After liberation, he set to work again and rebuilt it successfully. However, he suffered severe depressive periods, and a few times had to be admitted to hospital for treatment of psychotic symptoms. Mrs C's mother was a paranoid woman, always bossing her husband around and criticising him for his lack of feelings for her. The patient's father had always sought comfort with Mrs C, who was proud of their relationship and what she meant to him. This aroused her mother's jealousy and thus made her childhood very unhappy. The mother refused her virtually everything: she had to wear old-fashioned clothes in which she felt utterly ridiculous and was not permitted to further her education in a good secondary school, although she had the ability. Her teacher visited her parents in order to plead her cause, but in vain. The father was unable to counter the mother's constant aggression, being too depressed to interfere.

> Mrs C's parents had rejected the idea of another pregnancy. However, they felt that their son, born just before the war and having survived as well, needed a companion. They tried unsuccessfully to adopt two young cousins who had lost their parents in the war. Then, four years after the war ended, Mrs C was born. Immediately afterwards, Mrs C's father entered a psychotic phase and had to be hospitalised. He suffered from nightmares in which he saw long rows of children entering gas chambers in Auschwitz, where he believed himself to be present.

> In Mrs C's pathology, the wish to make up for her parents' lost objects played a central role. She accepted the aggression of her mother and gave her father comfort. The Oedipal constellation was strong but could be taken up in the transference. Mrs C was not aware of her own Oedipal

guilt feelings, the way she annoyed her mother by becoming the apple of her father's eye.

The father himself, Mr C, was put under my care because Mrs C found his attendance at a day centre insufficient. He was depressed but led an independent life, ignoring as best he could his ever-nagging wife. When, however, his physical condition deteriorated and the task of nursing him at home became too burdensome, he was admitted to a nursing home for the elderly. At first he was in high spirits, enjoying his rest and the presence of companions with whom he could play bridge, but after a few days he became depressed and entered a psychotic state. Again he had delusions of being in a concentration camp and was heard to exclaim, '*Nein, mein Herr, ich bin zurückgestellt!*' ('no Sir, I have an exemption'). Attempts to get him out of his psychosis by means of medication took some time, and only then could I discuss with him what had happened. He had no recollection of his emotions but was vaguely aware of a feeling of great misunderstanding. When I reminded him of the sentence he had shouted in German, he suddenly remembered feeling that the SS wanted to kill him, although he had made it very clear to them that he belonged to the group of survivors. We concluded that his central problem was his refusal to admit that in the end none of us survives. Certain associations he made between the nursing home and the concentration camp were explained and dealt with. And, finally, an immense difference in interpretation was established: that in this home he would not be murdered but could live his last days as he intended. His efforts to avoid acceptance of himself as an old man in the final stage of his life and to resist this new identity were part of his triumph of having survived persecution and now this triumph was being shattered with the imminence of death. Coming to terms with his feelings made Mr C more calm and his nightmares disappeared. He died a week later.

The ageing process in Holocaust survivors has been the subject of many studies. Some of these have dealt with the biosocial aspects of ageing. Assael and Givon (1984, p.35) studied Holocaust survivors who came to Israel and who, according to Winnik (1967), '…showed a relatively painless social and vocational adjustment. Often the breakdown is acute and progressive after a successful career, stable economic status and good integration in society'. In this study of 72 patients who were over 60 and hospitalised in an Israeli psychiatric institution, the Holocaust survivors differed from a control group of newcomers by their poorer prospects of total remission. In the Netherlands this was confirmed by Kuilman and Suttorp (1989) in a study of 100 Second World War survivors. In the US, Honigman-Cooper (1979) found more vulnerability in elderly survivors to, 'the stresses that go hand in hand with the process of aging' (quotation from Aarts *et al.*, 1996, p.56). These authors mention as well the case histories of elderly people for whom psychotherapy turned out to be very efficient. Aarts *et al.*. (1996, p.55) demonstrate that senescence is errone- ously considered a stage of the life cycle in which, '...each individual's mental and physical resilience to cope adequately with former and present experiences and emotions diminishes gradually'. By quoting much pertinent research and literature, they refute the idea that the elderly suffer more psychiatric disorders than other age groups, that their coping capacities deteriorate as a consequence of old age and that they are more vulnerable to trauma. They also illustrate the fact that there is no proof that the late onset of post-traumatic disorder is due to retirement, children leaving the parental home, the death of relatives or friends, physical illness or hospitalisation. These normal life events get their traumatic significance only from a prior disruption of the psychic integrity of the patient.

Here we are faced with a seeming contradiction in the findings of two different disciplines. In reported cases of psychotherapy with elderly people (Coltart, 1991; King, 1980; Sandler, 1984), retirement, for instance, is found to be a major source of distress and trauma, as are the other events which Aarts *et al.* could not prove from psychological research to be traumatic. This is not surprising because from a psychoanalytical point of view, retirement is not a cause in itself but a new enactment of an old conflict, of which the patient may have no conscious awareness.

From my own experience with ageing Holocaust survivors, chiefly in observing the benefits that psychotherapy may have for them, I am inclined to agree with the views of Aarts *et al.* that later and late psychopathology in the elderly is not a consequence of negative aspects of old age, but of post-traumatic character disturbance. This perspective shows a recognition that among elderly people the same conflicts that have persisted over the years now show themselves in new ways; the problem for elderly people lies in their projection of these long-standing conflicts onto their being old. In her 1991 paper, Coltart describes how in her patient of nearly 70 years the pain of retirement, that is the feeling of not being useful any more, gradually gave way to the enjoyment of spare time and freedom, but as a result of the clearing up of deep sources of depression which had spoilt the life of this patient long before he entered his last stage of life. The message is that with reasonably healthy people one can discuss in a personal way the disadvantages and advantages of old age, but that in the depressed and, even more so in the severely depressed, such an approach will be productive only if the hidden source of the depression is successfully identified by the therapist. This may only be possible with a small number of the people with whom one is working, but the number is greater than is often assumed by those who are giving care to the elderly.

It is of course impossible to illustrate from a few observations the complicated totality of life-cycle vicissitudes in Holocaust survivors and their offspring. However, I should like to point out a certain determinant factor visible in the process, namely the connection between the Oedipal constellation in the childhood of this group and the role of guilt in the survivor's development of identity, throughout its various stages.

The Oedipus complex, being the central pathogenic factor in neurosis, includes the concept of survivor guilt. In the fantasy of killing the rival parent it is not only the fear of retaliation that makes the child ambivalent about achieving success and hampers the feeling of triumph in this battle. It is also the deep love he/she devotes to this parent and the idea of missing him/her that brings forward a feeling of unhappiness. As is well known, this conflict is solved, or at least alleviated, by identification. When a boy (to choose an example) is like his father, it becomes simultaneously impossible and unnecessary to dispose of him. It is the best kind of survivorship one can imagine, to have the other whom one has survived in fantasy, inside oneself.

During the Holocaust the development of babies or very young children took place under great stress, for the parents, traumatised by the persecutions, were already unable to satisfy the psychic needs of their children. Mothers will have impressed upon their children their depressive moods. In order to cope with this intrusion the children will have resorted to hysterical mechanisms which are, in Khan's (1974, p.155) words, '...the technique to remain blank as if absent from oneself, with symptoms which are substitutes permitting the camouflage of this absence'. At this point, the tendency towards hysterical identifications sets in. Consequently, the Oedipal development of these children will reflect the tensions inflicted upon them at the time.

The second generation of Holocaust survivors will suffer even greater malformations in their Oedipal structures. As children, many of them had fantasies about reunification with their parents when they were in a camp (or other exceptional circumstances). Their feeling of exclusion from their parents' intimacy is here extended to a whole period in history, to a world that has been destroyed, never to return. Some parents kept the memory alive by a never-ending talk of this old world. They assigned their children roles in it, such as keeping a dead relative's memory alive, roles they could never fulfil. Mrs C was to keep her grandparents' memory alive by living up to their old-fashioned, now totally inappropriate, educational principles. From the second generation's behaviour we can discern how much survivor guilt was transmitted to them by their parents.

When confronted with the problem of survivor guilt, especially in acute cases, we must bear in mind that the context is of the destruction of a whole world. The survivor suffered not only the loss of his or her beloved ones, or the beloved ones of parents, but all that existed before the Holocaust. The immensity of these losses would have been insurmountable but for the less well known factor of survival triumph, which is the silent pride one takes in having survived. As Nietzsche (1930, p.265) wrote in *Die Fröhliche Wissenschaft:* '*Der Sieger glaubt nie an den Zufall*' (the victor never believes in luck). So thought the survivors in their fantasy, that it was after all their surviving capacity that had made them survive.

During the life cycle, guilt and triumph are in balance, a balance sometimes maintained by transmitting parts of the conflict to one's children. Mrs C was very much affected by the guilt feelings her father had transmitted to her. During her therapy, she obtained a good position as a management consultant but was unable to send her clients a bill. A discussion of this issue, taken from the perspective of guilt feelings, was ineffective. This only changed when I spoke about her triumph over me and my worthless interpretations; her father's feelings of triumph, transmitted to her, for having survived his 'stupid sisters'. In reality, the father had never made such remarks about his dead sisters being stupid, but he was highly critical of his other sister who had survived: he disregarded everything she did. This attitude was most striking coming from a friendly man who, indeed, never criticised anyone, unlike his wife who was forever degrading people. My interpretation was at last effective and Mrs C started to improve in handling the commercial side of her work. And, as a most remarkable follow-up, the father stopped his derogatory attitude towards his sister, without one word having been spoken about it in the family.

The diachronic trauma, illustrated here by a young post-war mother traumatised by her identification with the mothers whose children were killed in the Holocaust, involves identifications Freud would have called hysterical. In *The Interpretation of Dreams* he writes (1900, p.149):

> What is the meaning of hysterical identification? It requires a somewhat lengthy explanation. Identification is a highly important factor in the mechanism of hysterical symptoms. It enables patients to express in their symptoms not only their own experiences but those of a large number of other people; it enables them, as it were, to suffer on behalf of a whole crowd of people and to act all the parts in a play single-handed.

Survivor guilt and triumph find, in the diachronic trauma, at the same time both their denial and their expression.

From this perspective, traumatised people, upon entering old age, are confronted with two different pathogenical impacts. First, under the influence of impending death, their feeling of triumph vanishes. The balance between guilt and triumph cannot be maintained. Second, the identification with dead people becomes more prominent. But in this there is a lot of in-built aggression: this identification is not made with people who have completed their life cycle, who have departed in peace, but with people who have been murdered. This leads to much anxiety, discord and bizarre symptoms.

Mrs Q, whose history was briefly mentioned at the beginning of this chapter, had to keep up her position as a nurse who cared for her patient and was overwhelmed by the patient's misery. This is very illustrative of what I mean by diachronic trauma. She found all kinds of pretexts for not seeing me at home, where I practise. I was to come to her (which I did) and was then given a treat. Her struggle against the oppressing awareness that she was now the patient (a poor, lonely old woman with hardly anyone to care for her), involved several bizarre rituals in our relationship. She asked for anti-depressants but showed me later that she had never touched the pills. I then had to praise her and tell her that in fact she did not really need them. But, as I was told by her maid, she had actually copied the prescription and obtained another set of pills from her neighbour who had the same prescription from her doctor.

As I have said earlier, the reality of this patient's life as an old, lonely woman, for many things dependent on others, was by no means a misfortune that befell her in old age alone; all her life she had suppressed whatever longings she had had for love and care. As the clinical vignette may illustrate, her defences and adaptations were rather bizarre and brittle, and no effort was made to do away with them. On the contrary, I tried to reinforce them, waiting for a sign that she herself had become aware of her inability to receive instead of to give. It should be emphasised that psychotherapy with the elderly is liable to the same restrictions as psychotherapy at other ages, and professional enthusiasm for complete success must be recognised as a reaction against prevailing beliefs that there is an age-limit for psychotherapy.

Of central importance in the psychotherapy of the elderly is attention for their narcissistic frustrations and satisfactions. Giving them credit for what they achieve – even if this means only for what they are able to tolerate – can enhance the effectiveness of what we as therapists try to convey to them and form a good introduction to going more deeply into their problems. In the words of Sadavoy and Molyn (quoted in Cath, 1990, p.143): '...the needs for affirming, mirroring and soothing functions of the self-object are as great as, if not greater than, at any other time'.

In what way did we fail to offer to Mrs Q the help she needed, when she came back from the nightmare of her deportation?

An important issue of help has hitherto remained unmentioned. As a child psychiatrist 50 years after the liberation, I ask myself in amazement why a link was not found with a principle that had been common knowledge in child psychiatry long before: that a child, staying in a bad family which is detrimental to his or her development, cannot be helped by psychotherapy, but should first be provided with the loving care of a good foster family. If necessary, psychotherapy could later help the child to adapt to living in the foster family and to whatever other problems may arise from integrating the new life. Psychotherapy can never serve any other purpose than to help somebody to make better use of what is available to him or her; it cannot supply what is lacking. It can help you, so to speak, to prepare your food and make it taste better, but it cannot replace your food if you do not have any.

It has been the main failure of the professional helpers of Holocaust survivors directly after the war that they did not take heed of this. They failed to recognise that at the time the survivors resembled children who depended on the outside world to have their world that had been destroyed compensated for and, to some extent, restored. One must, however, bear in mind that the problems were measureless, that the helpers themselves were often in no better condition, that governments had other things to worry about in the light of having to govern totally disrupted countries. It took many years before this all changed, and it was as late as the 1980s that in some countries efforts started to offer homely facilities to survivors, as described elsewhere in this book (see Chapters 8 and 9). In the Netherlands, too, this work came fully into being only in the 1980s; meeting centres for survivors were created, discussion groups with and without experts were started. We had, in the meantime, learned something about the nature of loss and especially about the losses of survivors from the Holocaust: that it was not only the loss of their own family members that counted, the loss of their relatives and so many people dear to them, but that the individual feelings contained much that could not be expressed in therapies. The utter senselessness of it all was so painful and their feelings were still those of enforced living in a destroyed world. The neighbours, the shopkeepers, places that had been known and had changed, but also the disappearance of someone's personal possessions such as books and toys turned out to be deeply felt losses. At the same time, however, these losses could not be mentioned to anybody in the shadow of the still open graves of millions of people. In the course of time, we nevertheless found that many survivors whose parents and other family members had been saved were in no better health than others who had lost everything. Even parents and siblings could not make up for the total annihilation of the lost culture.

We learned another lesson: providing facilities for contact and the creation of communities on the one hand, and psychotherapeutically helping people to make proper use of them on the other, are not contradictory, but supplementary, activities. No expert can work without a deeper feeling of care and warmth for his client, and neither can a provider work without knowledge and expertise.

For Mrs Q the facilities came too late. As a young girl, having survived the horrors of an extermination camp, she found her whole world gone and nobody and nothing in its place. She struggled lifelong to make up for it, as a nurse helping to alleviate people's sufferings, and in so doing was symbolically indicating what she herself most needed but did not get. She was not aware that she was doing this. Her inclination to turn passive wishes into active deeds became second nature to her. It ruined her marriage – because in marriage both parties are alternatively helpers and helped. Even now, she cannot really yield to a helper, but must keep up a stiff upper lip while taking her medicine. It is impressive how she is able to keep up this strength in old age. It has also another meaning: by her behaviour Mrs Q is giving herself the credit that was lacking during her life, the credit for what she had been achieving, never asking anything for herself but all the time trying to help others.

Helping Elderly Survivors

As has been stated above, giving somebody the credit he or she has never obtained before is one of the powerful tools we have in treating elderly survivors for their psychopathology. This can directly be observed when one enters a Jewish old people's home: among the residents there is sometimes a hierarchy according to their war experiences. Who has gone through the worst ordeal gets most respect. Once there is a relationship with the therapist, his or her admiration of how the client survived though enduring terrible things, may be of great value.

Of course there are many other functions a therapist can fulfil for an aged client. One of these consists of representing reality to the client, hoping that he or she will be healthy enough to adapt to it once convinced. I remember a man of 75 who visited me because of a depression that had developed because he was unable any longer to be the director of his big paper firm. I was lucky enough to convince him that, at his age, being a director of a big firm was driving things a little bit too far, and why could he not take up a somewhat lighter job, if he still felt the need to work? Four weeks later he sent me a postcard from Africa. He had applied for a minor job in another paper firm, turned out to be the best papyrus connoisseur they had in their service and had been sent abroad at once. The depression had gone. Nowadays in old people's homes, there are social workers in charge who can see ways in which people can maintain a level of activity, albeit one that is less than when they were younger. As a psychiatrist one meets many older survivors who all their life have struggled to remain independent and who now cannot cope with a reduced level of function. A sensitively handled referral to social work facilities may be helpful as a means of accessing appropriate and meaningful alternative activities.

A particular activity one can sometimes successfully undertake is the resolution of conflicts between clients and their children which have led to the children no longer visiting their aged parent(s). Many so-called 'second generation problems' may block contact between these clients and their offspring. Some of these may be resolved in a meeting of client, child(ren) and therapist.

The main work with older survivors has been in discussing with them what happened in previous stages of life. In this respect they are no different from any other client one sees. Old problems come to the fore and the therapist can clarify how their faulty resolution has influenced the following stages of life, notably the present stage. Contrary to what is generally believed, this work can be very rewarding. Of course, old people have no long-term future and they no longer have the feeling that for them there is eternal life, like young people have. But for older people the remaining time is precious, and often they spare no pains to have repaired whatever is possible.

References

Aarts, P.G.A., Op den Velde, W., Falger, P.R.J., Hovens, J.E., DeGroen, J.H.M. and Van Duijn, H. (1996) 'Late onset of Post-Traumatic Stress Disorder in aging resistance veterans in The Netherlands.' In P. Ruskin and J. Talbot (eds) *Aging and Posttraumatic Stress Disorder.* Washington DC:American Psychiatric Press Inc.

Assael, M. and Givon, M. (1984) 'The aging process in Holocaust survivors in Israel.' American Journal of Social Psychiatry IV, 1, 32–37.

Cath, S.H. (1990) Review of Sadavoy and Molyn (1987) 'Treating the elderly with psychotherapy: the scope for change in later life.' Psychoanalytic Quarterly 143–147.

Coltart, N. (1991) 'The analysis of an elderly patient.' International Journal of Psycho-Analysis 72, 209–220.

Freud, S. (1895) Project for a Scientific Psychology. Standard Edition I, 281–398. London: Hogarth Press.

Freud, S. (1900) The Interpretation of Dreams. Standard Edition IV, 149. London: Hogarth Press.

Halberstadt-Freud, H.C. (1993) 'Postpartum depression and symbiotic illusion.' Psychoanalytic Psychology 10, 3, 407–423.

Honigman-Cooper, R. (1979) 'Concentration camp survivors, a challenge for geriatric nursing.' Nursing Clinics of North America 14, 4, 621–628.

Khan, M.R. (1974) 'La rancune de l'hystérique.' Nouvelle Revuede Psychanalyse 10, 151–158.

King, P. (1980) 'The life cycle as indicated by the nature of the transference in the psychoanalysis of the middle-aged and elderly.' International Journal of Psycho-Analysis 1, 153–161.

Kuilman, M. and Suttorp, O. (1989) Late onset post-traumatic spectrum disorders in survivors of Nazi-terror: a retrospective study of 100 patients. Unpublished paper.

Nietzsche, F. (1930) 'Die fröhliche Wissenschaft.' In F. Nietzsche, Werke, Alfred. Kroner Verlag. *Leipzig 1,* 245–287, 265.

Olshansky, S. (1962) 'Chronic sorrow: a response to having a mentally defective child.' Social Casework 43, 190–194.

Sandler, A. (1984) 'Problems of development and adaptation in an elderly patient.' Psycho-Analytical Study of the Child 39, 471–493.

Thomä, H. and Cheshire, N. (1991) 'Nachträglichkeit and deferred action.' International Review of Psychoanalysis 18, 407–429.

Winnik, H.Z. (1967) 'Further comments concerning problems of late psychological effects of Nazi persecution and their therapy.' *Israel Annals of Psychiatry* 1–16.

Further Reading

Erens-Hofman, N. (1995) Ver Verleden Dichtbij (Remote Past Coming Near). Thesis, Catholic University Nijmegen, the Netherlands.

CHAPTER 8

Café 84

A Social Day Care Centre for Survivors and their Children

Hedi Fried

Dan was born in Poland in 1927. He survives the Holocaust in Russia and arrives in Sweden in 1949. He builds up a nice business for himself, marries, has a son and feels completely adapted to Swedish life. His first visit to the centre is in 1987, when his wife dies. He is 60 years old. He is desolate and threatens suicide. He does not want to join the activities of the centre, but accepts the invitation to join a smaller group of people, who all have recently lost their partners. During these meetings his need for individual crisis therapy becomes more and more urgent and slowly he agrees to see me in individual sessions. He also feels abandoned by his son and this increases his suicidal urge. The son married a gentile girl who is now pregnant and Dan feels that his son does not care for him any longer. Not even the prospect of a grandchild gives him solace, as he cannot accept a gentile baby. His own feelings in connection with the loss of his parents come up, and for the first time he talks about his experiences during the Holocaust. After 12 sessions the crisis therapy is concluded and Dan joins the Friday activities. One year later he is a proud grandfather, with a normal relationship with his son and a new relationship with a woman.

Dan is only one of those who survived the Holocaust and, given a chance for a second start, was hoping to forget all about the past. Once again it turned out that a person cannot get rid of past traumas. You can repress these for a while, but they will surface more and more as time goes by.

The writer of this chapter is also a survivor, born in Romania and transported to Auschwitz from Hungary in May 1944. After the liberation of Bergen-Belsen on 15 April 1945 she arrived in Sweden, together with 10,000 other sick people, with the help of a Swedish rescue organisation called the White Buses. After two months' convalescence she started to work and after a career of household, factory and office work, she married. With three small children she started her studies in psychology at Stockholm University, interrupted by the death of her husband in 1962. During the following 15 years she developed a small business in medical supplies. Thereafter she took up her studies, receiving an MA and the authorisation to work as a psychologist.

Café 84

The majority of survivors who arrived and stayed in Sweden started working immediately. Most of them achieved good careers and started families. While starting their new lives, people decided to forget the past and banish all the bad memories from their consciousness. However, the memories kept haunting them at night, often resulting in poor sleep and nightmares. As time passed, with people getting older and children leaving home, the memories became stronger and at times debilitating. Increasingly survivors complained of depression, anxiety, alienation and psychosomatic ailments, and became more and more disabled. In the early 1980s, the social workers of the Jewish community realised that something had to be done to help these people. As social workers in Sweden are not authorised psychologists, the writer was engaged to develop activities to this end. In 1984, she became the Director of the newly founded social day care centre called Café 84. The opening of Café 84 brought relief to a large number of suffering people.

After having worked some years with the survivors, it became obvious that communication between parents and their by now middle-aged children was often very poor. Most parents had kept silent about their camp experiences and some, in their endeavour to shelter the children, had even said little about their Jewishness. It emerged that parents who had invested so much in their children were very disappointed by what they experienced as ungratefulness and lack of love. This prompted the work with the second generation (2G) and the 'Dialogue' that started in October 1990.

Concept and Structure

The concept behind Café 84 is to offer survivors a meeting place in a warm and accepting atmosphere, a forum that gives the possibility of opening up a dialogue (see Figure 8.1). The survivors would be allowed to go at their own pace: they could talk or not talk about their experiences, while the psychologist would take an existential approach, pursuing the here-and-now and adopting a wait-and-see policy. During the daily meetings, with the psychologist present between 2.00 and 5.00 p.m., coffee, tea and cakes are served, while newspapers in Yiddish, Polish, Hungarian and Swedish are available. These meetings, though not directly therapeutic, permit members to reveal themselves and to choose the moments they are ready to talk. In addition, a rolling programme of daily activities is offered. The programme works therapeutically, although no classical psychotherapy technique is used, and the week looks like this:

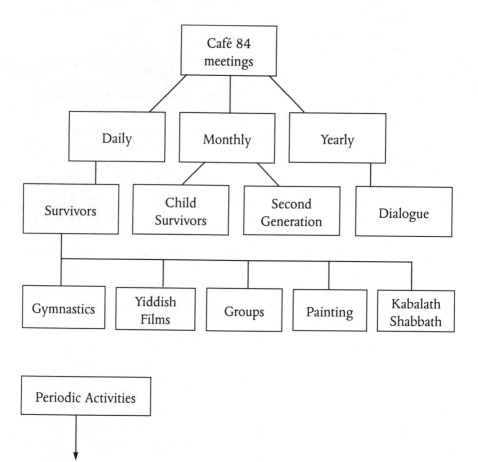

Going to the movies, theatres
Birthday celebrations
Celebration of holidays
Ourim, Chanukkah
Big yearly party
Twice yearly excursions
Summer camp

Figure 8.1. Café 84: a centre for survivors and their children

Monday: physical education is given by a Russian immigrant with knowledge of yoga-gymnastics. This is very much appreciated and is beneficial for the aches and pains of elderly bodies.

Tuesday: films with a Jewish content are shown, often in Yiddish.

Wednesday: group discussions are held, with the possibility of raising questions about problems, feelings and current events.

Thursday: painting sessions are available under the guidance of an artist.

Friday: there is Kabbalath Shabbath every Friday, with the lighting of candles, Kiddush, blessing over Challa and refreshments. Entertainment is provided by different artists or speakers. As this centre is the only place in Stockholm that offers Kabbalath Shabbath for those who have no family, this is the most appreciated part of the programme. Attendance amounts to between 60 and 70 people.

Further events include the members' birthday celebrations whenever these occur; the celebration of holidays, such as Chanukah and Purim; a big yearly party to celebrate the anniversary of the centre; cinema and theatre visits; excursions twice yearly by bus and/or boat; and ten days' stay each summer at the Jewish summer camp of Glämsta.

The psychologist also offers the opportunity for individual discussions, of which people often take advantage. However, the need for individual therapy normally surfaces in connection with acute traumas. Personal problems are not usually ready to be worked through until a new loss occurs to one of the group members. At that point, crisis therapy is provided.

The goal of the existential approach is to promote courage and to help members accept life as it is. Traumas of this magnitude cannot be healed, they can only be learned to be lived with. The role of the psychologist is to encourage people to share their memories and to contain the surfacing emotions. During this process the psychologist has been given the role of the 'good mother', while the assistant has been identified with the bad object, thus establishing a balance that suits members. Positive camp experiences re-emerge; the members establish bonds and take care of one another.

One of the lessons the psychologist has learned over the years is that elderly survivors are very reluctant to accept psychological help. People who have been on their own during the greatest difficulties of their lives feel that they must also manage the memories. However, with patience and skill it is possible to help them open up. With the help of a book, a painting or a piece of music, it is possible to start a discussion about 'what memories does this bring to you?; how does this apply to your experiences?'. Very often the people enjoy talking about their pre-war memories. After using this method for a while, it seems easier to go into the camp experiences as well. It is important that the psychologist is open and empathic and feels the way along the thoughts of survivors. The psychologist should never press for answers. The survivor should feel that he or she is in control.

The importance of giving testimony has been widely discussed. With the passing of the years, more and more people have come to the point of telling. However, there is a big difference between older and younger survivors. Child survivors are more prone to tell about their experiences, they are also better educated and have a better command of the language. It has also been noted that giving testimony also serves to give some relief to the person, as some of the case studies will confirm.

All survivors who visit the centre automatically become members. In the initial phase, attendance was free, but members expressed their wish to pay a membership fee: SwCr 100 a year (about £8). At the start the only paid member of staff was the psychologist, and survivors provided voluntary help. One of the male survivors took the responsibility for opening and closing the centre, making the coffee and welcoming members. Others volunteered for other chores. It slowly emerged that these activities gave their lives another meaning. The other members noticed improvements in their mood, their sleep and even in their health. This has been confirmed by their children, who observed less dependence in their parents. The survivors often stated that the centre was their second home – some even said that it was their real home.

Café 84 members consist of retired male and female survivors, heterogeneous regarding both Holocaust experiences and countries of origin. This is not just a self-help model. As Café 84 is led by a professional psychologist who herself is a survivor, trained to facilitate groups and to carry out individual psychotherapy, she is able to help members with their ongoing struggles and to intervene in crisis situations. The programme provides members with the opportunity to scrutinise their own past and come to terms with it. Participation in the centre also allows members to compare with each other their relationships with their offspring and thus gain an understanding of how to improve their interactions.

On the emotional level, the activities of Café 84 provide an environment that is conducive to members coming to terms with survivor guilt. The Holocaust also becomes a somewhat less overwhelming trauma. It becomes a part of their personal history which they can now share with others with greater ease. This was evidenced when a group of 30 survivors who attend Café 84 were asked if they agreed with the idea that the second generation of victims should start meeting the second generation of the perpetrators. Twenty-five answered yes, three said no, two did not reply. In comparison, a group of 15 other survivors who do not attend Café 84 were asked the same question. This group unanimously answered no. They did not even want to discuss this topic and stated that it was too early to start thinking of reconciliation. To their mind, any communication between offspring of perpetrators and offspring of victims will have to wait for four or five generations to pass. For Holocaust survivors who do not have an opportunity of ongoing support for their traumatic past and losses, that part of themselves is still personally overwhelming. Certainly the thought of resolving issues with outsiders is outside the realm of possibility.

The following case studies show the importance of establishing this type of survivor support:

> Sam was born in Romania in 1931. As the only survivor of his family, he was liberated from the concentration camps at the age of 14. He is taken to Sweden and immediately hospitalised with TB. After several years in sanatoria he settles down in Stockholm, living alone. He has no relatives whatsoever, and his only contact with the outside world is a social worker involved with the Jewish community. Although he wants to get married, he does not succeed in finding a relationship with a woman. He feels persecuted because of being Jewish and gets more and more depressed. The social worker tries to convince him that he needs therapy, but to no avail. He does not want to see a psychologist or go into hospital. He is one of the clients that makes the Jewish community understand that they need a psychologist and, as a result, Café 84 is started.

> Sam takes part in the activities of the centre from the first day of its opening and from that time on becomes a daily visitor. It is the first time he feels that he belongs, and after a few days he declares that it is the only place he forgets about his loneliness. He is the first one to arrive and the last one to leave and he complains about the centre being closed on Saturdays, Sundays and holidays. During the year of 1986, Christmas Eve and New Year's Eve fall on a Tuesday and Twelfth Night on a Friday. This means, for Sweden, five days' public holiday for Christmas, five days for New Year and three days for Twelfth Night. Accordingly, the centre is closed during that time. This is too much for Sam and weeks in advance he complains that he will not survive all those days being all alone. It is not the first time that he uses these words and we work with these feelings in therapy sessions. At the beginning of the Christmas week he is taken ill and is brought into the hospital. He has had a minor heart attack, but he is discharged after Christmas. However, the thought of spending another five days alone precipitates another attack and once again he is taken to the hospital. He does not recover and dies a few weeks later.

> Ruth was born in 1920 to a big family in a small town in Czechoslovakia. She marries in 1944 in the ghetto, survives Auschwitz and Bergen-Belsen and is brought to Sweden after the liberation. She has TB and goes

through several operations. After recovery she settles down in Stockholm, keeping in close contact with the Jewish community. She has no relatives, has never worked and lives on social assistance, although she receives German retribution money that she saves, piling up a fortune. The social worker in the Jewish community notes her continuous complaints regarding her health, complaints that get more and more paranoid: 'The neighbour enters her flat, he takes her belongings, he lets gas into her bedroom'.

Ruth is also one of the first members of Café 84. She arrives on the first Friday to our Shabbath celebrations. She is reluctant, very suspicious and knows nobody else but the social worker who brings her there. When the meeting comes to its end, she talks animatedly in Yiddish and sings happily along with the others. She comes only on Fridays, but stays on after the others have left to thank the psychologist for this opportunity, as she says, 'to get away from her gas chamber'. She goes on talking and complaining, and slowly agrees to come to the centre on weekdays too, so that her problems can be worked on. Proper therapy cannot start as she is not capable of a dialogue. She goes on with continuous monologues about her sufferings. She pretends that even in the camps she was better off, because there everybody shared the same suffering. Her paranoia increases. In the hope that medication can help she is taken to a doctor, but she will not take any pills. To break her isolation it is suggested that she moves into sheltered housing, which she does not accept.

She has no insight. Her headaches are caused by the gas that the neighbour lets in. Items she cannot find have been taken by him. The radio or the refrigerator that does not work have been destroyed by the same neighbour. Her home looks like a rubbish heap. Around a worn-out sofa and a table with two chairs, there are rows of cardboard boxes and plastic bags neatly tied together, piled up along the walls up to the ceiling. When she leaves her house, she takes her most important belongings, her money and bank book, her jewellery and so on. in a shopping bag on wheels, surrounded by plastic bags tied together with string. She looks a real bag-lady. When seen in Café 84, she gives a completely different impression. She forgets all about her ailments, looks serene and happy, and repeats on and on her satisfaction about being able to frequent this place. When her peers try to persuade her to leave the shopping bag at home she does not answer, but later complains that they cannot understand the necessity for it. She adds that she feels humiliated by having to carry these bags and by not being able to dress properly (the neighbour tears her dresses).

From time to time she calls the police to help her with this evil neighbour, resulting in the police taking her into hospital. There she calms down, but will not stay and everything starts anew. She asks for help but the only help she can think of is the removal of the neighbour. She is offered a new flat, which is not accepted because, 'mine is much better. I want to keep my flat, the neighbour has to move'. By 1991 both her physical and mental health have deteriorated. She gets more and more confused and has different ailments. A physical check-up diagnoses a minor heart disorder, but nothing serious is found. One day she falls in the street and she is taken to the hospital with a broken arm. The doctor who takes care of her notes her confusion and sends her to a mental hospital. The procedures at admission with all her belongings being taken away remind her of her arrival at Auschwitz and she fights her way out of the hospital. However, her heart condition gets worse and once again she is hospitalised. She protests, saying, 'this is exactly as it was in the concentration camp, I do not want to be there again'. After some persuasion from a nurse speaking Czech, which is also Ruth's native language, she accepts the single room offered to her and stays until she gets discharged. When she next visits the centre, she seems completely normal and none of her peers notices her confusion. Outside Café 84 she has difficulty in containing her anxiety and she is confused in her conversations. Time passes but she cannot be persuaded to see a doctor. I try to persuade her to take the formerly prescribed tranquillisers but her answer is, 'pills are poison'. She lives more and more in the past and her notion of time becomes blurred, but she continues to frequent Café 84. I see her regularly on Fridays, when she stays on, and she talks about her childhood, bringing up memories she has never mentioned before. One Friday in March 1992 she promises to come on Monday to continue our conversation, but she does not show up. The following Friday she is absent and there is no answer to the phone. When I call social services I find that Ruth had been found dead the day before by the young woman who used to help her out.

In conclusion, these case studies show that therapy, in its classical form, is not always appropriate for survivors. The therapeutic setting of Café 84 led by a psychologist, with the peer support present, alleviates the pressure and can slowly pave the way for work with memories. We can see how much strength survivors get from the unorthodox methods used. Once again the feeling of family togetherness emerges, the peers taking the place of the lost siblings and the leader that of the mother. It also shows that no healing is possible but that survivors can learn to live with their traumas. The model of Café 84 can also help prevent retraumatisation because the staff are more observant; they work in the environment of the survivor and have a better understanding of their reactions. If the doctor admitting Ruth to the hospital had known about her background, it might have been less traumatic. If the hospital had kept Sam for the whole period of the Christmas holidays he might have lived, and in this case it can be said that the psychologist, too, shares some of the responsibility, for not having arranged for Sam to spend the holiday with a family.

The case of Dan, mentioned at the beginning of this chapter, shows that the threat of suicide is somewhat easier to deal with within this setting. The psychologist can appraise the seriousness of it by knowing more about the survivor. There are experiences that are impossible to live with when there is retraumatisation; suicide seems to be the only solution, for example the case of a person who worked in the crematoria or a mother who had to watch her child being smashed into a wall.

Child Survivors

The participants of Café 84 were all adults at the onset of the Second World War and today they are all retired. Those who survived as children, born between 1930 and 1945, are still active and thus meet only once a month. This is a group that accepts therapy more easily, and the aim of the group meetings is to allow them to start talking about their so far untold experiences and to have these acknowledged and documented.

Second Generation Group

This is an open support group, meeting once a month from 1.30–6.00 p.m. The first part of the meeting is a lecture on Jewish culture and religion given by a professional, while the second part is the group meeting itself. Out of the initial 30 people there are still ten who continue to attend after four years. The process has been very slow. Many individuals have attended regularly for several years, without volunteering to talk. For this group, too, the approach is existential and the role of the therapist is mainly encouraging and containing. The aim of the group is to reconcile, to accept the parents as they are, to strengthen their newly discovered Jewish identity, and to transform the lessons of the Holocaust into creativity.

The 'Dialogue'

This is a yearly seminar for survivors, the first generation, and children of survivors, the second generation. It aims to break the silence, to bring parents and children closer to each other, to enable them to talk and to increase their understanding of each other. The ultimate goal is to enable parents to talk openly to their own children.

The set-up is somewhat different each year and again the work is very slow. At the first seminar (in 1990) the first generation had difficulty accepting the existence of a problem. They could not acknowledge a possibility of transgenerational effects of the Holocaust. During the second meeting, in 1991, the pain of the second generation was acknowledged and, in 1992, people were ready to start working on their emotions. Today the 'Dialogue' is an intensive, therapeutic group led by the writer, who belongs to the first generation, and another therapist, Judith Beerman-Zeligson, from the second generation. The work with Café 84 and the child survivors on the one hand, and the second generation group on the other, provides continuity between the yearly seminars. The group consists of 40 men and women, half of them belonging to the first generation and the other half to the second generation. The age range for the first generation is 60 to 70, while the second generation are mostly middle-aged adults with their own children. Some participants may have had an earlier experience of the 'Dialogue', some have not.

There follows now a description of the 'Dialogue' that took place in October 1993:

The seminar took place over a weekend. The aim of the first day was to meet for a social gathering, listen to music and poems, have coffee and prepare mentally for the second day.

On Sunday morning the programme started by the random division of the group in half, with ten first generation and ten second generation in each. The two groups were in separate rooms and led by the two psychologists. A presentation followed, where the parents introduced themselves with the name and characteristics of their child, while the children gave the name and characteristics of one of their parents. This put everybody into the middle of the problem, without having to formulate it explicitly. After the introduction the central themes were noted on the blackboard, to constitute the basis of the afternoon work.

The themes that surfaced were:

- exaggerated love
- the feeling of never having been acknowledged
- parents who take up too much space
- fear of emotions
- fear of causing pain
- difficulties in understanding the pain of each other
- lack of respect
- exaggerated sense of responsibility

- ° over-protection
- ° food as a central issue
- ° guilt feelings
- ° fear of a new Holocaust
- ° identity problem.

Next, in order to get closer to each other's fate, the following sociometric exercise was given to the entire group of 40:

The members were asked to sit on chairs in a circle. People belonging to the first generation who were in Auschwitz and those of the second generation whose parent was in Auschwitz were asked to step into the circle and look at each other. Next, people who were in other specified camps and those who had lived in hiding were asked separately to do the same thing. Finally, those of the first generation who had discussed their experiences with their young children were asked to join those who, during their youth, had been told of their parents' experiences. In this instance, only five people entered the circle. This confirms again what Helen Epstein (1988) calls 'the conspiracy of silence'.

After this exercise the two sub-groups once again gathered in separate rooms, with the instruction to ask each other questions they would want to ask their own parent/child. These questions centred round the themes that had surfaced early in the morning. Some of the dialogues are quoted here:

Second generation: 'Why can't you see me as I am, why do you want to change me?'

First generation: 'I only want the best for you and it hurts to see that you waste your talents'

First generation: 'Why do you push me away, why am I not allowed to help you in your household?'

Second generation: 'I cannot depend on you all my life, I want to take my own responsibility'

Second generation: 'Why did I never get any Jewish education?'

First generation: 'I wanted to protect you so that you would never get into the same predicament as I did for being a Jew'

The post-seminar evaluations showed that deep processes surfaced among several of the attendees, processes which developed and reached resolution during this intensive day.

Ron, a middle-aged married man, did not really belong to the second generation. He signed up for the seminar with the explanation that, as a child, he lived very close to Holocaust survivors and was very interested both personally and professionally in the problem of the second generation. Initially he was not accepted but then, because of a late cancellation, he was allowed to attend. In the morning he had apparent difficulty in presenting himself in the role of his stepmother. The words came slowly, with long silences in between: 'I am not a real mother, I am a stepmother. My name is Rivka Steiner. I was born in Poland and taken to Auschwitz where I was a Capo. After the war I came to Sweden and married the widower, Johan Benson, who needed a wife and a mother for his children'. He stopped abruptly, saying this might be enough.

Ron was very silent during the day, and late in the afternoon stammered a very poorly formulated question of the following content: 'Is it usual for the first generation to hit their children?'. He tried to pose a neutral question but evidently this was very personal, because he burst into tears and could not continue. Crying more and more vehemently, he forced himself, between the bouts of sobbing, to talk about the stepmother who battered him throughout his childhood. He said that all his life he thought that he was exposed to 'stepmother behaviour' and had never thought of himself as belonging to the second generation. Slowly the story of the seven-year-old Ron took shape. He lost his mother during the birth of his sister and was then confronted with the woman his father married later. Authoritative and demanding, she insisted that he take care of his baby sister. He was hit with a leather strap for the least offence. She hit him while abusing him, calling out, 'this you shall have because of the child the Germans killed, because I had to marry your father, this for all the beatings I have had'. In vain he turned to his father for protection, yet the father was in turn forced by the woman to hit his children. The group got very involved. Both generations were trying to support Ron with comments such as: 'You should never forgive her', 'You must hate your father', 'Maybe she would not have hit you if you had been her own child', 'It must have been her experience in camp that made her behave in this way'.

After he calmed down, Ron continued to say that he had never spoken about these experiences, not even with his family. Not before the role-playing in this seminar did it occur to him that what happened during his childhood was a second generation problem.

Ron's comment at the end of the day was that he now felt strong enough to tell his family about his childhood. The next day I found out over the phone that indeed this had happened and, although exhausted, Ron felt good. He was relieved and he felt better than ever.

Anna, a child survivor born in Hungary, signed up together with her son, Lars, aged 30. They were placed in different groups and the process they went through was presented by Anna during the evaluation. Lars approached his mother during the coffee break with the question: 'Why did you never tell us about your experiences?'. 'Why did you never ask?' was the reply. 'Because father had strongly forbidden such questions.' Anna got very upset by this initiative of the father, as she had taken the absence of questions as a lack of interest. Now she prompted all first generation present to talk to their children and not wait for questions. She herself confirmed her promise to her son to tell all she remembers. She observed that although the children know a lot about the Holocaust, they must become aware of the history of their own family.

The 'Dialogue' has proved a very effective short, intensive therapy for both generations. With a small input it seems possible to reach important goals. Fifty years ago, when the gates of the concentration camps opened, there was no knowledge about crisis intervention. Today we know how important it is to work through deep trauma. As it turned out, keeping silent did not heal the wounds. On the contrary, the wounds only deepened, causing pain not only to those who were directly injured, but also to their offspring. According to research, the transgenerational transmission will continue to future generations if the silence is maintained. The second generation, which fights with the shadows of the past, needs to receive help to work through their Holocaust issues so they can become whole persons and thereby produce a healthy generation.

What Scaturo and Hayman (1992) wrote about multi-generational family therapy for Vietnam veterans is valid also for the 'Dialogue':

> ...such discussions would be the opportunity for the grown up children to know and understand their parents as real people with traumas and stresses in their lives which make them capable of errors, rather than being viewed only as the internalized misrepresentations of childhood perceptions and idealizations. For the parents, the opportunity to be known, understood and forgiven in this way may provide a much needed corrective emotional experience.

Projects for Café 84

The writer sees a great future for this type of social day care centre. However, more staff and more space are necessary to pursue the above-mentioned programme. Due to financial shortages, only one psychologist is regularly involved. As soon as more staff can be appointed, the possibilities for individual treatments will increase. Increased space is also required for this. Plans are afoot to find money enough to build a Survivors' Home where people can live and spend their remaining years together. Survivors feel understood only by each other, and the older they are the more important it is for them to stay together.

Summary

Café 84 started out as a rehabilitation centre for aged and lonely survivors and has grown into a social day care centre with several offshoots:

1. Café 84 proper, with recurrent daily programmes.

2. Group meetings of child survivors.

3. Group meetings of the second generation.

4. Dialogue between the first and second generations.

All these programmes have turned out to be very important and beneficial for their members. The model could easily be applied in other countries.

References

Scaturo, D. and Hayman, P. (1992) 'The impact of combat trauma across the family life cycle.' *Journal of Traumatic Stress 5*, 2, 273–287.

Epstein, H. (1988) *Children of the Holocaust: Conversations with Sons and Daughters of Survivors.* New York: Penguin.

CHAPTER 9

From Victim To Survivor

The Possibility of Healing in Ageing Survivors of the Nazi Holocaust

Judith Hassan

Rachel is a widow in her early sixties. As a child of ten years she saw her parents being arrested by the Gestapo, from the vantage point of a cupboard in which her mother had hidden her. She never saw her parents again. They were murdered in Auschwitz. Friends of the family placed her in a convent in which she was hidden until the end of the war. She was fed, but was otherwise left alone in a cold cellar. The point of referral to myself was her feeling of helplessness as she watched her own daughter slowly killing herself – she is a drug addict. The vulnerability she felt reactivated her own experiences as a child in the Holocaust when she had been powerless as a victim of Nazi oppression.

I first met Rachel informally in the self-help group she attended. She therefore did not find it difficult to come and see me professionally, as she was familiar with the setting and knew others who were in counselling with me. Rachel had to decide whether she wished to return to the trauma of her past to deal with the present. We used her creative ability in art and writing, as well as talking. The first year of weekly meetings was offering a nurturing experience which she lacked because of her extreme deprivation as a child. I worked on her strengths and coping mechanisms which had enabled her to survive until now. The second year focused on the unfinished mourning related to her family – with no gravestones, they had never really been buried.

She decided to erect a memorial stone for her family, and a rabbi colleague of mine said the ritual prayers at the cemetery. Rachel said this was the moment of her 'liberation', not when she was set free from the convent. Throughout this mourning period of nine months, I supported Rachel both practically and emotionally. She was then able to move on from the past to the present and look towards her future. Though the emotional scars remain we try to ensure that the patterns of the past do not have to repeat themselves in the present. She was still able to do something for her family, and the powerlessness was converted into more constructive efforts to make a life for herself in which she was no longer the victim.

This survivor had carried the burden of her past around with her for over 46 years. As with many survivors, she found a world unwilling or unable to listen to the atrocities she had been through, and so she learned to be silent. Though the survivors themselves felt that the meaning of their survival was inextricably bound up with giving them an opportunity to tell the world what had happened so that it should never happen again, in reality, they were encouraged to forget.

Rachel, like many other survivors, coped by suppressing the traumas. She followed hedonistic principles – she wanted to have fun to make up for the missing years of her childhood. However, her marriage was brief and unsatisfying, and gave her no security. Her post-liberation experience carried its own traumas and therefore gave her no opportunity to express what she had been through. Nevertheless she managed to work and look after her daughter and make a life for herself with no outside professional help.

There has been a naive assumption on the part of many professionals that survivors had overcome their trauma, and indeed the majority of survivors were leading very successful lives. There developed what became known as a conspiracy of silence, and a wasteland developed between the survivor and the professional. This process of silence was compounded by the medical and psychoanalytical world which viewed the survivor as sick, suffering from syndromes and symptoms, the best known perhaps being Survivor Syndrome, as seen, for example, in the work of Henry Krystal (1984). According to this classification, survivors were seen as having been damaged irreparably by their experience, and this conveyed a very pessimistic view about healing. There was an emphasis on diagnosis rather than understanding the nature of extreme experience. This approach was exacerbated by the fact that compensation claims could only be made after a psychiatric assessment, which reinforced the image of the sick survivor. Needless to say, many survivors did not claim this money.

To the survivor who did ask for professional help, there was a feeling of being neither heard nor understood. Professionals were on the whole trying to fit the survivor's experience into existing theoretical and practice frameworks, and yet the fit was not quite right (see, for example, Arlene Steinberg's review of clinical literature on Holocaust survivors and their children, 1989). In my work today, we continue to see survivors who have been from therapist to therapist, yet the Holocaust experience has never been addressed. When we enter the world of the survivor, we enter a world of chaos. The camp experience, for example, was a mad world, a world in which the unimaginable happened. The abnormality and extremity of the experience is beyond the comprehension of those of us who were not there. The discomfort which this experience brought to the professional resulted in a retreat into familiar ways of working which were not meaningful to the survivor or, at worst, the Holocaust experience was totally ignored.

Not surprisingly, therefore, survivors generally were reaching old age having never been able to open up and look at the wounds which remained with them. As age increased these wounds began to fester again. It is a normal part of ageing for memory to return to earlier events and the trauma to be re-experienced. Usually there is a current trigger which brings back events from 40–50 years earlier.

Yael Danieli (1981 p.197) emphasises that, 'old age in itself is traumatic for survivors. They may experience the sense of abandonment, isolation and loneliness common among ageing people in this country [USA] as a repetition of being shunned and dehumanised during and right after the Holocaust'. Many elderly survivors I have spoken to emphasised that they have no model for ageing and growing old, as their parents were murdered by the Nazis. The old were among the first to be gassed because they had no usefulness as workers in the camps. Their dependency and vulnerability were a death knell. Consequently, retirement and redundancy may bring back memories of their dispensability. Loss of work can bring an overwhelming sense of despair and bring back a sense that the meaning has gone from life. 'And when life has no more meaning in old age, the will to meaning is lost; when life no longer seems to be worth living, some people who have experienced disasters and are unable to cope, may throw their lives away' (Wilson, Havel and Kahane 1988).

Loss of work, however, is only one possible trigger for memories to return. Loss of health, for example, could bring back a sense of vulnerability and powerlessness which in terms of a death camp experience meant extermination. Bereavement and the loss of someone close may bring back memories of massive losses of family and even entire communities. With ageing a greater number of friends and family also die, and the closeness of these people serves as a vivid reminder of the brutal murder of loved ones so many years earlier. One survivor aptly described this experience of remembering when she said that her, 'nights were invading her days'. With age, there is less control over what thoughts return to consciousness. With ageing there is more time to reflect and to re-experience the traumatic past.

However, I would like to stress at this point that just as no two elderly people are the same, so no two Holocaust survivors are the same. There were many variables which affected how they coped and adapted to the trauma –

experiences of early childhood; the age of the person when the Holocaust began; whether they were with their family or not; what happened to them during the incarceration; what happened after liberation. Seeing the survivor as an individual opens up the possibility of exploring the strengths and coping mechanisms which may be functional in the current re-experiencing of trauma. David Guttmann, a survivor as well as someone who has made it his life's work to promote the needs and understanding of older people, has emphasised that coping with negative events is directly related to the resources (internal and external) that people have at their disposal. In general, he says, the more resources are available to the older individual, the less his/her vulnerability to stress, as these resources act as a barrier to stress (Guttmann, 1994).

Knowing what these resources are within each individual survivor is the task of the therapist to discover. The Holocaust is part of the whole life history of the survivor. It is not encapsulated, but is linked inseparably with events before and after.

The ageing survivor offers the professional a 'second opportunity', as one survivor put it to me, to address the unfinished business from their traumatic past. As death approaches, the urgency of bearing witness increases. The survivor must ensure not only that what happened to them is known about, but also needs to speak for those who perished. In more general terms, this last phase of life is a time for consolidation and a preparation for letting go. If we forget, or if we are forgotten, it is as though we never existed. To remember, and to be remembered, are perhaps the two most important elements to growing old.

Where Does This Work Begin?

Just as the journey to old age follows a developmental and sequential process from childhood, through adolescence, adulthood and lastly becoming old, so our therapeutic work with survivors needs to mirror this journey. For many elderly survivors, the idea of asking for counselling for their Holocaust experiences as a first step, would be anathema. My early work with elderly refugees from Nazi persecution had taught me that most would refer themselves for practical reasons, for example, housing problems related to age, loneliness, financial or health problems. Other contributors to this volume note the same thing. Jewish Care was seen as an agency providing such resources, and hence it would be permissible to use these services. It was only when I really listened to the hidden agenda, of what had brought that person to me at that moment in time, that I could begin to address the unfinished business from their traumatic past. I increasingly realised, however, that survivors who had been in Europe during the war were not coming forward to ask for help of any kind. It seemed curious to me that, as their suffering in the camps, in hiding, as partisans in ghettos or living under false papers had been so extreme, they were not in need of professional help. That was a naive assumption on my part. I have since learned why survivors kept away from organisations such as the one in which I was working.

First, many survivors felt an animosity towards the Anglo-Jewish community for not having done enough to help them when they needed it after they arrived in this country. Second, asking for help implies weakness and vulnerability, which in terms of a death camp experience meant extermination. Third, institutions and authority were equated with Nazis in their experience, and hence it was preferable not to bring attention to oneself by turning to such an organisation.

Survivors were suffering, but could not be reached. The community was dying without being heard. My tools (social work training and experience) were mostly inadequate in reaching survivors. I sensed the need but seemed helpless in knowing how to deal with it.

Mutual Support and Self-help as Meaningful Responses to the Effects of Extreme Trauma

The turning point which was the beginning of the therapeutic journey came when an elderly survivor came to see me, not as a client but seeking my help to set up a self-help group. She knew about six survivors who wanted to come together and meet socially. They did not want counselling or therapy but to be mutually supportive. They would not need to explain why they were there. In this self-help group I became an honorary member (a non-survivor).

My usual professional role was not functional in this situation. As they shared their experiences with each other in this informal social setting, in a venue of their choice, I could hear the hidden agendas but had no authorisation to deal with them. I observed, I listened, I learned – survivors came to know me personally. Not only was I individualised to them, but I began to see each one's experience as unique. This was not a homogeneous group: they had different experiences, came from different countries and had different mother tongues. My willingness to cross the professional boundary and act as a facilitator in this group played a major part in all the subsequent work which followed. It was an experience that bears a strong resemblance to Fried's work within Café 84 (Chapter 8).

What I realised in that experience in the two years and more that I spent with these people, was how this approach was much more meaningful for the survivors (who had reached 40 in number) because the mutual support aspect of it mirrored the camp experience. Many survivors in other groups have felt themselves 'outsiders' – in this group they belonged. The non-clinical informal atmosphere in which we had refreshments together, and shared in parties, was a more acceptable environment for the therapeutic work to take place, and they felt 'normalised'.

In this group there was music, there was laughter and enjoyment. They celebrated being together, yet the Auschwitz number was clearly marked on some of their arms. What this taught me was how amid horror and adversity it was possible to sing, to share a joke, and this passed one more minute in the hell that they had been through. What worked in the past experience in the camp seemed to have relevance today. The past was acknowledged, but the focus shifted to being actively involved in the group. The survivors strengthened each other, and helped me to look for the creative side of the survivor that had helped him or her to cope.

The Holocaust Survivor Centre

Thus emerged the image of the survivor free from the victim label. The empowerment which the mutual support generated in this first self-help group laid the foundation for the philosophy of the Holocaust Survivor Centre, which was subsequently opened by Jewish Care and World Jewish Relief in London in January 1993. In this centre, survivors are not merely recipients of services, but are actually involved in its fund raising and in its public speaking programme, which includes going into schools and colleges and talking about their Holocaust experience to children; they are also involved in the user group, befriending each other and recording their testimony for posterity. This is a social centre in which the most popular events are playing cards and eating in the café. The importance of 'play', particularly for those who lost their childhood in the Holocaust, needs to be understood. It is not a second childhood in the sense often associated with the elderly in a negative way, but a new opportunity to compensate for what was lost earlier in life. It offers a foundation on which to rebuild emotional development.

These survivors celebrate the Jewish festivals together. Together they commemorate Yom Hashoah, and together they warn others where fascism leads. Their ability to enjoy themselves, to find a collective voice, to ensure their Jewish identity is continued, and to have dignity and respect, are all victories over the Nazis. For the Nazi intention was to dehumanise, degrade and ultimately annihilate the entire Jewish population. These survivors now find the strength to rebuild a community. This is an essential ingredient as they reach the last stage of their lives. As old people often experience increasing isolation and loneliness, survivors feel this even more acutely because their families were often wiped out. They would otherwise have had to face the return of horrific memories in the solitude of their own homes.

The Holocaust Survivor Centre also offers another essential component for these ageing survivors, namely an institutionalised form of memoralisation.

Their testimonies will be kept for posterity, and there will be no fear that their suffering will be forgotten. The security of knowing that their suffering will not die with them seems to help to release many survivors of the burden of returning to the past repeatedly to keep the memories alive. In the art class, for example, many elderly survivors are finding creative potential they never knew they had. However, with one exception, they do not paint images of horror or of their suffering. They produce beautiful images from nature or their imagination, and this medium forms a release and escape from the 'dark shadow' which hovers over some of their lives.

This centre is not a replica of other day centres for older people. We always have to be aware of the meaningfulness of the programme related to the survivors' experiences. They are not only actively involved in the Holocaust Survival Centre, but act as educators, and take on a political role in warning others about the rise of fascism. They dispel many of the myths related to the elderly generally, and turn on its head the idea that the old should be looked after and die quietly. Their active involvement has produced power struggles, but it is this very dynamic which makes these elderly survivors feel alive.

The Model of a Therapy Centre Adjacent to a Social Centre for Holocaust Survivors

The ego strengthening which goes on in the Holocaust Survivor Centre then allows some of these elderly survivors to seek out the services of the team in Jewish Care's therapy centre next door to the centre, namely Shalvata. The model of a therapy centre next door to a social recreational centre has developed into a concept which has been developed in other countries. My work has taken me in particular to centres in Eastern Europe. I cannot overstate the importance of allowing people who have been severely traumatised an opportunity of coming together for mutual support. For the majority of survivors, this opportunity is enough. However, to ease the transition from the centre to Shalvata, the latter had to be a place in which survivors would feel comfortable. Being part of a social work organisation meant we could provide a non-clinical atmosphere in Shalvata. The decor and facilities reflect a non-institutionalised feel. The doors which once divided the two centres are now opening up. Survivors recommend one another. I also spend time informally in the Holocaust Survivor Centre, and it is during these times that survivors get to know me and ask for help. I maintain that if I had remained sitting in my office expecting survivors to come for counselling I would still be waiting.

In Shalvata, the same approaches to working with the long-term effects of trauma apply as in the Holocaust Survivor Centre. The emphasis is on the strength of the survivor, the healthy side rather than the pathological. There is a shift in emphasis from helper and helped to a more equal relationship. The survivor is seen as the teacher, guiding the therapist along the lines which will be helpful. Some survivors wish to explore the past, some want strategies for coping with the present. Some may express their experiences using metaphor, especially child survivors whose memories of trauma may be fragmented. Survivors very quickly get a sense of who can help them, and react negatively to the notions of authority and expert. Personal information from the therapist about connections to the Holocaust may enable a survivor to feel more at ease. Robert Krell (1989, p.224), who himself is a survivor as well as a therapist, points out that, 'in the therapy with Holocaust survivors/and or their children, the therapist may be sought out for precisely those reasons that make them feel some degree of intimacy is possible'. Not only do older people sometimes feel that a younger therapist cannot possibly understand what they are going through, but older survivors feel that if you have not gone through the experience of the camps how can you understand the suffering? My answer is always that, 'I cannot possibly understand, but I would like you to teach me'.

Case Study

I would like here to introduce an example of someone I have worked with.

Mrs E came to the Jewish Welfare Board in the 1980s, originally at the point when her husband died. This was the current trigger to memories of her past trauma. She was seen by a social worker who offered her bereavement counselling and wanted to help her to mourn – this was the limitation of the tools available to her from her training. Mrs E could not make use of this counselling and terminated her contact. I then met Mrs E six years later in the self-help group for camp survivors mentioned earlier. We got to know each other informally in this group. She later asked if she could come and see me as she would like to write down what had happened to her during the Holocaust. She had never been able to tell her children what had really happened to her in Auschwitz-Birkenau, and she wanted them to know. As she was growing older, there seemed to be an urgency to record this.

We met regularly over several months, and she would talk to me about her life before the camp, during the incarceration and after liberation. She thought her English was not good enough to write it down herself, so she would speak and I would write it up for her in the first person. Her imagery was vivid and contained the essence of her experience, as this brief extract from her testimony shows:

> One day I was ordered to search through some clothing and chanced to find a diamond hidden away in a shoulder pad. Yet I could so easily discard it – it had no usefulness to me – it could not get me what I needed – the food which would sustain me. The diamond had no value in that

world. The beauty of the diamond only reflected me as I really was –
dirty and full of lice.

As well as the recording of the survivor's story, it was also the process which
was therapeutic. Mrs E was able to give something to me – she was helping me
understand the incomprehensible. My recording seemed to demonstrate the
success of her teaching. We shared the painfulness of what she recalled, and
for the first time she felt heard. As a result, Mrs E was able to go on a trip back
to Auschwitz with her daughter and a group of young people. The willingness
of this group to listen to her in the watchtower in Birkenau gave meaning to
her survival and she felt she had not survived in vain.

Mrs E's ego had been strengthened sufficiently, through the self-help group
and her informal contact with me, that this journey back could happen. It linked
the past, including her childhood, to the present. Having recorded her testimony, she was then able to move forward to her future. Mrs E now participates
in the Holocaust Survival Centre, and has produced wonderful images through
her art. She is also involved in public speaking and education programmes. She
enjoys playing cards and participating in celebrating the Jewish festivals and
anniversaries. I turn to her for advice about the centre. I tune in to her strength
and sense of justice and humanity. I owe a great debt to what she has taught
me about survivors and surviving. Her dignity conveys a much more hopeful
message to professionals than the pathological images referred to earlier in this
chapter.

To undertake these journeys with Holocaust survivors necessitated a professional adaptation to take place. This involved using a much more informal,
personal side of myself; crossing professional boundaries; addressing issues
about my own Jewish identity and issues related to the finite nature of my life;
being more accessible to survivors than just in the therapeutic hour; and
allowing for social networks to develop simultaneously with the therapy.

To accompany the survivor the therapist also needs to undertake his or her
own journey in preparation for entering the survivor's world of extreme trauma.
A personal metamorphosis needs to go on for the therapist to open up and
enter this 'world beyond metaphor'. I needed to look at my own personal
connection to the Holocaust, my mother having come to this country as a
refugee from Nazi persecution in 1939, and my grandparents being interned
in a camp in France. My initial wish to make reparation for the suffering
survivors had experienced only allowed me to see them as victims. Liberating
the survivor from this sick, pathetic victim category involved a process of
liberation for myself from the theoretical, practical and organisational constraints that were holding me back.

To be able to work constantly with traumatised people needs the infrastructure and support of a consultant as well as organisational backing. The 'feeding'

which nourished me to undertake this work could then be passed on, not only to the survivors, but also to my team who were working with me. As a team we take on the role of replacement family. In the work we undertake at Shalvata, we have art material at our disposal as well as musical instruments. This broadens the options available to us, and may allow us to reach survivors for whom the spoken word may be difficult. Choice is an essential therapeutic component working with people who were victimised. The more in control the survivor feels in the therapy, the less chance there is of repeating the victim experience. The beginning of the journey we undertake with a Holocaust survivor may include looking at a map and tracing the journey the survivor made from home to ghetto to camp.

The powerlessness and helplessness which present themselves to the therapist from the survivor can be counteracted through focusing on what can still be done and what strengths have helped the survivor to reach this stage. When a survivor asks to see me, I want to know who is this person, which journey have they been on, and which route are they currently on which has brought them to me at that moment in time? How this is put into practice can be seen through the description of the work with Rachel that began this chapter.

For other survivors, suicidal thoughts and severe depression do not release them from their traumatic past. As they grow older they feel they are living on borrowed time; their own parents were dead by the age they are now. These survivors may feel that to give up their suffering may be a form of betrayal to their families who were murdered. However, it is not always as clear-cut as that. We have to understand whether emotional problems affected them prior to the Holocaust, and also what their post-liberation experiences have been. Family issues may come into this dynamic, and we are now seeing at Shalvata an increasing number of families of survivor parent/s and their adult children. Sometimes permission is being sought from the therapist to release the survivor from haunting memories. We use all the resources available to us as a team as well as the input from the Holocaust Survivor Centre to support these survivors for whom death lurks close by. We also work closely with other professionals outside the agency. The coming together of the 'helpers' serves to give some strength to survivors who feel fragmented by their trauma.

For other ageing survivors, choosing to remember or not to remember is beyond their control. As longevity increases, there is a greater number of people suffering from Alzheimer's disease and dementia. The loss of control over what can and cannot be remembered is like a nightmare for the survivor – he or she is once again incarcerated and at the mercy of an ever-wandering mind. Is it fantasy or reality which is so haunting? This is the theme of Elie Wiesel's book *The Forgotten* (1992). In this novel, Elkanan, a Holocaust survivor, is losing his memory and needs his son Malkiel to record everything so that it will not be forgotten:

'I'll tell you everything if God lets me. Are you listening? Try to remember what I tell you because soon I won't be able to tell you anything' (p.27)...'soon', he said 'I will be absent from myself. I'll laugh and cry without knowing why' (p.62)... The doctor tells Malkiel his father is suffering from a 'sick' memory...and nothing can save it. With increasing senility there would be a loss of identity as well as orientation.

'Soon' says Elkanan 'I will envy the prisoner, though his body is imprisoned, his memory is free, whereas my body will always be free but...' (p.51)... For Elkanan it would seem that his fear is that if he cannot remember the dead will be forgotten. He will have failed in his duty not only as a survivor but as a Jew. 'For a Jew, nothing is more important than memory. He is bound to his origins by memory... Those wounds exist; it is therefore forbidden and unhealthy to pretend they don't' (p.71)... Without this connection through memory the link in the chain is broken and the danger of the past repeating itself is increased.

Malkiel becomes for Elkanan his 'Memorial Candle' (Wardi 1992). This is sometimes a heavy burden for the second generation. The more involved we become as therapists, and through the Holocaust Survivor Centre, with survivors, the less the second generation has to carry this on their own. Some are burdened by not knowing what happened to their families. There are concerns among some professionals that there is a 'second generation syndrome' because of the transmission of the unfinished business of the survivors. Because we came into the work with the first generation so late, there has been some transmission, and as a result we offer a group once a week at Shalvata for the second generation.

However, instead of pathologising the effects of the Holocaust, I feel we should be working with the positive contributions that the second generation can feed into the Holocaust Survivor Centre – both in terms of professional skills, and their energy and vitality in helping to ensure that the activities, the fund raising, and any other aspect of the Holocaust Survivor Centre, are developed. In this way, intergenerational communication is enhanced without necessarily returning to the trauma. Instead of calling them children of survivors – the term most often used – I believe it more appropriate to refer to this generation as adults whose parents were survivors of the Holocaust. As often happens in ageing, there is a role reversal between parent and child. Viewed positively, this enables an opportunity to be created whereby the survivors can be nurtured by their adult offspring, either directly, or indirectly through the Holocaust Survivor Centre. Again, this more active care-giving role counterbalances the popular view of their 'children' being the victims of their parents' transmitted experiences in the Holocaust. The vicious circle of this approach causes me concern and often leads those who adhere to this view to talk of a third generation of victims.

Spouses of survivors, who are also ageing, find it increasingly difficult to deal with the returning memories of their husbands or wives. They find it difficult and disloyal to share with friends/family, and need each other to talk about the issues related to being married to a survivor. A group is therefore offered at Shalvata for this purpose. As our services develop, we are constantly looking for needs which we may not be meeting. A group of people who were hidden during the Holocaust and escaped imprisonment felt they needed a facilitated discussion group at Shalvata, as their experience could not be shared with camp survivors.

In homes for the aged and in hospitals, there needs to be an awareness of what it means to a survivor to be in an institution, given a number on the wrist as in the camp, feeling helpless and dependent on people in uniform. Those who were experimented on medically in the camps may react particularly strongly, and this has in my experience led to a psychiatrist being called. All too often a diagnosis of paranoid schizophrenia is made without taking into account the reality of the experience the survivor has been through. Survivors, as Frankl (1987) has emphasised, are reacting normally to what was an abnormal situation. Being old, as well as a survivor, often means that you are not listened to, and hence many misdiagnoses are made. My job is to raise awareness of these issues both within our organisation and outside it.

Awareness of the particular needs of survivors is essential in day centres and homes for the elderly, where reminiscence therapy is widely used. Reminiscence with elderly people is useful if there are good memories to call on. For survivors, especially those who were young in the war, there may be no good, warm memories to hold on to and sustain them when they look back on their lives. Their childhood and their families were torn away from them, and they felt abandoned and helpless. Reminiscence for them, particularly by staff who do not follow up the work, can be more of a nightmare than a blessing. The appropriateness and extent to which the survivor wishes to recall and remember events earlier in life must be individually discussed, rather than being included in a general programme. It is a point which Coleman and Mills expand upon when they caution against the indiscriminate and insensitive use of reminiscence groups (Chapter 12).

Whatever approach is used, its usefulness depends on whether the survivor feels helped. Elie Wiesel (1992) wrote: 'Listen to survivors, listen to them very well, they have more to teach you than you them'. If we do this, we begin to establish a good track record with survivors and we are more likely to meet their needs.

The 50th Year After 'Liberation'

This 50th anniversary has given the ageing survivors permission to speak publicly about their experiences of extreme trauma, and they have corrected many of the myths, including 'lambs going to the slaughter' in the Holocaust, and of the perpetual sick victims in the present. The survivors speaking for themselves give a much broader picture of their experience. Their memories include small acts of kindness of one prisoner to another, not only the acts of violence and bestiality. They include acts of sabotage in the Krupp factory which used slave labour, and not just pictures of submission and weakness. They portray pictures of children 'playing' in the camps, an image taken up in the film *Schindler's List*, in which children were seen using the spades for burying the dead as a see-saw. For the survivors, while they want the atrocity to be remembered, to remember only the atrocity would be another victory for the Nazis.

Though 50 years ago prisoners were physically set free from incarceration, many of them remained emotionally imprisoned. The work we do now with survivors is urgent and essential in helping this last stage of their journey to be reached. The 50th year has been about remembering, but also about celebrating survival. We work with survivors to find their collective voice and to find meaning in this last stage of their lives. When survivors' experiences become part of each one of us, then the survivors' goal will have been reached. The ageing survivor may be able to let go, having found some peace of mind (the meaning of the Hebrew word 'Shalvata'). To do this, we as practitioners need to remember and to help the elderly survivors to be remembered.

References

Danieli, Y. (1981) 'The ageing survivor of the Holocaust.' *Journal of Geriatric Psychiatry XIV*, 2.

Frankl, V. (1987) (ed) *Man's Search for Memory*. London: Hodder and Stoughton.

Guttmann, D. (1994) Personal communication.

Krell, R. (1989) 'Alternative approaches to Holocaust survivors.' In P. Marcus and A. Rosenberg (eds) *Healing their Wounds: Psychotherapy with Holocaust Survivors and their Families*. New York and London: Praeger.

Krystal, H. (1984) 'Integration and self healing in post traumatic states.' In S.A. Luck and P. Marus (eds) *Psychoanalytic Reflections on the Holocaust. Selected Essays*. New York: Ktav Publishing House.

Steinberg, A. (1989) 'Holocaust survivors and their children: a review of the clinical literature.' In P. Marcus and A. Rosenberg (eds) *Healing their Wounds: Psychotherapy with Holocaust Survivors and their Families*. New York and London: Praeger.

Wardi, D. (1992) *Memorial Candle*. London: Routledge.

Wiesel, E. (1992) *The Forgotten*. New York: Summit Books.

Wilson, J., Haval, Z. and Kahane, B. (1988) *Human Adaptation to Extreme Stress: From the Holocaust to Vietnam*. New York. Plenum Press.

Further Reading

Wiesel, E. (1982) *The Holocaust Patient*. Address to Cedars Sinai Medical Staff, Los Angeles.

PART THREE

Starting from Old Age

The next four chapters and, indeed, the chapter by Gibson in Section 4, are all written by professionals whose routine work is with older people. The perspectives are from social work, nursing and psychology. What these contributors have in common is their recognition, in the course of working with older people who were experiencing difficulties in old age, that for some older people the origins of their current dis-ease lay in unresolved business from the past. The emotional and psychological 'luggage' they were carrying into old age was becoming intrusive and interfering painfully, and at times almost overwhelmingly, with the present. Although in some instances, this intrusion was a more prominent and forceful presence of something that had been 'around' but in the background in earlier adult life, the stories of other older people suggested that the intrusion was something new, unexpected and occasionally inexplicable.

A further point to stress is that the contributors came across instances of unresolved trauma in the course of their *routine* work with older people, their *everyday* research or practice. As Davies says, he was not expecting or even thinking that events of 50 or so years ago would be significant in what was, for him, an unexceptional, run-of-the-mill referral to his outpatients clinic. Coleman and Mills describe the occasionally painful impact of reminiscence therapy upon just one member in an 'ordinary' reminiscence group. Both Sutton and Miesen and Jones write about one individual receiving services in 'ordinary' residential or nursing home facilities. None of the older people written about came with a known problem from the past, although they all had physical or psychological problems which had resulted in their referral to outpatients, day care or residential care. Each of the contributors in this section is therefore writing about the gradual understanding of the presence of the past in the present – an understanding which in some cases could be shared with the older person but in others was used to inform the management of difficult behaviour so as to promote feelings of greater security and well-being. As Sutton graphically describes, such feelings are equally important for staff, for if they lack confidence in their ability to cope, they will not be able to respond constructively to distressed and troublesome behaviour.

An underlying question posed by the chapters in this section is – why now? Why, for some people, has past trauma become so significant in their old age? What social, psychological, physiological and spiritual reasons may, singly or in combination, account for the domination of late life by one or more events from the past? And how, in the context of old age, can help be offered? Many possible answers have already been suggested in this book from staff working in specialist settings. The suggestions of this group of contributors arise from work in less specialist settings and complement those which come before. Issues such as hidden histories and the proximity of death are put forward. Between them, the contributors offer ideas and early answers which may help us deal with our own ignorance.

A significant point made by Miesen and Jones and, earlier in the book, by Crocq and Hassan, is that physiological change within the brain alters cognitive functioning. Miesen and Jones are writing about the more extreme dysfunctions caused by the disease process of dementia, but in normal ageing we know that the ability to receive, store and retrieve short-term memory becomes less reliable, while long-term memory remains more intact for longer. The impact of dementia accentuates and hastens this process and, in Miesen and Jones' view, presents the older person with the additional challenge of managing the consequences of the disease which interact with the experiences of the past. But whether we are talking about dementia or normal ageing, the conclusion is the same: if the present memory becomes less secure and past memory remains firmer, then we cannot be surprised that the past assumes more importance in the present.

But to take a purely physiological stance is an oversimplification. Davies reminds us that most of the current population of older people in Europe have war memories of some kind or another. Not all were unpleasant, as Coleman and Mills show. Many were shared by large numbers – the bombing of towns and cities, imprisonment in prisoner of war camps, invasion, occupation and evacuation. However, and this is a theme of other chapters in this book, the public versions of such events have not always been consistent with the private experiences, which for some people were of shame, fear, disgust and guilt rather than heroism, fortitude and mutual support. These private stories were not for sharing; not only were they by their very nature difficult to tell, even to a sensitive listener, but the actual telling was officially discouraged as unpatriotic and potentially harmful to individual and national well-being. The greater chronological distance from the war that we now have, and the wider under-standing of the management of trauma, have altered the societal context of these wartime survivors and this has perhaps contributed to there now being an easier environment in which to talk. But the presence of old age is arguably also of importance.

Ageing brings social change, not least a reduction in the amount of time spent in the roles of worker, parent and carer. These roles are absorbing and demanding and can be effective distractions from unwelcome memories. Their reduction, and often cessation, as Brainin and Teicher earlier say, leaves a gap which may be difficult to fill, especially if disability, poverty or widowhood inhibits opportunities for social interaction. Fewer defences against the painful past therefore exist, allowing it to surface in ways that may not be manageable. We also do not fully understand the significance of the nearness of death. Does this produce an urgency, conscious or otherwise, to put things right, to achieve the 'integrity' that Erikson (1950) writes about in his representation of old age? He suggests that this is the phase of life when the individual faces either the despair of an unfulfilled or unsatisfying life or the state of 'ego integrity' when the rewards and the failings of that life are equally acknowledged and accepted. Many carers of older people can recall someone dying not long after something troublesome had been sorted out. To draw from Sutton's account of her work with Joan, is tackling the dominance of something unresolved from the past part of the preparation needed in order to say goodbye? If so, the responsibility of carers to listen and to facilitate and to refer for specialist help if necessary is a major one.

Sutton's work with Joan, Davies' work with Mrs Smith and Miesen and Jones' account of the story of Mrs De Bever all illustrate that private experiences of a domestic nature – as a child, spouse or parent – can be no less difficult to share. Like the personal histories of the war which contradict the public versions, physical or sexual abuse within the family contradicts the vision of childhood as a time of happiness and innocence and of the family as a safe and nurturing environment. Child abuse and domestic violence make both child-hood and family life less safe than we would like them to be. The history of professionals not wanting to see the presence of abuse is well established in respect of children and women, while the abuse or maltreatment of older people has still to be widely recognised as a serious social problem (Rowlings, 1995). However, largely due to the growing literature of personal accounts of surviving child abuse, we have a better understanding of the ways in which the abusive experience promotes secrecy, shame, guilt and becomes a story often too difficult to tell. Again, as with survivors of the war, society's attitudes are changing and becoming more sympathetic to those who have been abused. But when Joan, Mrs Smith and Mrs De Bever were younger, this was not the case, just as it was not the case for Mary in Chapter 3. Thus in their way, they too have been discouraged from telling their stories. In Sutton's words, they have been 'living in silence' – as indeed have so many of the older people written about here and elsewhere in this book.

For whatever reason or reasons (and we suggested some earlier in this chapter), the older people appearing in these chapters are breaking out of their silence. They have used different ways. Mrs Smith was well able to benefit from a conventional programme of treatment for phobias and to talk about her experiences. Joan literally acted out aspects of her story, as did Mrs De Bever, though neither wanted nor was able to share more than what seemed a very partial account, and for both a therapeutic environment was essential to 'hold' them, sometimes literally, in their distress. What emerges in these accounts is the importance of staff in nursing homes, residential or day care units being able to respond, individually and collectively as a staff group, to the meaning of both words *and* behaviour, to recognise the meaning in either form of communication and to engage with that meaning, however it is expressed and however best they can communicate with the older person. Very similar messages came from the chapters by Hassan and by Fried, although their day centres were established for specific purposes that mark them out from the non-specialised day and residential units described in this section.

Frequently, such care staff will not be specialists in dealing with trauma or post traumatic stress syndrome. They may be experienced workers but have had few opportunities for study and training. And in any case, the type of work that is the subject of this book is not well articulated in books or in teaching material on training courses. But, as Coleman and Mills point out, staff in long-term settings have more opportunities to talk and to be, in all senses of the word, with residents than many other professionals whose contact will be more episodic. In the conclusion to their chapter, they outline some principles for care which enable staff and residents to come together over stressful and difficult issues. Where problems seem more intractable, then outside support and consultation, such as that provided by Sutton, is an example of the way in which a specialist service can be provided in an indirect manner. As others have found (Coulshed; 1980), working through nursing or care staff can sometimes be a more efficient and effective use of scarce specialist time than for the specialist to provide the service him or herself.

To conclude the introduction to this next section, it is important to heed the cautionary messages that come out of these chapters. Reminiscence groups are not by definition therapeutic; Coleman and Mills give examples of individual members who are not reassured and validated by past memories, and in these cases individual and sensitive help must be readily available. Not everyone wants a complete resolution; Mrs Smith was quite clear with Davies that once her past trauma had become less important in her present life, then that was sufficient and she did not wish or need to continue with therapy. The point is emphasised even more clearly by Miesen and Jones when they consider the lessons to be learnt from the experience of working with Mrs De Bever. They prefer the goal of 'continuing progression' rather than resolution, and although they are relating this to working with grief, the wider message would seem to hold true. Continuing progression also allows for success in small particulars to be properly acknowledged, and this indeed is the encouraging message to come from these chapters. Staff *did* help, they *did* learn to understand apparently incomprehensible meanings and they *did* provide greater comfort, security and self-esteem. Older people *did* become less anxious, less consumed by the past and more at peace with themselves and others. Such progressions happened even when the deterioration caused by dementia was evident. But they happened, as Miesen and Jones argue most forcefully, because the professional response was tailored to the capacities of the older person to achieve individuality and to express identity, be this through verbal means or through private and social activity, which allowed self-expression and contact with others, however momentary that might be. On that important note, it is timely to move to Miesen and Jones' chapter as the first one in this section on 'starting from old age'.

Cherry Rowlings

References

Erikson, E. (1950) *Childhood and Society.* New York: Norton.

Coulshed, V. (1980) 'A unitary approach to the care of the hospitalised elderly mentally ill.' *British Journal of Social Work 10*, 1, 19–22.

Rowlings, C. (1995) 'Elder abuse in context.' In R. Clough (ed) *Elder Abuse and the Law.* London: Action on Older Abuse/Age Concern England.

CHAPTER 10

Psychic Pain Resurfacing in Dementia
From New to Past Trauma?

Bère M.L. Miesen and Gemma M.M. Jones

People with dementia always experience losses, which we believe to constitute new trauma, in their old age, arising from the very nature of their disorder. For some, however, there is also a resurfacing of loss or problems from the past (old trauma) and these may lead to psychological or emotional difficulties or to pathological grieving.

This chapter presents a framework in which to understand and explain psychic pain in people with dementia and thence to plan intervention. It is built around the history of Mrs De Bever which serves to illustrate two important points. The first is the nature and development of her awareness of what is happening to her and the emergence of her feelings of loss. Second, it will be seen that not only the level of care provided had to be revised to take account of her changing needs, but the type of therapeutic help had also to be tailored to her ability and willingness to address directly her very obvious anxieties and sadnesses.

Mrs De Bever

Mrs De Bever was born in 1905. She was the second child, but oldest daughter of eight children. After primary school, at the age of 11, she cared for the whole family. At 16, she left home to work in a factory, until her marriage in 1923 to a farmer when she was 18 years old. (She had previously been in love with a man whom she was not allowed to marry because of their different religious convictions.) The marriage to the farmer was precipitated by her pregnancy following an incestuous relationship with her father, and her oldest son, John, is in all probability the child of this relationship. Twelve other children were born during the marriage. Her (younger) daughters have always been frightened by the aggression and sexual advances of John. They describe him as less educated, aggressive and an alcoholic. John is suspected of sexual abuse and violence against his mother, especially since 1986, the year of his father's sudden death. John has always lived at home. The other children stopped visiting their mother because John's behaviour frightened them.

The cognitive deterioration of Mrs De Bever dates from approximately 1990, when she was diagnosed as having Alzheimer's disease. In October 1993 she began attending a psychogeriatric day care unit twice weekly in a nearby village. In January 1994 she was given two extra days of day care in an old people's home in her own village and then in September went to live in a residential home in a nearby village. This arrangement proved unsatisfactory, and in December she was admitted to a psychogeriatric nursing home in her own village. During the two years since first receiving day care, she had become seriously cognitively impaired, with little awareness of time or where she was.

In 1993 she was offered therapy for her severe anxiety and depressive periods. By 1995, due to her deterioration, the therapeutic goal became more palliative in nature, concentrating on social and emotional support.

This brief chronological summary presents a familiar pattern that derives from the chronic and irreversible nature of dementia. From a cognitive perspective, memory dysfunction is the core symptom, but psychologically speaking the effects of the disease are as complicated as they are tragic. Not surprisingly, therefore, difficult questions have to be faced, by families and professionals alike, about appropriate interpersonal interventions. Too often, because of the inadequacy of our knowledge and understanding, the choice we make tends to be somewhat 'hit and miss'. How, for example, can we understand and respond to the pain of the former high ranking naval officer who, as a younger man, used to be violent to his children? He is now consumed with guilt and wants to put things right, but how might we help? Then there is the case of the woman who was regularly sexually abused by her brother-in-law after her husband died. She is now in a nursing home and she panics each time her brother-in-law visits. Should he be asked not to visit? How can she be helped to overcome that abusive experience, which still distresses her, when her recall and her ability to explain herself have become impaired due to dementia?

Before we can begin to help Mrs De Bever and the two individuals to whom we referred above in passing, we have to be able to understand them better. We need theoretical perspectives that will make sense of their experience and guide us in how we might respond. As a starting point, it is useful to regard their past experience and, arguably, their present circumstances as 'trauma'. Trauma can occur throughout the life span and in many forms. In some cases, it may be caused directly by other persons; sometimes it is through inadvertent neglect or through circumstances beyond anyone's direct control. Generally trauma can be seen as a condition in which the individual has no power, no supportive structure, and hence no protection. The feature common to all trauma sufferers is the isolation and alienation from others and, ultimately, from themselves. In this respect, the experience of progressive isolation resulting from dementia is an example of trauma – a cluster of circumstances producing inevitable isolation and psychic pain.

All trauma potentially leads to fear, apathy and aggression. These are also common behaviours arising in dementia, and following Bowlby (1969, 1973, 1980) we suggest that they can be linked to each individual's history of attachment and loss (Miesen, 1992b).

To take these ideas forward, we explore aspects of Mrs De Bever's situation in greater depth, in an attempt to provide a theoretical framework within which the influence of the painful past upon the present can be better understood and responded to, despite the existence of cognitive impairment.

Past Trauma, Psychic Pain and Dementia

The progress of Mrs De Bever's dementia and an accompanying increase in her concern with her parents was clearly evident from the psychological assessments carried out during the two years since she began day care and from notes made by nursing and care staff. The account illustrates how, over time, past experiences became more intrusive and distressing for her, surfacing at a time when her grasp of what was happening around her was becoming less secure:

> Six months after Mrs De Bever started day care twice a week in her home village and twice a week in a nearby village, she began to speak a lot about her oldest son. On one occasion she said: 'He is worried if he doesn't know where I am. I must do what he wants, or else he spanks me on my bare bottom'. And in the same month, but at a different time, she described how: 'Sometimes I feel like I'm a visitor in my own home. I would like to have a place for myself, on my own. Now and then I like being alone'.

> In May she said: 'He often comes home drunk. Then I make sure I go away. I'm glad that I'm able to get out. Here, I can be myself. Here I'm finding a bit of a home, too'. But in June and July, she was tired and not very talkative. By August she had become confused and emotional. One afternoon in the day care unit she mistook a visitor to the unit for a boyfriend from her youth, but this man ignored her. His 'rejection' made her very sad, because she had hoped for a 'reunion'.

When she was admitted to the residential home in September, she was relieved but also angry. Relieved, because of the freedom and having a place for herself; angry, because she had to leave her house, as she described it, 'on the run', while her son remained there. From the beginning of her stay, panic, sadness and death wishes increased. She refused invitations to speak about her feelings, but seemed glad of the opportunity to talk about them whenever she chose to raise them. As long as nothing was said about her family, she felt well.

Otherwise, she was frightened and sad, and often wandered about the streets. Three months later, in December, she was admitted to a psychogeriatric nursing home. Especially in the beginning, she was continually afraid of going back home to her eldest son. She often said: 'He is doing it again, and I don't want him to do it'. Her moods were full of fear, then full of sadness. She spent much time searching for her mother (long since dead) and she was very angry at her father (also dead). Her poor vision put her in constant danger of falling. If one tried to restrain her in a chair to protect her, she became panic-stricken.

The phenomenon of *increasingly remembering or thinking* of a parent/parents, while realising that one or both are indeed dead is called 'parent orientation'. *Believing* that one or both dead parents are alive is called 'parent fixation'. The terms 'parent orientation' and 'parent fixation' come from POPFiD theory: parent orientation and parent fixation in dementia (Miesen, 1985, 1990, 1996).

In 1993 Mrs De Bever's short-term memory store recall was moderate and her long-term memory store recall was good. Indeed she was able to reproduce much new information and almost all earlier stored information. All other cognitive functions were nearly intact. She demonstrated moderate parent orientation and fluctuating parent fixation. Sometimes she thought frequently about her parents. She knew that her mother had died and sometimes she thought that her father had died, but mostly she believed he was still alive. She said: 'Father was my friend' and, 'I'm often confused, then I think my parents are still here. This I want to unlearn because such thinking stays too long and too much inside my head. It makes me very tired'.

By early 1995, her short-term memory store recall was absent and the long-term memory store recall was only moderate. She was not able to reproduce new information and only moderate amounts of earlier stored information. Other cognitive functions were also declining. She demonstrated strong parent orientation and fluctuating parent fixation. She also said: 'I love my daddy very much'.

In the summer of 1995, she said at one moment: 'I don't know if my parents have died. As far as I know, they are doing well'. Then the next moment she said: 'You want to know if my parents have died? I can't say for sure. But I think so'. She started crying and added: 'When my mother died, I lost everything'. It was striking that she often had monologues where she talked to give herself courage. To the question: 'Are you unhappy?' she answered: 'I'm often worried about myself. I'm worrying more than I'm allowed to'. About the large family she has, she said, among other things: 'I used to cry when I was pregnant again. I mean about the whole situation, not about the children'. According to staff observations using a systematic checklist, between 1993 and 1995, Mrs De Bever's behaviour became increasingly lacking in emotion and more restless, suspicious, sad and anxious.

Later in this chapter, we will return to Mrs De Bever and how care staff attempted to help her. First, though, we address the question of how we conceptualise and analyse the psychic pain of people with dementia. This takes us through the development of POPFiD theory and the impact of the experience of dementia upon the individual concerned.

The Assessment and Analysis of Psychic Pain in Dementia: The Development of POPFiD Theory

Three key cognitive changes occur in dementia: the capacity to store new information permanently decreases; recent events become increasingly difficult to retrieve from memory; and, eventually, even the retrieval of early memories will become impaired. Raaijmakers and Shiffrin (1980) and Jones (1990), among others, have identified that people with dementia also have severe attentional deficits.

The result of these changes is that at some point in the dementia process, a person does not acquire new memories; they seem to live in a 'forever now' state. Jones and Burns (1992) refer to this as a 'collective' or 'cumulative' reality, with the remembered events of a lifetime superimposed loosely onto one another. In other words, at a certain point in their deterioration, people with dementia become disoriented with respect both to present reality and to chronological time sequencing. Thereafter, such persons do not know how old they are and often think themselves to be young again, except during 'lucid' moments when they realise they have become old, but are not sure of their exact age. Their apparent age regression can be to any point in past time, but frequently it is to the pre-adult years.

This shift or transfer to the past coincides with a progressive decrease in the ability to store new information permanently (progressive short-term memory dysfunction), attentional dysfunction, and increasing social isolation in present reality. This social isolation may be explained alternatively as a result of their limited ability to have meaningful attachments to people, animals and things in the immediate environment, and/or as a result of being 'abandoned' by those in present time who cannot understand or accept their cognitive and behavioural changes and who therefore distance or separate themselves so as to avoid meaningful contact. Behaviours that are particularly difficult for both lay and professional carers to understand include searching for deceased parents; wanting to care for their young children who have already grown up; and referring to whatever setting they are in as if it were really the parental home from by-gone days (Miesen, 1985).

Although the above account of this aspect of dementia has been widely observed and accepted, the extent and significance of its occurrence has not been examined. It was this gap that led to the development by the main author of this chapter of what has become known as POPFiD theory – an explanation of the importance of the theme of parents to people with dementia.

POPFiD theory has its roots (Miesen, 1992a) in the Jungian concept of 'parent archetypes' and their 'importance' during periods of limited levels of consciousness. Additionally, however, reminiscence theory, with its acknowledged therapeutic element, would lead us to expect that the theme of parents would arise from time to time in the process of connecting present experiences and problems with past ones (Coleman, 1986; Merriam, 1980; Molinari and Reichlin, 1984/85). Finally, attachment theory (Bowlby, 1969, 1973, 1980) highlights the importance of attachments, the changing nature of attachments through the life span, and how individuals react when they suffer the loss or separation from their affective ties or relationships. Indeed it is not uncommon for an individual suffering a significant bereavement to search intensively for the dead person. They may have persistent memories of them and 'see' them in the street or 'feel' their presence in the room. Such experiences in the early stages of grief are normal; it is their persistence and unabated intensity that makes them pathological.

Bowlby's work on attachment theory does, however, require some additional explanation. Although he never worked directly with older people or older people with dementia, his work sheds light on the 'searching for parents' behaviour within dementia. Bowlby speculated that the care-giving behaviour which is complementary to attachment behaviour, happens not only between children and their parents, but also between care-givers and older adults. The latter situation arises particularly under conditions of reduced health, stress and in very old age. He also identified what he described as 'proximity-seeking behaviour' in situations where fear is experienced and meaningful and familiar 'attachment figures' (persons with whom there is a close affective tie) are absent. Such behaviour refers to a range of psychological and physical strategies which try to bring the important person back again.

Fear is experienced in situations of real, perceived or threatened loss and danger. Sooner or later, each individual experiences loss, and with it the reactions which follow particular stages in the grieving process (Kübler-Ross, 1970). Bowlby would say that psychopathology in later life has its roots first in disorders of the development of early attachment patterns between the child and its parents and second in the consequences of pathological grieving in childhood due to early experiences of perceived or threatened loss.

In suggesting, as we did above, that dementia is a loss process which gradually isolates or separates a person from everything which is familiar in present reality, one needs to find out what replaces the present reality. In short, it seems to be that memories of 'safe situations' in the past begin to resurface individually and collectively. As the dementia progresses and memory for recent events becomes increasingly impaired, past memories seem to be re-stimulated and, unlike the memories talked about in normal life review, become the present. Bearing in mind that, for the present generation of elderly people, the mother was the first and key attachment figure in early life, one would expect mothers to play an important part in the memories of people with dementia. And so the research suggests, providing that the early relationship with their mother was a good one. Memories of fathers are nearly as common, and thereafter those of one's own children, as children. This early research (Miesen, 1985) and clinical observations showed that behaviour progressed from a 'talking about parents' to a more active 'searching for parents', as the dementia worsened. Broadly speaking, this shift coincided with the marked cognitive and behavioural changes from early to moderate dementia. 'Talking about' parents was described as parent orientation whereas parent fixation denotes the 'searching' for parents and the increasingly stronger search for, and attempts to 'hold on to', someone (or something).

However, in this search for a theoretical understanding of parent orientation and parent fixation, we have to address a further question – what part does dementia play in explaining the presence of this behaviour? And, linked to this, what does this behaviour mean or represent?

Dementia and its Significance in the Searching for Parents

In their study of the management of terminal illness in hospital, Glaser and Strauss (1965) introduce the concept of 'awareness context'. They showed that, irrespective of whether or not they had been officially told about their prognosis, the terminally ill people in their study frequently had some aware-ness or understanding of the seriousness of their condition. Glaser and Strauss argued that such knowledge was essential if these people were to be able to complete the essential tasks of bringing their life to a conclusion and mourning for its impending loss. There is both clinical and empirical evidence to show that people with dementia also have an awareness context and that they normally remain aware of what is happening to them for longer than researchers had believed to be the case (Miesen, 1992a, 1995).

The researches of the first author have found a strong correlation between parent fixation, the level of cognitive functioning and attachment behaviour. This can be explained by understanding the experience of dementia as a journey into a 'strange situation' in which the person feels unsafe for long periods of time and over which he or she has no control. Additionally, people with dementia have to cope with the same feelings that come up in situations which resemble separation, homelessness or displacement. Many secondary symptoms of dementia, such as fear, restlessness, sadness, aggression and apathy can be explained as being reactions to loss (Miesen, 1990, 1993).

What we have, therefore, are two explanations for behaviour. On the one hand, there is the decreasing cognitive functioning which follows from changes within the brain. These are the symptoms of the cerebral disease. On the other hand, there are other behaviours which fit into the experience of loss and fear, based on the person's awareness context, their 'knowledge' that something is 'not right'. These behaviours are a response to the *consequences* of the disease, rather than being symptomatic of the disease itself.

The reduced ability to keep new information in long-term store causes a person's awareness context to move from 'continuous' to 'momentary' awareness. The sufferer slowly drifts into a 'strange situation'. This process is a downward spiral, for the awareness context of a person with dementia will always proceed from a more or less permanent state to a temporary or momentary one.

The changing awareness context activates the experience of feeling unsafe; the process of separation from persons and things in present reality and subsequent abandonment is started (Miesen, 1990). In this way, a person with dementia gradually loses everything and slowly loses control of him or herself, becoming more and more what might be termed a 'displaced person'. The need to feel safe is activated, the need for proximity, the need to have and hold on to attachment figures. At the same time, the person experiences attachment figures as being less and less present. The diminishing capacity to keep new information in long-term store also causes the person with dementia slowly to lose awareness of the presence of, and emotional response from, attachment figures. Hence people with dementia can no longer find safety and well-being with friends, family or those around them.

What must be emphasised here is that progressive short-term memory failure and diminishing attachments in the present, result in earlier episodes of life being experienced more frequently. Unresolved loss, or past trauma, become conscious and come to the surface. Why such loss or trauma was unresolved at the time it happened is beyond the scope of this chapter. However, we contend that the key to understanding present loss behaviour will be by reference to the person's attachment history. Thus, to return to Mrs De Bever, we can trace how her behaviour may be understood and responded to in the light of her history of attachments and loss and in the context of her progressive dementia.

From 1992 onwards, Mrs De Bever exhibited anxiety, feelings of displacement, panic and occasionally a wish to die. The anxiety and the depressive feelings grew worse over the next few years. Psychological assessment shows that during this period there was a steady cognitive decline, so that by 1995 her cognitive impairment had become moderately severe. Her awareness context progressed from being continuous to only momentary. Thus her anxiety levels became raised as the momentary awareness context led to present feelings of being unsafe which, in turn, reactivated the old feelings of being unsafe which went back to childhood, the sexual abuse she had suffered from her father and then later possibly also from her son. Thus the new, ongoing trauma of her dementia again brought to the fore interacted with the old trauma from the past.

We already know that trauma or psychic pain can come from many sources (self-infliction, infliction by others or from external pressure such as illness or disaster) and that its outcome may also differ depending on whether it is sexual, physical, mental or spiritual. But whatever its origins or nature, all trauma leads to stress or fear which in turn causes isolation, anger, guilt or shame. Loss of self, loss of identity and the transfer of control from inside to outside oneself are the end result. In response, the individual can fight or fly (Selye, 1956). Flight can end in despair, withdrawal, apathy and depressive behaviour; fight in aggressive behaviour and rebellion. For some the reaction will be evidenced through chronic anxiety, manic depression or extreme agitation. Mrs De Bever exhibited many of these signs: sadness, fear, anxiety, anger and restlessness (it will be remembered that she often wandered the streets after she was admitted to the residential home). Her attachment to her mother was relatively strong, but to her father it was ambivalent. She talked of having had to 'stand on her own two feet' too early in life, suggesting that she had not experienced the support or security normally provided by parents to their growing children.

Matching Treatment and Care to Changing Needs

In the early stages, in 1993, because Mrs De Bever still had some capacity to learn and her cognitive impairment was less severe, she was offered psychotherapy to try to resolve her past trauma. This was provided in combination with day care which emphasised a reality orientation approach. Various social activities were available, as was one-to-one validation therapy whenever she felt particularly sad or anxious. However, she refused to take part in psychotherapy and in any form of structured life review. Some resolution of her psychic pain might have been achieved had she consented.

But her behaviour did not change and in 1995, because her capacity to learn had virtually disappeared, the decision was made to end reality orientation work with her and instead to involve her in validation therapy. On her admission to the psychogeriatric nursing home, she joined one of the groups there. The goal was now palliative: to provide as much emotional comfort and support as possible. Social activities continued to be available and music therapy was also offered.

This approach has had some success. Mrs De Bever appears to enjoy company and she increasingly joins in singing songs and reciting familiar poems. From time to time, she searches for direct support from the nurses and this is provided through a one-to-one validation approach. She still, on occasion, has felt useless and sad and has said she wants to die, and treatment with an anti-depressant has failed to alleviate her general anxiety and sorrow. But in spite of this, Mrs De Bever now has more frequent periods when she seems overtly happy and able to join in communal activity.

The care of Mrs De Bever poses questions but also offers learning. Among the questions are significant ones for society and for professionals within health care systems. Caring for Mrs De Bever and others like her is not cheap and it is not easy. Does our health care system want to provide such care? Can the systems provide the kind of care that is needed? If the answer to both these questions is 'yes', then what are the goals of intervention?

We suggest that the starting point has to be with the assumption that everyone has suffered some degree of abuse in life. We cannot specify the degree of abuse or suffering because we cannot retrospectively quantify negative stress reactions or their cumulative effects on the conscious/unconscious psyche or on the body. Resolution is possible – but we question whether resolution should always be the only goal of intervention or of providing care. Might we not instead speak in terms of helping people with a continuing progression through the grieving process?

The range of goals in planning interventions to help a person to continue working through the grieving process include:

- the achievement of insight into the past, to reach the stage of acceptance and possible forgiveness and to achieve resolution of one's life story

- the experience, as often as possible and either alone or in groups, of moments of overt happiness (indicated by smiling, laughing, singing or dancing)

- the development of feelings of being more at peace with oneself, with others and with the environment, leading to contentment and to meaningful relationships (even if these are only momentary)

○ the maintenance of maximum orientation and alertness

○ participation in meaningful activity.

The achievement of these goals is related both to the stage of the dementia and to the specific cognitive (dis)abilities of the person concerned.

The first goal, active interpersonal therapy to reach resolution, is possible if there is still a capacity to learn and be oriented in reality. The person has also to be willing to engage in such work (Mrs De Bever, as we saw, had the cognitive capacity early on to undertake such work but was unwilling to do so). The other goals are chosen if the first is not appropriate or does not work, and they can be regarded as palliative psychological treatment. This leads to safety, optimal sensory and mental stimulation and a predictable routine – all providing psychological comfort.

The interventions for care-giving in dementia must fit the stage of the dementia process and the same techniques can be used for different goals. The core goal is always the same: to realise the 'ownness', 'individuality' or 'identity' of the person; to enable him or her to trust others and to feel trusted; and to facilitate psychological or emotional safety. Techniques such as dynamic psychotherapy, reality orientation, reminiscence work, structured life review, validation therapy, music therapy, psychomotor therapy and so on may all be appropriate, either singly or in varying combinations (Jones and Miesen, 1992; Miesen and Jones, 1996). However, if we are to find a way to match the types and the degree of psychic pain to the best treatment modality, we need more research of both a retrospective and longitudinal nature. Critical evaluations of pilot therapies have in the past been lacking, yet are much needed. Links with Post-Traumatic Stress Disorders, using both literature and clinical experiences, need to be established with behaviour in dementia.

Dementia as a Model for Understanding Psychic Pain and Trauma

We conclude this chapter by proposing that the dementia process itself could be a model for the study of psychic pain, for the sufferers always experience alienation, displacement and separation. Because of their cognitive deficits, they have no means of understanding, controlling or suppressing the psychic pain caused by these experiences. They cannot maintain a sense of their past, their present or their future, and are faced with a totally new reality that can only be properly described as traumatising.

In some sufferers, the process of separation and alienation reactivates unresolved pain (stemming from past trauma), be this having survived the Japanese concentration camps; or having lost a future (Jewish) husband who was first hiding and later murdered; or having participated in the underground Resistance; or in hiding Jewish children during the war; or to have been 'kidnapped' as an adolescent girl to work hundreds of miles away from home in the war industry of the occupying army and never returning home; or, as was shown with Mrs De Bever, to have survived physical, sexual and emotional abuse within the family.

Dementia itself always brings new trauma and causes psychic pain. Dementia is in itself a trauma and the experience of this new trauma can bring back trauma from the past. When it happens that someone brings with them past trauma, the suffering and the amount of psychic pain appear to increase exponentially.

The tragedy is that the trauma of dementia is chronic and usually unacknow-ledged. It is our challenge to understand dementia syndrome as the beginning of a new chronic trauma which, for some elderly people, is heightened and intensified by the return of trauma from the past.

Acknowledgment

The authors gratefully wish to thank Petra Dekker for her help in preparing this chapter.

References

Bowlby, J. (1969) *Attachment and Loss, Vol. 1: Attachment.* London: Hogarth Press.

Bowlby, J. (1973) *Attachment and Loss, Vol. 2: Separation: Anxiety and Anger.* London: Hogarth Press.

Bowlby, J. (1980) *Attachment and Loss, Vol. 3: Loss: Sadness and Depression.* London/New York: Hogarth Press/Basic Books.

Coleman, P.G. (1986) *Ageing and Reminiscence Processes: Social and Clinical Implications.* Chichester: Wiley.

Glaser, B.G. and Strauss, A.L. (1965) *Awareness of Dying.* New York: Aldine Publishing Company.

Jones, G.M.M. (1990) The cholinergic hypothesis of dementia: the effects of lecithine and nicotine on human memory and attention. PhD Thesis, London: Institute of Psychiatry, University of London.

Jones, G.M.M. and Burns, A. (1992) 'Reminiscing disorientation theory.' In M.M.J. Jones and B.M.L. Miesen (eds) *Care-Giving in Dementia: Research and Applications.* London/New York: Tavistock/Routledge.

Jones, M.M.J. and Miesen, B.M.L. (eds) (1992) *Care-Giving in Dementia: Research and Applications.* London/New York: Tavistock/Routledge.

Kübler-Ross, E. (1970) *On Death and Dying.* New York: Macmillan.

Merriam, S.B. (1980) 'The concept and function of reminiscence: a review of the research.' *The Gerontologist 20*, 5, 39–50.

Miesen, B. (1985) Meaning and function of the remembered parents in normal and abnormal old age. Paper presented at the XIIIth International Congress of Gerontology, New York.

Miesen, B. (1990) Gehechtheid en dementie. Ouders in de beleving van dementerende ouderen. Dissertation, Almere/Nijkerk: Versluys/Intro.

Miesen, B. (1992a) *Dement: zo gek nog niet.* Houten: Bohn Stafleu van Loghum.

Miesen, B. (1992b) 'Attachment theory and dementia.' In M.M.J. Jones and B.M.L. Miesen (eds) *Care-Giving in Dementia. Research and Applications.* London/New York: Tavistock/Routledge.

Miesen, B. (1993) 'Alzheimer's disease, the phenomeon of parent fixation and Bowlby's attachment theory.' *International Journal of Geriatric Psychiatry 8,* 147–153.

Miesen, B. (1995) Awareness in Alzheimer's disease patients: consequences for care-giving and research. Paper presented at the IIIth European Congress of Gerontology, Amsterdam.

Miesen, B. (1997) 'Attachment behavior in dementia: parent orientation and parent fixation (POPFiD) theory.' In Pollock, G.H. and Greenspan, S.I. (eds) *The Course of Life Vol VII.* Madison: International University Press Inc., pp.197–229 (in press).

Miesen, B.M.L. and Jones, M.M.J. (eds) (1996) *Care-Giving in Dementia Vol II.* London/New York: Tavistock/Routledge.

Molinari, V. and Reichlin, R.E. (1984/85) 'Life review reminiscence in the elderly: a review of the literature.' *International Journal of Aging and Human Development 20,* 2, 81–92.

Raajimakers, J.G.W. and Shiffrin, R.M. (1980) 'SAM: a theory of probalistic search of associative memory.' In G.H. Bower (ed) *The Psychology of Learning and Motivation: Advances in Research and Theory, Vol 14.* New York: Academic Press.

Selye, H. (1956) *The Stress of Life.* New York: McGraw-Hill.

CHAPTER 11

'Out of the Silence'
When People Can't Talk About It

Laura Sutton

In March 1992, an article was published in a British newspaper, *The Independent on Sunday*, entitled, 'Out of the silence' (Heller, 1992). Survivors of the Second World War were trying to speak out about what they witnessed, but sometimes they could not:

> When they try and speak of it the memories overwhelm them and they fall silent. The British servicemen who saw Auschwitz from the inside, as prisoners of war, can never forget its horror. Nor is it possible for them to understand why, when they came home as young soldiers almost fifty years ago, no-one wanted to hear the story of what they had witnessed. Even to-day, survivors share the feeling that still no-one is listening (p.2).

When I meet people who have been through traumatic experiences which have rarely, if ever, been talked about, or that they have not been allowed to talk about, the feeling that no one is listening can be very strong (and they may not be listening still). It is a kind of silent memory. There is then a double burden, of witness and of silence. People may have long lost sight of what it is to speak out:

> There's this young chap who's also from Northwich – he was at Auschwitz but he ended up going to a mental home. Now he's in a bedsitter on his own – but you couldn't talk to him about what happened to him because he's gone...gone too far you see. I could have gone the same way. When I used to meet him, we'd talk about it – but we'd never tell anyone else because they wouldn't believe it. It was ridiculous really. Arthur Dodds (quoted in Heller, 1992, p.4)

It is difficult to estimate how many people who have been traumatised in their younger days now live in residential care, and who may be 'living in silence' still (Kaakinen, 1992) with unattended mental health problems (Kitwood, 1990).

For the older person in this position the road home is not easy. It is fraught with uncertainties and obstacles. Often there is fear, and there are few signposts along the way. It is even more difficult if the person is unable to speak of what she or he endured or to put into words what is wrong. It is almost impossible to recover from severe early or compounded traumatisation on one's own (Bass and Davis, 1990; Keenan, 1992), and those supporting the person need to offer some signposts and to some extent to journey with the client. This chapter takes the setting of residential care and looks at the role of the specialist in these instances, which is to help the support workers establish these signposts and to develop with the client. I would like to do this with a journey and development of my own, in supervising Ann, the owner of the rest home where Joan lived.

Joan

Joan was 66 when she was referred to me by the Consultant in Old Age Psychiatry at the end of October 1990. She was living at St David's, a rest home for people with dementia, and had been there for two years. She had apparently been diagnosed as having dementia during the time she lived in a rest home in the north of England, near one of her daughters. It seems they could not manage her, and Joan was moved back down south, to St David's, to be near her other daughter. Joan did not have dementia, however, although she might have been described as 'out of her mind' in other ways.

The consultant noted that Joan had had a depressive illness previously, with a serious suicide attempt in 1987, and was a 'new woman' for six months following ECT. He felt that her current rest home was well below her potential, if she could ever get properly well. Her behaviour was said to be 'quite complex'. She was said to be refusing to talk about her feelings, and to be very afraid of formal psychiatric involvement. Rather, she apparently denied that her difficult behaviour was anything to do with her at all. Recently she had become aggressive, which brought new fears for Ann, the matron, that she would not be able to contain the situation and that in anger Joan would attempt to commit suicide. The consultant felt that Joan was very afraid of rejection by the home. In all, he felt that Joan needed a way of expressing her feelings without loss of security so that staff could enable her to settle down – but then if that happened she would probably be 'too good' for St David's. The consultant also suggested that in Ann I would find a very willing and insightful person with whom to work.

Meeting Ann and Joan

I went to meet Ann and Joan at St David's in November 1990. Ann was a warm and compassionate woman experienced in working with particularly disturbed residents, but she was finding it very stressful indeed with Joan. She described how Joan would be sitting in the lounge and suddenly jump up, go over to the clock on the wall, move the hands forward and then sit back down. When Joan was questioned about this, she apparently denied doing it. She was soiling and smearing her room with her faeces and stole food from the kitchen, all of which she was said to deny. Ann said Joan, 'puts up a wall which nobody can get through'.

I asked if I could meet her. Ann introduced us, leaving us to meet privately in Joan's room. Joan seemed reluctant to talk. Actually she looked paralysed with fear in my presence, her body rigid and her eyes fixed in a frightened glaze. At one point her look turned vicious (staff said that, 'if looks could kill, Joan would be lethal'). I could see how people could be afraid of her. There were photos around the room which I assumed were of her family so I asked her about them. Joan's body eased and she talked more easily: about her daughter, Marianne, up north with two children, her daughter Ruth here with her two children, telling me about their fortunes and misfortunes. She spoke less about her son who lived elsewhere in England. In time, I was able to explain to Joan who I was and why I was there; that I would like to help her if I could. She declined my offer outright; neither did she wish myself, Ann and she to meet together. However, I explained that Ann did feel in need of support and Joan, to my surprise, was not averse to my meeting Ann to support her in caring for Joan.

Ruth, Joan's daughter, was also at the meeting with Ann that day and talked openly about her difficult relationship with her mother, for whom she felt responsible. Ann wondered whether Joan had been abused as a child because she seemed so afraid of men, touch and adults. Both described her as 'frightened like a child'.

Thus a picture was emerging of someone who was very afraid and childlike, unable to control her feelings and thereby her behaviour; and in that confusion unable to hold on to what she was doing. Feelings were running high generally; staff felt out of control too.

Containment

When feelings are running high there is a need for 'containment'. Kitwood (1990) writes about the metaphor of 'containment' in therapy, which, 'carries connotations of safety, reassurance, boundary and strength' (p.50). He suggests that, 'with adequate containment a person comes to sense that powerful emotions…are not going to turn into demons, or overwhelm and shatter the self: it is "all right" to experience these things' (p.50). This was true for staff too.

First, discussing Joan's behaviour with Ann, Ann suggested that staff could literally 'manage' it, that is, clean up her faeces without particular mention. It is important to do this without risking reinforcing the behaviour through inadvertent attention, positive or negative (see Zarkowska and Clements, 1989). Ann could also begin to set boundaries of what was, and was not, acceptable behaviour and could communicate this to her staff so there was consistency, again a very important behavioural principle (Zarkowska and Clements, 1989).

We agreed that, at the moment, the placement had not actually broken down. Indeed they had been coping after all for two years so far. We could take time to understand what Joan was going through, though we had to be prepared for a rough ride along the way. In an emergency, Ann was to contact the consultant. We agreed to work to the '4 + 12' format of cognitive-analytic therapy (CAT; Ryle, 1990), meeting weekly in the first instance and then for review. The 4 + 12 format has four 'assessment' sessions, followed by 12 'intervention' sessions. Although CAT was designed for working with independent clients in individual therapy, it was useful as a broad conceptual framework for Joan's dilemmas as it addresses the 'borderline personality states' and issues of transference and counter-transference which were important in Joan's case.

From Diagnosis to Understanding

I visited roughly weekly over the next month. Each time I visited, staff would give me example after example after example of the bizarre, unseemly or difficult things Joan was doing, from the changing of the clocks, to the soiling and smearing of faeces, and stealing of sweets from other residents, to incontinence, aggressive outbursts ('temper tantrums') 'suicidal vibes', 'The Wall' (see below), looking frightened, 'freezing over', agoraphobia (Ann said Joan had not gone outside St David's in two years), depression, 'laziness' and so on. I felt overwhelmed by this: I took it that this was how staff must be feeling. 'Transference' is a concept in psychodynamic psychotherapy whereby the client transfers feelings and constructions on to the therapist (for example, Genevay and Katz, 1990; Knight, 1996). Just as Joan was 'offloading' on to staff, so staff were offloading on to me. It is important to 'hand back' people's feelings to them, as it were, so that they are enabled to own them and to work them through. This was the same for staff as it was for Joan.

I suggested to them that, in giving example after example after example of what Joan was doing, it can seem overwhelming, and that it was time to classify these behaviours as they seemed to fall into three distinct 'states' (Ryle, 1990). One was what Ann and I termed her 'survival' state. This was where Joan seemed to exist in some sort of suspended animation. There was a sense of numbness about her as though there was nothing 'in there': 'The Wall' came up and she was unreachable. The second was what we termed her 'regressed' state. Like a child out of control and desperate, she would throw tantrums, refuse food, soil and smear and steal.

The third state was what we termed her 'real self'. It was easy to lose sight of this, given all that Joan was doing, but it is very important in working with severely distressed people to be sensitive to the potential for personal growth. McCormick (1990) discusses this within the CAT approach in terms of the humanistic concept of the 'seed self'. Like a seed, in order to grow and to develop and thrive, we need the right conditions. It is not difficult to grow and develop in the right conditions; rather when we are deprived of light, warmth and sustenance, literally and metaphorically, we fail to thrive. Like a plant, we can wither and die. With Joan, through her devastation – through all the examples of what she was doing – we would catch glimpses of the lovely person she was: 'the way she was 40 years ago', as Ruth put it. Staff would sometimes mention her lovely character, her beautiful beaming smile and her sociability when at ease.

Meanwhile, staff intimated that Joan would switch rapidly between these 'states' with no apparent (for instance, conscious) connection (Ryle, 1990). In terms of how best to be with Joan when she was like this therefore, I asked staff to consider, for each state in turn, if they were feeling like that, how would they like people to be with them? I encouraged them to work from their own intuitions (just as Joan was having to follow hers).

By now the feeling was emerging that there was something terribly wrong for Joan. She was not 'just a difficult person', or 'lazy' as her daughter proposed. Indeed her behaviour would make sense in terms of the long-term effects of past abuses. I drew this in a diagrammatic form (Figure 11.1) adapted from Ryle (1990). Figure 11.1 shows how original experiences of humiliation or degradation can bring fear and soiling and shock.

This shock brings a numbness of feeling and, for some, of memory with anger suppressed (Bass and Davis, 1990). Joan was left in a state of severe anxiety, with anyone more powerful than she, particularly men, and any adult in an authoritative position triggering her 'core pain' (Ryle, 1990): as a kind of memory, or 're-enactment' of what went on before (Miller, 1990). Her fear and degradation emerged in her self-abuse and she would numb over: 'The Wall' was up. There she was safe, as if no one could get to her, the suppressed anger bubbling like a volcano. Bass and Davis (1990) describe well these means of psychological survival. Once the threat was over, Joan was free to emerge once again, vulnerable but with a possibility for growth.

It was as if time had stood still for Joan, so strongly symbolised by the clock: no matter how hard she tried, she could not move time on. Seeing Joan's

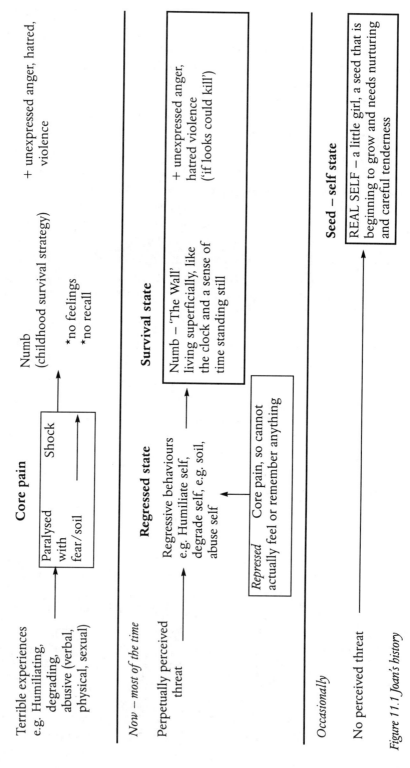

Originally as a child and adolescent

Core pain

Terrible experiences
e.g. Humiliating,
degrading,
abusive (verbal,
physical, sexual)

Paralysed   Shock
with
fear/soil

Numb
(childhood survival strategy)

*no feelings
*no recall

+ unexpressed anger, hatred,
violence

Survival state

Numb – 'The Wall'
living superficially, like
the clock and a sense of
time standing still

+ unexpressed anger,
hatred violence
('if looks could kill')

Now – most of the time

Regressed state

Perpetually perceived
threat

Regressive behaviours
e.g. Humiliate self,
degrade self, e.g. soil,
abuse self

Repressed   Core pain, so cannot
actually feel or remember anything

Seed – self state

REAL SELF – a little girl, a seed that is
beginning to grow and needs nurturing
and careful tenderness

Occasionally

No perceived threat

Figure 11.1 Joan's history

possible history on paper like this brought a stark awareness to staff and to Ruth of the reality of the potential depth of Joan's traumatisation. With a great deal of courage, I think, Ruth hinted at enduring abuses of her mother by her father. He had died about five years previously and it was then that Joan had 'run away', apparently to her daughter's up north. Ruth knew little of her mother's earlier past however.

Meanwhile, Ann had been setting aside regular times to meet with Joan for 'quality time' but Joan was very unforthcoming about her past (or present) problems. Ann and I agreed not to press her or Ruth on these matters, but to listen, because it is extremely important to enable the client to maintain control of her or his own issues, as in abuse and maltreatment this is precisely what has been taken away (Bass and Davis, 1990).

We agreed that Ann should not see herself as 'a therapist' for Joan: if in time Joan would like to be referred for personal therapy then we would arrange this. Rather, it was in her capacity as matron of the home that she met with Joan, giving individual time for her resident. If Joan wished to disclose, then Ann would of course listen, but otherwise she attended to her care of Joan in other ways, such as encouraging her to develop her self-care or to develop interests in the home or garden, and so on; that is, to nurture the seeds of her 'real self' that had been hidden away so long ago.

In working with survivors of the Holocaust, Hassan (Chapter 9, this volume) suggests we have to stop diagnosing pathology and to start understanding trauma within a model of empowerment. We were going through this transition, moving from 'diagnosing' Joan's 'states' to understanding what she was possibly going through. Then we were able to create the conditions in which Joan would feel safe to learn and to develop. Gradually there came a sense of direction, with the setting of consistent boundaries of acceptable and non-acceptable behaviours, the containment of feelings and understanding of Joan's probable demise. In the words of Edith Horning, in surviving abuse: 'There is more than anger, more than sadness, more than terror. There is hope' (Bass and Davis, 1990, preface).

Surviving

Just before the last of the initial assessment meetings, Joan had an explosive temper tantrum. Ann was shaking, saying she did not know how to deal with the situation. I sat with her, giving her time to let her shock dissipate, allowing her anxiety to wax and wane in the warmth and safety of the room where we met, with a cup of tea. I advised her that Joan was probably scared and a bit shaken too; so the thing to do was to sit with her, giving her that space, making sure she was warm, in familiar surroundings and maybe have a cup of tea too.

That night Ann felt she had made a breakthrough. She had been up with Joan into the early hours as Joan wanted to talk. She talked not of abuse, but confided in Ann that, 'you know, when I get like this I just want to end it all'. Ann said she had been able to say to Joan that through talking problems are shared, that we knew something bad had happened to her, but that she was safe now. She said she got more out of Joan than ever before. The next morning the atmosphere was fresh, staff noticing a difference in Joan: the suicidal vibes, as Ann called them, had gone and were never to appear with such intensity again.

Just as Joan had not known whether she would survive, Ann did not know whether the placement (she) would survive: again the transference was coming through. Reflecting with me on this time in order that I could prepare this chapter, Ann felt that my advice to her that day was a turning point, in modelling how to be with Joan when she was talking about her fear of ending it all. Beck *et al.* (1979) discuss working with the suicidal client and Bass and Davis (1990) write very well on suicide, affirming for women survivors of childhood sexual abuse that we have lost too many women already. They reach out to survivors to let them know that they deserve to live: Joan in turn had broken through 'The Wall' to reach out to Ann.

My own support came from peer supervision with experienced psychotherapeutic and cognitive-behavioural practitioners. The importance of this cannot be overstated, because this provides the safe conditions in which the specialist her or himself can learn and develop from her or his own experience and that of others.

Ann and I resumed work in the New Year, meeting monthly for the remaining 12 sessions.

Working Through

At this point, the family issues surfaced more clearly. As Joan's main carer, Ruth had joined Ann and me for some or part of the sessions to learn about managing her mother's challenging behaviours. As our understanding of issues of abuse grew, these shared meetings became highly problematic, and difficult for Ruth who indeed had her own story to tell. We felt it important to secure confidentiality for Joan, yet support Ruth. A therapist from our team therefore offered support for Ruth, affirming that she was not responsible for what her mother did and encouraging her to set her own boundaries. I continued to support Ann. Ann found that this arrangement helped ease the tensions between herself and Ruth, enabling her to attend to Joan.

Ann noticed that when Joan 'opened up', for example starting to go out more, eventually 'The Wall' would go up again and the old anxieties would return. She was opening up old wounds, however, and the difficulty was that if Joan started to do more, this was taken as a sign of her 'getting better'. The pressure was then on her to 'get better': control was being taken away again. It is not easy to overcome the effects of abuse and staff were anxious too. Always we reaffirmed the need to proceed at Joan's pace: it was, after all, only March 1991, and still very early days.

If Ann found she was getting anxious about Joan's recovery, she was to try and remember that she did not have to 'cure' her: this was about Joan's quality of life; it was a palliative intervention. In her 'good phases', as Ann called them, we needed to realise that Joan was risking trust again. Daring to improve brings new fears (Bass and Davis, 1990), so Ann was to be aware of signs of stress in Joan and to validate her feelings to help her manage her anxiety. For example, she might say: 'You've done well lately and it's maybe running away with you a little, so how about easing the pressure a little, have a bit of a rest?'.

Over this period up to April 1991, Joan started to take more care over her appearance and Ruth remarked that she seemed to be 'more aware of herself as a personality'. She also lost a lot of weight (having been very overweight) and remarked that she could not believe she had let herself get so bad. From the psychotherapeutic point of view, she had indeed lost a lot of 'weight' from the tensions she had been carrying for so long.

Ruth felt that her mother should now be moved to another rest home where the residents were not so disabled. Ann and I considered that this was the wrong time. It was not Joan's wish and Ann and I felt that it was because she felt secure at St David's, possibly with residents with whom she empathised, that she was able to take these steps forward. Joan relapsed over this time, with some of her difficult behaviours returning, especially over mealtimes. She did not attempt to move the clock forward any more though, her mood this time being rather one of defiance. I was pleased to see this coming through for Joan, signalling the struggle from helplessness to anger, when anger is the 'backbone of healing' (Bass and Davis 1990, p.122). However, it meant that Ann was being tested out once more and she had to reinstate the behavioural boundaries firmly.

Through Joan's difficult behaviours, especially when so regressed, it was tempting to see her as a child. It was important not to collude with this feeling (Genevay and Katz, 1990) but to stand back and look at the whole. We always tried to affirm and reaffirm Joan as a mature woman of great resources, albeit one who at times was scared.

Joan continued to improve and 1991 saw a 'marvellous summer'. She was going out more, with improved relationships with other residents and staff. She also began to disclose to Ann abuses by her brother when they were young, and issues of her difficulties or fear of men arose. Ann and I explored the issues around listening to disclosures and understanding the vulnerability the person can feel afterwards (see Bass and Davis, 1990) and, to maintain the control with Joan, Ann did not disclose the precise confidences to me.

Joan was beginning to come 'out of her silence'. Her difficult behaviours had abated, and she went from strength to strength. Her good periods were getting longer. It was lovely for Ann to see her so happy, smiling and laughing. She had gone back to her gardening, too, which she had so loved and about which she was so knowledgeable. At times she was vulnerable, but Ann was practised now in setting limits and it was easier to maintain a stability in the home from the behavioural point of view.

Ending

It was time to put limits on Ann's work, and a volunteer companion was arranged for social time for Joan outside of the home. It was October 1991 and also time to look ahead to the end of my support of Ann. Issues of 'termination', of endings, are extremely important in psychological work and need to be prepared for. Indeed it is important to be aware of this from the beginning, where loss, including facing the loss of one's own life, is very much a part of working with older people (Genevay and Katz, 1990; Knight, 1996; Worden, 1991). We arranged the final three appointments into Christmas and the New Year. In the November one of the residents died and Joan cried. I wonder if this was when she started to feel again. She went on to join a social club where she formed friendships and met up regularly with other members.

In the January of 1992, Joan began to talk of her hatred of men. Ann felt confident in her support of Joan through this. I finished my visits as planned, with the understanding that Ann could contact me if the need arose, with a follow-up planned for six months' time for October 1992. There I discovered Joan had maintained her gains, and had visited her daughter up north, travelling on her own by train. She was more sociable and would now come to Ann if she was upset.

I remember the words of the consultant, who hoped that Joan could find a way of expressing her feelings without loss of security so she could be enabled to settle down. I think this is what happened; and now there was a real possibility that one day Joan might be able to move on to a different rest home.

Mental Health through Mental Health Problems ('Strong at the Broken Places')

Joan died in her sleep in August 1993 at St David's. When I visited Ann, I learned that Joan had built on those early days and difficult times. Her difficult behaviours had not returned. On the Wednesday she had spoken on the phone to her son, whom she had not seen for many years. They had arranged to meet the following Wednesday and Joan bought a new dress. 'Laura, she looked radiant,' Ann said. Joan died on the Monday, two days before the reunion.

Ann and I talked about the timing of her death and whether these were the preparations she needed to make in order to say goodbye. Joan was courageous to the end. Courage through fear and despair is rarely accorded to people who, when they are older, show severe disturbances. Rather there is an artificial dichotomy between those who are seen as in good mental health, with notions such as 'successful ageing', and those seen in terms of 'mental health problems'.

In work on elderly 'mental health problems', for instance, the focus is on obsessional problems, phobias and anxiety states, hypochondrias, the border-line personality and psychotic problems, and so on (for example, Gearing, Johnson and Heller, 1988). Texts on mental health in later life refer to ego-integrity, wisdom and self-worth drawing on Erikson's work (Erikson, Erikson and Kivnick, 1986; Coleman, 1988). What, however, of the mental health of older people with mental health problems? That is to say, what of the wisdom, ego-integrity and self-worth of those in fear and despair, particularly for people as disturbed as Joan? We need to secure an understanding of this in order to understand what it is to be 'strong at the broken places' to secure the foundations of work with survivors (Sanford, 1990).

Thus Ann and I reflected upon what we learnt, particularly in terms of the role of the specialist as a supervisor to staff working with older traumatised people in residential care.

Ann as the Matron of St David's

Important lessons for Ann were that people *can* change and that, however little time they have left to live, it is worthwhile. This is the issue of 'a good ending' in later life, with the right to be allowed the issues of one's age, at any age. Ann felt the full force of her grief following Joan's death, haunted by the image of her degraded body in death. I felt that this stemmed partly from the 'violence' done to her by Joan over their time together. I encouraged Ann to take the image to the tree in the garden which Joan's daughter had given to St David's to commemorate her mother, and finally to lay Joan to rest as if reuniting mind and body. I encouraged Ann to think of her own healing. Ann said that this had been very important to her in saying goodbye to Joan and that now, two years on, she herself is at peace. Spirituality in the broadest sense is often important for survivors (Bass and Davis, 1990), just as it was for Ann.

Ann reiterated that both she and Ruth had been astonished at the diagram formulating the issues within the CAT framework. They were shocked at how well it described Joan and how I could understand Joan so well just from what they said, from their experiences in the here and now. Ann considered that the supervision had been important in preparing her to liaise with Ruth better, through the concept of the boundaries of our different responsibilities. Ann, too, had felt prepared for the time she sat with Joan when Joan told her how she just wanted to end it all when she was like this; Ann said she came to understand how the feelings she had could be what Joan was feeling.

Ann suggested that as a specialist I had been able to 'put it all into words', taking her, 'from the behaviours to understanding the person'. Joan was not a 'mental patient' she said: she had had an image of Joan as a mad woman running down the corridor changing the clocks, when all that it meant was that time had stood still for her. Ann said that interpretation made her realise that Joan was normal. She said that supervision helped her not to give up. It helped her to sustain the reality of the situation: that this was real, that the situation was as bad as Ann thought. She was not imagining it all or 'making a mountain out of a molehill'. Supervision apparently helped Ann with her own feelings of inadequacy, disbelief and numbness.

She said that in the end she and Joan became friends; that the quality of their relationship changed from a parental one to a more equal one. Ultimately, though, Ann said she learned about limitations, of the pain that Joan was in but of which she could not speak and where we could not help her, and of what we shall never know.

Myself as Supervisor

For my own part, I learned of the expansiveness of work with survivors, from beginnings in containment and initial understandings and how this can develop into issues of surviving, anger and working through and ending; and of final ending in death and the aftermath for staff. Moniz-Cook and others have talked about how, 'as therapists we may have to free ourselves from a need for structure, if we are to understand the experience of people who have suffered much, but said little' (Sutton and Moniz-Cook, 1995, p.19).

An understanding of the wilderness that some people seem to be living in, and an awareness of the importance of the metaphors that people use, non-verbally as well as verbally (in body and mind), can help in relating to those whose experiences have been without the conventional realm (Keenan, 1992). Moniz-Cook, for instance, draws on techniques from drama and archetypal work to relate to older people, 'through the language of images' (Sutton and Moniz-Cook, 1995, p.18) when they may have refused to speak for long periods and are severely depressed or catatonic.

The therapist-supervisor needs to be comfortable with strong feelings. Because of this, the notions from psychotherapy of transference and counter-transference (what the therapist brings into the encounter of her or his own) (Genevay and Katz, 1990; Hausman, 1992; Knight, 1996) in particular can be a source of support throughout the work, helping the supervisor maintain staff's ownership of the situation.

Having said that, in its association of the 'working through' of issues, the aim of psychotherapy, as Kitwood (1990) explains, is conventionally to help the person to lower her or his defences so that the pain is exposed and then it may be worked through. For people as traumatised as Joan, however, this is not advised. Rather the aim is for a 'supportive psychotherapy' in which the person's defences are not challenged (Bloch, 1977). Psychotherapy was originally developed for people with 'neurotic' problems rather than the more traumatised. In other words, it was developed for people for whom a basic belief in the humanity of persons has not been thwarted; who have not experienced a challenge to the point of their existence by another and so still have a familiarity with feelings of safety and security. This cannot be assumed for survivors. For them, the establishment of conditions for safety and security, and for feeling in control, are of paramount importance. This I could not give to Joan: it is what Ann gave, in her rest home with its warm, supportive milieu.

In the residential context, to support staff I attend to them in the same way as I attend to the client. In other words, from their words and their own body language comes an understanding of the weight they are under and the weight which they need to clear away. They really may have gone 'beyond the point of no return' and cannot actually cope any longer with the disturbed resident. It can be important to discuss whether or not this is the case for them. Usually, however, staff feel that although the referral has come at a point of crisis, it is worth at least trying to carry on. Then, if they fail and the placement breaks down, they feel they have done all that they could. In other words, there is usually some hope. Securing emergency cover (for example, knowing whom to contact for an inpatient admission) can be an important safety net, enabling staff to feel more secure should the situation change.

Staff often have a great need to be listened to. They often need to 'offload' a great deal, over and over and over before they can attend properly, because of the stress of working so closely with people as traumatised as Joan amid the difficulties of residential care generally. Through this comes the time for trust to develop; the specialist is after all a new person to them and an unknown quantity with unknown and untested methods, and it really is not known whether the specialist help will be useful in this instance.

As staff talk, I often begin to realise that part of the problem is that they are finding it hard to put into words what is going on; they do not seem to have a language or the constructions for what they are trying to say or do. They have no 'signposts' themselves. Very quickly I find myself reflecting back to them what they seem to want to say ('yes Joan is worth it, because she is a human being') and what seems to be going on ('yes, this is a crisis – you are in the emergency phase', as Bass and Davis (1990) might say) and we need to work with that, helping them 'stay in the moment'.

It is important to maintain this simplicity throughout the work. Our anxieties for the resident to 'get better' can lead us to think of the future. However, all of the pieces of the jigsaw do not have to fit; if we stay focused on the present, with what is presented now, we can draw on appropriate approaches to support it (and the future tends to take care of itself). In Joan's case we drew from behavioural and cognitive-analytic approaches. Others may be useful. For instance, some survivors cannot relax because if they do bad memories would resurface, be these mental or physical (Bass and Davis, 1990). When I am working with people who are suffering panic attacks or storm phobias going back to wartime bombings and raids, and it is hard for such people to find a focus, learning various slow breathing techniques can help them to ease their panic. This enables them to feel more in control of their situation (Beck, Emery and Greenberg, 1985; Holden, 1988; Trickett, 1992) and, as a result, they are able to work in their own time.

However, care is needed in learning about past trauma from the war or from childhood. I would, for instance, be more cautious now in the use of the CAT diagrammatic reformation because I am much more aware of how it is depicting extremes of human suffering for people such as Joan, and it is difficult to know if one is working sensitively enough. It is important not to minimise the potential harm of our well-intentioned approaches and to be aware that we can easily do so, given the minimisation in society of the suffering of some survivors (Bass and Davis, 1990; Masson, 1990; Miller, 1990).

It is therefore important to have some grasp of what people endure in trauma over time; what they had to do to survive (literally and psychologically) and what it is like living in the aftermath, experiencing the silence of others and of society. Bass and Davis (1990) and Keenan (1992) write very well in this respect, and of the difficult decision to try and trust again and to start the road back. As Keenan (1992, p.297) explains:

> Humanisation is a reciprocal thing. We cannot know ourselves or declare ourselves human unless we share in the humanity of another. Finding our way back from the animal condition imposed on us was no easy task... We needed the stimulus of another person, his sympathy, his critical judgement to help guide us. We needed his assurance that the world was worth the effort.

This is true for staff, too. If, like Ann and her staff, they have worked closely for a long time with a resident who is severely distressed, finding their way back is no easy task. They too need the stimulus of another person, her or his sympathy and critical judgement to help guide them. They too need the assurance that their world is worth the effort.

Conclusion

As Ann said, we are left with an awareness of our limitations, with what we cannot solve and do not know. We of course touch upon only a fragment of people's lives. More than that, however, some people cannot talk about it because they do not know what 'it' is. How can someone talk about that which is much bigger than they; about experiences that were never constructed or acknowledged by society (Middleton and Edwards, 1990; Miller, 1990) but which hurt them so badly? People can, however, say or show that 'it hurts'; in the end, however complex things may seem in theory, there can be a simplicity of practice.

Contrary to what is often thought, older people can be more motivated to change, for, 'it is as if time has run out and the person is keen to find peace at the end of the journey' (Sutton and Moniz-Cook, 1995, p.19). As a supervisor, herself retired, said to me once, it is not that it has all come too late – it has come just in time.

References

Bass, E. and Davis, L. (1990) *The Courage to Heal. A Guide for Women Survivors of Childhood Sexual Abuse.* London: Cedar.

Beck, A.T., Emery, G. and Greenberg, R.L. (1985) *Anxiety Disorders and Phobias. A Cognitive Perspective.* New York: Basic Books.

Beck, A.T., Rush, A.J., Shaw, B.F. and Emery, G. (1979) *Cognitive Therapy of Depression.* New York: Guilford Press.

Bloch, S. (1977) 'Supportive psychotherapy.' *British Journal of Hospital Medicine,* July, 63–67.

Coleman, P. (1988) 'Mental health in old age.' In B. Gearing, M. Johnson and T. Heller (eds) *Mental Health Problems in Old Age.* Chichester: Wiley.

Erikson, E.H., Erikson, J.M. and Kivnick, H.Q. (1986) *Vital Involvement in Old Age. The Experience of Old Age in Our Time.* New York: WW Norton and Co.

Gearing, B., Johnson, M. and Heller, T. (1988) *Mental Health Problems in Old Age. A Reader.* Chichester: Wiley.

Genevay, B. and Katz, R.S. (1990) *Countertransference and Older Clients.* London: Sage.

Hausman, C. (1992) 'Dynamic psychotherapy with elderly demented patients.' In G. Jones and B.M.L. Miesen (eds) *Care-Giving in Dementia. Research and Applications.* London: Routledge.

Heller, Z. (1992) 'Out of the silence.' *The Independent on Sunday,* 15 March, 2–4.

Holden, U. (1988) 'Hyperventilation.' In U. Holden (ed) *Neuropsychology and Ageing. Definitions, Explanations and Practical Approaches.* London: Croom Helm.

Kaakinen, J.R. (1922) 'Living with silence.' *The Gerontologist 32,* 258–264.

Keenan, B. (1992) *An Evil Cradling.* London: Vintage.

Kitwood, T. (1990) 'Psychotherapy and dementia.' *The British Psychotherapy Section Newsletter 8,* 40–56.

Knight, B.G. (1996) *Psychotherapy with Older Adults, 2nd Edition.* London: Sage.

Masson, A. (1990) *Against Therapy*. London: Fontana.

McCormick, E.W. (1990) *Change for the Better. A Life Changing, Self-Help Psychotherapy Programme*. London: Unwin.

Middleton, D. and Edwards, D. (1990) *Collective Remembering*. London: Sage.

Miller, A. (1990) *Thou Shalt Not Be Aware. Society's Betrayal of the Child*. London: Pluto Press.

Ryle, A. (1990) *Cognitive-Analytic Therapy: Active Participation in Change. A New Integration in Brief Psychotherapy*. Chichester: Wiley and Sons.

Sanford, L.T. (1990) *Strong at the Broken Places. Recovering from the Trauma of Abuse*. London: Virago.

Sutton, L.J. and Moniz-Cook, E. (1995) Working with older survivors', Psychologists Special Interest Group in the Elderly PSIGE Newsletter, 18–19 (note: this was published erroneously as Gildener, S. and Moniz-Cook, E.)

Trickett, S. (1992) *Coping Successfully with Panic Attacks*. London: Sheldon Press.

Worden, J.W. (1991) *Grief Counselling and Grief Therapy. A Handbook for the Mental Health Practitioner, 2nd Edition*. London: Tavistock/Routledge.

Zarkowska, E. and Clements, J. (1981) *Problem Behaviour in People with Severe Learning Disabilities. A Practical Guide to a Constructional Approach*. London: Chapman and Hall.

CHAPTER 12

Listening to the Story
Life Review and the Painful Past in Day and Residential Care Settings

Peter G. Coleman and Marie A. Mills

Introduction: Mr Clerkenwell

For most of us, memories can be a source of joy and wonder, and of entertainment and instruction for others. When we listen to older people, this is also our common expectation, that we will hear stories that, although not always of happy events, will be meaningful for the teller and rewarding for us too. It can be a jolting experience to be confronted with raw memories of traumatic events from the past, still unresolved and unintegrated into the person's total life story.

Mr Charles Clerkenwell was a moderately demented 81-year-old man living with his wife in the community and attending a psychogeriatric day centre three days a week. There he enjoyed talking about his present interests such as drinking his home made beer while sitting in his sunny conservatory and listening to his music. He also enjoyed reminiscing about times past, the remembrance of Christmas as a small boy, his older sister comforting him when he was ill and his mother 'who was always singing'. These simple and pleasant reminiscences, however, would often slip into painful recall of his war experiences. Mr Clerkenwell still had memories of his traumatic time as a prisoner of war in the Japanese camp at Changi, during the Second World War. Some 50 years later, the remembrance of the brutality of his captors was vividly alive in him. He could not come to terms with their cruelty.

As he told his stories of the camp, he occasionally screamed orders in Japanese. It was as if he relived those days, and heard, once again, the voices of those guards who had been in total control of his life. The progression of his illness appeared to have little effect on his memories. At the age of 83, he

was eventually admitted to a long-stay psychogeriatric ward. During a visit by
the second author, he was discovered sitting in a wheelchair in the day room,
slumped to one side of the chair and gazing at the floor in an unfocused manner.
He was not wearing his glasses or his hearing aid and appeared to be unhappy
and disconnected from his surroundings. However, without hesitation he began
to recall his war experiences:

> So we used to get a rice ration which was crawling with maggots... So
> we did the only thing possible, we ate the bloody things!...We thought
> we'd better stay on the right side of the Japanese. They were
> obviously...from the start, they were obviously...cruel people...

He told a long and detailed story of the brutal treatment of women prisoners:
'...there were twenty-odd people, women... And they were locked up, and
they were raped, one by one, whenever the Japanese felt like it... Not very nice!
You got to remember that they are completely and utterly different'.

When asked whether he felt that he couldn't understand the Japanese, he
replied: 'Oh [they are] very very different! When they are on a different end of
the spectrum, you know...'.

He died three months after this conversation, leaving unresolved his memories of the war and of his captors, whom he continued to see as alien beings
whose behaviour was impossible to understand.

Attending to the Meaning-of-Life Stories

Mr Clerkenwell's case provides a good example of how unresolved memories
from the past may intrude without warning in ordinary care work with the
elderly. How is one to respond? Although reminiscence is now a well-recog-
nised form of diversionary and therapeutic intervention in social and health
care, understanding of the principles of life review and skills in dealing with
persistently troublesome memories is much less well developed. We respond
with enthusiasm to older people talking about their sometimes unique, sometimes shared, life experiences when they are sources of satisfaction to the
speaker. But what are we to do when the process of recall takes us into deeper
and stormier waters?

We are at an important developmental point in reminiscence practice with
older people, and it is worth reflecting a little on the journey on which we have
come (Coleman, 1994). When the first author was investigating reminiscence
in residential homes and sheltered housing schemes in London in the late
1960s, the commonly expressed view of the matrons and officials in charge
was that encouraging reminiscence should be avoided if at all possible. To
reminisce was, at best, an escape from the present, at worst, an encouragement

of senile deterioration. They saw only a difference of degree with the repetitive reminiscences of elderly people with dementia. This negative view of reminiscence was also reflected in the textbooks of the time.

In the 1970s and 1980s these considerations disappeared in a wave of enthusiasm for reminiscence work, particularly in groups, within geriatric hospitals and homes. Reminiscence was seen as life enhancing, an antidote to depression and, above all, an especially appropriate activity for older people. In support of this view, much use was made of the theories of Robert Butler on life review (Butler, 1963) and of Erik Erikson on achievement of ego-integrity (Erikson, 1950) as developmental tasks of old age. An enthusiasm for reminiscence was also part of the general spirit of the time, with its interest in returning to roots and discovering one's origins.

However, although it was commonly observed that reminiscence was enjoyed by most older people, evaluative studies did not consistently demonstrate more substantial benefits to their well-being (Thornton and Brotchie, 1987). One can point to methodological limitations in these studies, such as small numbers and lack of control groups. But a more significant problem was the failure of many studies to distinguish between different types of reminiscence and the different functions that thinking and talking about the past could have, such as life review, confrontation with the past, keeping up a sense of self, and the teaching and entertaining role of the story-teller (Coleman, 1986). Some types of reminiscence (for example, 'integrative') could be beneficial, others not (for example, 'obsessive') (Wong and Watt, 1991). Unhappy memories play a major role in maladjustment to physical ill health in later life (Walker et al., 1990). Some types of reminiscence benefit from the larger audience of the group setting, others require sensitive individual attention. These issues are now well recognised, and more recent studies make explicit the nature and purposes of the reminiscence interventions that they investigate (Bornat, 1994; Haight and Webster, 1995).

But what has also emerged in the 1990s is a generally more cautious attitude to reminiscence and particularly to life review. The reasons are varied, but all acknowledge in one way or another the emotional power of the past and the danger of underestimating the lasting effects of traumatic memories. The discovery of, and heightened sensitivity to, child abuse and particularly child sexual abuse, in the last ten years, have led to a concern with the consequences for adulthood and also for late life, a time when losses may overcome previous defences and the shielding activities of a busy working life are no longer available. Also significant has been the resurgence of distress in the Second World War generation of children and young adults who are now retired. This has been commented on in a number of countries, and related to the anniversary ceremonies of recent years.

Older people themselves handle traumatic memories in different ways. Some may choose to leave these memories undisturbed, and this choice and these defences must be respected. We know that adjustment to emotional upsets in life may be prolonged, indeed may never be resolved (Bromley, 1990). Because they can distort the perception of other meanings, we need to tread carefully in arousing memories of these events. We should not confront people with painful memories without very careful consideration. But for others, the knowledge that they have an interested and concerned listener is enough to open the 'flood of remembrance'. For others still, the story will be told haltingly, over time, and presented in the fragmented format of an uncompleted jigsaw puzzle which has a constantly changing frame of reference, particularly at the early stage of life review. Yet others, like Mr Clerkenwell, will experience times when they are seemingly overwhelmed by the uncontrollable intrusion into their thoughts of previously repressed memories.

For many professional carers, listening to such stories is a difficult task and one that threatens their own defences. A common ploy in this situation is to 'block' or deny such disclosures by means of distraction or avoidance. Frequently such behaviours are partly unconscious and largely fuelled by fears of skill inadequacy and lack of psychotherapeutic training. However, carers' skilled use of empathetic listening remains highly therapeutic and it is to carers that older people turn when in distress. Practical experience within community and residential care settings suggests that older people will initially speak of emotional concerns more readily to their primary carer/key worker than to a perceived specialist in mental health care. Their reluctance to seek help from mental health services may be due to the negative stigma associated with such services from their youth, when only the severely impaired received help (Myers, 1990), a point also noted by Bergstrom-Walan in Chapter 3. Whatever the reason, it is evident that professional carers can become the major confidants to those they care for (Challis and Davies, 1986).

Traumatic Memories in the Community

As was the case with Mr Clerkenwell, war is a major element in the reminiscences of British older people. It is important to note that the outcomes are not necessarily negative. Trauma can be overcome. For example, men's accounts of the First World War played a large role in the first author's study of the reminiscences of older people living in sheltered housing schemes in the 1970s (Coleman, 1986). They have a powerfully emotional, often quivering and nervous character, which provides some indication of the degree to which these men were still affected 50 and more years later. The men who spoke at length about their experiences had learned to live with their memories of the war. They had constructed a personal story and could, for example, speak with empathy of the German soldiers who were their 'enemy'. They had transcended received accounts of that war, and were on the look-out for contemporary accounts to see if they told the 'true' story as they knew it. But there were also people in the sample who did not want to reminisce about the war and referred only in the most oblique way to their war experiences. Their needs were different.

A suspicion of enthusiasm for reminiscence work, without an awareness of its dangers, was engendered by this study and was reinforced by observations of insensitive use of reminiscence aids in day centres and elsewhere in the early 1980s. It was not uncommon for images of an Edwardian childhood to be followed, without interruption or warning, by photographs of First World War trenches, to the evident discomfort of many men present. It is now almost too late to help the First World War generation. But within the UK, greater sensitivity is at last being shown to the Second World War generation of service men and women, not to forget the many civilians who suffered the trauma of wartime bombing. This is not before time, and many opportunities for study of the consequences of wartime experience over the life span have been lost.

Fortunately much can be learned from the pioneering and ongoing longitudinal studies of Glen Elder and colleagues in the United States on the disruptive effects on career and the emotional sequel of combat in the Second World War (Elder, Shanahan and Clipp, 1994; Lee et al., 1995). There is clear evidence that exposure to combat decreases longevity, possibly through a breakdown of the immune system. More significantly, for its practical implications, it also appears that events that lower personal control, such as an automobile accident or the sudden death of a spouse or friend, markedly increase the risk of intrusive memories, especially in the later years. The key experience in combat exposure is the experience of death and dying of comrades and the enemy (Elder, personal communication). It is important that such knowledge, as it develops within life-span studies, is communicated to, studied by, and reflected on by care workers and those responsible for their training.

A major fault evident in reminiscence group work, and in wider society, is the attempt to reinforce stereotyped accounts of major events without attention to possible differences in experience, interpretation and meaning. War again often provides telling examples of this failing. Many traumatic war stories have never been told adequately. Often the reason is because people did not want to hear them at the time they needed to be told. In their place narratives of important events have been routinised. These do not capture individual experiences and serve rather to inhibit their telling. A commonly noted example is the retreat to, and evacuation from, Dunkirk in 1940. This has become part of the British 'mythology' of the war. Yet far from everyone has a story to tell of glorious retreat. The following case example may suffice:

A man in his 80s attending a day centre became emotionally aroused when the topic of Dunkirk arose in his reminiscence group. But it was only later, on his own with the group convenor, that he was able to tell his story. He had held the rank of Sergeant in his unit which had been among those forced to retreat. He had felt ashamed at the behaviour of the British troops in his unit in retreat and that he had been able to do nothing to stop them. After the war this experience had faded to some degree, but, on retirement and after the death of his wife, the memory had come back to haunt him. It was only when he met an old acquaintance from the war with whom he was able to discuss what really happened and his own sense of failure, that his feelings of shame and guilt began to lessen. He was still affected by the memory but less so.

One can imagine how much worse it would have been if he had been unable to find a suitable listener. Research in the USA also shows the importance of peer support (Elder and Clipp, 1988). The care worker may not be able to find such a person but at least can avoid colluding with the 'myth' by seeking to understand what is being told rather than imposing another vision of events.

We have experience both of individual life review work and groupwork reminiscence in community settings. Both provide possible modes of intervention for the care worker. A great strength of groupwork is the possibility it provides for sharing. The first author has experience over seven years of acting as a co-therapist in a weekly outpatient open group for elderly people recently discharged from hospital after treatment for severe depressive illness. Records were kept of the group's proceedings. Reminiscence played a major part in the group, and worked most positively to produce a sense of solidarity through the recounting of experiences which could easily be shared or empathised with by fellow members. The Second World War played a not insignificant role in this, featuring in approximately 20 per cent of the sessions. Virtually all of the male attenders had dangerous wartime incidents abroad to recall, but the women also recounted many civilian stories of bombing.

A question frequently raised was 'had it all been worth it?'. The balance wavered at times. But generally the answer was a resounding affirmation of the rightness of what had been done, and pride in their own achievements. Perhaps because of their recent depression, the implicit, sometimes explicit, contrast was with the present. For example, in a last group before the summer break, each in turn recounted their war service: working on a secret project in the country, night-time filling of shells with cordite in a war factory, secretarial work in Whitehall and telephone operating. The British had been at their best in the war. No one was lonely, people cared about one another. On many occasions, comment was made about the exhilaration of life during the war and the great sense of comradeship. One did not worry about coping because everyone joined in, and also older people were useful. People wanted to be together and one could walk the streets in the dark without fear. One man repeatedly commented on his view that death in the war would have been more appropriate and that he would have been less afraid. It would have given him a good feeling to die 'as a hero' with one's companions around. The explicit contrast was a lingering death at home alone. The same theme of heightened living was repeated by new entrants to the group. One woman, rather quiet in most of her first year of attendance, became especially talkative during the war reminiscence session. It was the excitement of the war that kept people going, she thought. She herself had 'got a thrill' from her time in London as a fire watcher.

The opportunity the group provided for shared experience and camaraderie was much appreciated. For some it was the 'highlight' of the week. With persistence and patience it was possible to include even the more withdrawn members. But reflection on it also reveals the difficulties of incorporating the memories of those which jar with the dominant mood and themes. Davies (Chapter 13) expands on this in respect of the experiences of civilian evacuees but it also applies to those directly involved in the fighting. One man had served in the merchant navy, enlisted in the army 1940–42, but had then been transferred back to the merchant navy. He spoke vividly of his experiences of trembling with fear at the danger of attack and the possibility of being sunk. These fears had now come back to haunt him. Unfortunately he did not remain a member of the group for very long. Problems with alcoholism and physical disability had led him into residential care and although he was brought on occasions by the owners to attend the group, he later gave up attendance altogether.

Although groupwork can provide major benefits of its own, for example, in helping to resocialise isolated individuals, we believe that life review requires one-to-one attention. For an individual to reveal his or her innermost thoughts and possibly shameful past, it is necessary to have one listener only. The principles of life review we have applied are that, as well as being individualised, it should also be structured and evaluative (Haight, Coleman and Lord, 1995). By 'structured' we mean that it should cover the whole life course, not necessarily in chronological order, but that the opportunity should be provided to cover every period. The sessions should not be hurried and should be spread over a time span as long as six weeks. 'Structured' also means, most essentially, that there should be a major opportunity for summary at the end, where the actual integration can take place, often after much repetition, rehearsing and reintegration of material. 'Evaluative' means providing the opportunity to weigh and value life's events, which is particularly important for troublesome events which may need to be evaluated more than once.

Such 'structured life review' has been well tested and evaluated in the USA (Haight, 1988; Haight and Dias, 1992), and has been shown to be effectively used by home health aides with elderly people living at home. An evaluation of such a process has been carried out with a sample of older women attending a day centre in the south of England, and has shown beneficial effects on self-esteem which had not been evident as a result of other forms of intervention such as enhanced attention during craft activities. Closer analysis suggested the benefits came from being able to talk to someone about the painful things in life, which in this study revolved around childhood trauma, such as mother's dying 'too soon', a violent father and the experience of 'being given away'. It appeared that this form of life review counselling had given participants the opportunity to work through unresolved issues related to loss, which was not otherwise available to them (Haight *et al.* 1995).

Life Review in Long-Term Care Settings

Although life review work in long-term care settings requires workers to cope with the additional problems caused by increased frailty including dementia, it also provides opportunities for more intensive and long-term work. One can see the results of any attempted intervention, and not just over a short time period. The possibility for close confiding relationships engendered by the provision of personal care services in the community will apply even more so to residential settings. These encourage the development of confidentiality and trust which aid disclosure of deeply felt life experience (Mills and Coleman, 1994). The following case study provides an illustration from the second author's experience of residential care practice:

> Mr Terence Ennings had moved into a residential home when he was 85 and a recent widower. A few months following admission Mr Ennings was seen by the local psychogeriatrician, who diagnosed early senile dementia of the Alzheimer type. According to those who knew him well, his lapses of memory were apparent before the death of his wife, although this loss obviously exacerbated the problem. As so often happens due to the trauma of relocation, his short-term memory appeared to decline rapidly in the first few months following his admission to the home, although his memories of a more distant past remained clear. He found some sympathetic listeners among the staff and regaled them with parts of his life story. These were repeated at frequent intervals, sometimes after a gap of only a few minutes. Staff found them repetitious and wearing. It was difficult to listen with interest time after time. However, these stories contained a common theme. They were all stories of events in his life when he had been a hard-working and very well-respected member of the community.

Other stories concerned his early childhood. His father had died when he was only a few months old, supposedly of tuberculosis, and his mother had returned to live with her widowed father and older sister. It was a joyless household. His grandfather appeared to be a Victorian autocrat whose frightening temper was legendary. Mr Ennings recalled that he and his mother always tried to be quiet and self-effacing in his presence. His aunt was very jealous of his mother and her son, and her tongue, too, was spiteful. The spectre of TB loomed over him and he was forbidden many of the experiences that other children enjoyed. He was protected against all sources of infection and over-exertion. He said, with some understatement, that: 'This period of my life was a most unhappy time'.

Miesen (1992, 1995, Chapter 10, this volume) gives some understanding of how early attachments from the past influence the present. The present period of Mr Ennings' life was filled with uncertainty and grief. This appeared to have triggered early memories of loss and the need to be 'good' at all costs. This in turn gave rise to the repeated accounts of his 'good and useful' endeavours. In addition, these stories gave him identity and a sense of self-respect. The manager of the home encouraged all staff to listen to him with empathy, but sought, herself, to develop his sense of self-worth, drawing on her own training in counselling. This was done through continued discussions of the immensity of his achievements when set against his miserable childhood, where he felt in a constant state of tension and low self-esteem. They frequently spoke of these times in some depth.

As this resident gradually became familiar with the home, his anxieties slowly began to abate. Over a period of many months his repetitious stories, too, lessened, but would always return during periods of stress and worry. However, the content had in part altered. They had become, in some way, richer and more mature accounts of the past. He recalled them in more detail and he spoke of these times with a sense of enjoyment, accomplishment and acceptance. For some years, this client was able to lead a relatively full life in his new home. He took daily walks, visited his son and friends, went into the nearest town unaccompanied and attended services at the local church. Moreover it was noticeable that he continued to draw considerable benefit from his relationship with the manager of the home and sought her out at every opportunity. She had become associated with the role of a nurturing but non-controlling parent, a non-critical authoritarian figure. This is frequently the role played by empathetic members of a mature staff team in social and health care services for older people. It can be of vital importance to residents' recovery and well-being, as was described in Chapter 11 and the account of how Ann, the matron of the home, sustained Joan.

Mr Ennings' memories, although of experiences that were not so traumatic in the same sense as those of Mr Clerkenwell mentioned at the beginning of this chapter, were also, in their own way, concerned with survival, the psychological survival of the self. Those who listened to his stories of early life with empathy, reported experiencing themselves feelings of fear, oppression and unworthiness. The memories of emotional abuse in childhood, therefore, may frequently reappear, together with their associated emotions, most strongly in a dependent and demented old age. The ability of these two elderly men to 'tell their story' does not, however, minimise the problems associated with this type of work within residential care. Many older people are now entering residential and nursing homes with greater levels of physical and mental frailty than before. Studies indicate that older people with dementia are still able to speak of their troubled past (Hausman, 1992; Mills, 1993, 1995; Sinason, 1992; Sutton, 1994). However, increased frailty leads to the need for increased practical tasks to be performed by care staff.

Listening in these circumstances may be time-consuming and difficult. Nonetheless, residential care settings provide opportunities for more intensive and long-term work. Staff will see residents frequently during the course of their shifts. Carers and residents will talk to each other during those private and individual occasions when personal care is offered. There are fewer time constraints and, as the case of Mr Ennings shows, it is possible to see effective and long-term change take place.

The therapeutic benefits for older people in speaking of past experiences and/or evaluating these events are many. For other older people who live in residential care and who become more cognitively impaired by their illness, their stories or narrative are kept alive by those who care for them. The ability of staff to absorb and retain these stories may facilitate the psychological well-being of people whose memories are fading. One woman, aged 95 and with diagnosed Alzheimer's disease, has lived in a residential care home for the last five years. Although very mobile, she is profoundly deaf and has impaired sight. Staff are aware that she cared for her blind husband for many years and with much devotion until his death. They had no children, which was always the cause of great anguish for them both. She still retains a great love of babies and children. All visitors with children to the unit are encouraged to take them to meet her. She greets them with evident enjoyment.

Another elderly woman with dementia who was a professional actress used to tell her carers of London theatres where she appeared and the parts she played. Although her acting career has now faded from her memory, staff are still able to remind her of her former triumphs and she takes pleasure in this momentary recall. Of more significance is the lack of self-confidence that she has, due to an emotionally starved childhood and an autocratic husband. Knowing this, staff are aware that in a very dependent old age, she needs to be told that she is valued and loved. This particular resident also allows others to be made aware of what can help the person with dementia to achieve well-being in dementia. She has told staff: 'Things don't matter. People matter, and good kindness. We are very lucky. This place is full of good kindness'.

Thus the various strategies which facilitate work with people with dementia benefit from a knowledge of their personal narratives. We believe that the sharing of such a narrative reinforces carer attitudes of respect, understanding and acceptance. In this sense, therefore, the personal narrative of people with dementia need never be lost.

Conclusion: Principles for Care Practice

Not all older people will have memories of trauma associated with life-threatening experiences, but all possess a life history or narrative which may contain painful and/or unresolved memories from the past. To understand the person in the present it is necessary to see them in the context of their experiences over the life span. Simple reminiscence allows older people to give pleasing glimpses of these experiences to the listener. This type of recollection is encouraged by effective listening skills which encompass empathy, respect, genuineness and non-judgemental interest. Such skills also aid more complex evaluative recollections of the past when aspects of a whole life are examined by the elderly person in order to achieve resolution and acceptance. For some, this evaluation is a comparatively easy task. For others, who are not so fortunate and whose memories are painful to them, it is more difficult.

The experience of listening to older people review their lives in both community and long-term care settings suggests that certain characteristics are required of both care staff and the environment. This is as true in cases where the past was painful, even traumatic, as it is when the earlier life was happier and more fulfilling. First, there must be a genuine commitment by the environment to allow this review to take place. This is not as simple as it may sound. Many long-term care settings perceive practical care tasks as having greater priority at all times. This is not always the case. Routines and processes may need to be adapted to allow older people time to tell their story and, perhaps, to evaluate their lives. Further, it must be remembered that older people, in common with other age groups, need time to get to know/trust possible recipients of their confidences. This applies equally to older people who have dementia (Mills, 1995).

Skills of effective listening, too, need to be taught to carers, perhaps within existing training courses. Again, it is too easy to be dismissive of this valuable skill. Not all carers are effective listeners but may rather act as effective advice-givers. The unsolicited giving of advice has little place within the practice of attentive and effective listening. Indeed, the hallmark of this skill is that the listener 'listens'. This skill, which forms part of basic counselling skills, is of immense value within long-term care settings. It could be argued that all standard care courses should incorporate the teaching of this therapeutic strategy, as well as the theory and practice of the more usual and necessary practical care tasks. However, not all tutors/trainers are effective listeners themselves. It may be necessary to 'train the trainers'.

Finally, we should remember that in hearing the stories of older people's lives, we are hearing that which has given their lives value. When we listen to them review their past and learn to revalue their accomplishments and experiences, to forgive themselves their own failures and transgressions and those of others, we see a late growth and flowering of personality. In many respects this courageous and definitive blooming has a singular beauty which may be unmatched in other life stages.

Acknowledgement

We should like to acknowledge the contribution to the work reported in this chapter of the following colleagues: Carol Harding, Matthew Hunt, Kris Lord and Mary Millar.

References

Bornat, J. (ed) (1994) *Reminiscence Reviewed: Evaluations, Achievements, Perspectives.* Buckingham: The Open University Press.

Bromley, D.B. (1990) *Behavioural Gerontology: Central Issues in the Psychology of Ageing.* Chichester: Wiley.

Butler, R.N. (1963) 'The life review: an interpretation of reminiscence in the aged.' *Psychiatry 26*, 65–76.

Challis, D. and Davies, B.H. (1986) *Case Management in Community Care.* Aldershot: Gower.

Coleman, P.G. (1986) *Ageing and Reminiscence Processes: Social and Clinical Implications.* Chichester: Wiley.

Coleman, P.G. (1994) 'Reminiscence within the study of ageing: the social significance of story.' In J. Bornat (ed) *Reminiscence Reviewed: Evaluations, Achievements, Perspectives.* Buckingham: The Open University Press, pp.8–20.

Elder, G.H. and Clipp, E.C. (1988) 'Wartime losses and social bonding: influences across 40 years in men's lives.' *Psychiatry 51*, 177–198.

Elder, G.H., Shanahan, M.J. and Clipp, E.C. (1994) 'When war comes to men's lives: life-course patterns in family, work and health.' *Psychology and Aging 9*, 5–16.

Erikson, E.H. (1950) *Childhood and Society.* New York: Norton.

Haight, B.K. (1988) 'The therapeutic role of a structured life review process in homebound elderly subjects.' *Journal of Gerontology 43*, 40–44.

Haight, B.K. and Dias, J.K. (1992) 'Examining key variables in selected reminiscing modalities.' *International Psychogeriatrics 4* (Suppl 2), 279–290.

Haight, B.K. and Webster, J.D. (eds) (1995) *The Art and Science of Reminiscing: Theory, Research, Methods and Applications*. Washington, DC: Taylor & Francis.

Hausman, C. (1992) 'Dynamic psychotherapy with elderly demented patients.' In G.M. Jones and B.M. Miesen (eds) *Care-Giving in Dementia: Research and Applications*. London: Routledge.

Lee, K.A., Vaillant, G.E., Torrey, W.C. and Elder, G.H. (1995) 'A 50-year prospective study of the psychological sequelae of World War II combat.' *The American Journal of Psychiatry 152*, 516–522.

Miesen, B.M. (1992) 'Attachment theory and dementia.' In G.M. Jones and B.M. Miesen (eds) *Care-Giving in Dementia: Research and Applications*. London, Routledge.

Miesen, B.M. (1995) Awareness in Alzheimer's Disease patients: consequences for research and care-giving in dementia. Paper presented at the III European Congress of Gerontology, Amsterdam.

Mills, M.A. (1993) 'Hidden wealth within dementia.' In K. Tout (ed) *Elderly Care: A World Perspective*. London: Chapman and Hall.

Mills, M.A. (1995) Narrative identity and dementia: narrative and emotion in older people with dementia. PhD Thesis, University of Southampton.

Mills, M.A. and Coleman, P.G. (1994) 'Nostalgic memories in dementia – a case study.' *International Journal of Aging and Human Development 38*, 121–137.

Myers, J.E. (1990) 'Aging: an overview for Mental Health counsellors.' *Journal of Mental Health Counselling 12*, 245–259.

Sinason, V. (1992) *Mental Handicap and the Human Condition: New Approaches from the Tavistock*. London: Routledge.

Sutton, L. (1994) What it is to lose one's mind? Paper presented at the Tenth International Conference of Alzheimer's Disease, Edinburgh.

Thornton, S. and Brotchie, J. (1987) 'Reminiscence: a critical review of the empirical literature.' *British Journal of Clinical Psychology 26*, 93–111.

Walker, J.M., Akinsanya, J.A., Davis, B. and Marcer, D. (1990) 'The nursing management of elderly patients with pain in the community: study and recommendations.' *Journal of Advanced Nursing 15*, 1154–1161.

Wong, P.T. and Watt, L.M. (1991) 'What types of reminiscences are associated with successful aging?' *Psychology and Aging 6*, 272–279.

CHAPTER 13

We'll Meet Again

The Long-Term Psychological Effects on, and Intervention with, UK Second World War Evacuees

Stephen Davies

Mrs Smith: Coping with Civilian War Trauma

The day I first saw Mrs Smith had been a hectic one. My car had developed problems which were likely to be expensive to mend. I had to book an extra patient into my afternoon clinic because of mixed up appointments. So I was far from thinking about war when I ushered the well-dressed, elegant woman into one of the shabby rooms in the outpatients department of the hospital where I worked. Mrs Smith was a 66-year-old widow who had come for help with a long-standing fear of vomiting. The fear was most intense when travelling or even thinking about travelling on public transport or when anticipating a visit from her granddaughter. Mrs Smith imagined that she would vomit or, much worse, be vomited upon when on public transport or when her six-year-old granddaughter visited her. She avoided travel by public transport, particularly by coach, which meant that she could not go on holiday with her friend which she really enjoyed and she only visited her granddaughter when she could get a lift in a car. She also felt unable to invite her granddaughter to stay with her, something which had caused some family tension. She had discussed her fear with her daughter and had met with a hostile, dismissive response.

I gave Mrs Smith a questionnaire to measure how upset she was and this showed that she was mildly depressed. She further described how she had trouble getting to sleep some nights and that she suffered from some nightmares about her wartime experiences and her husband's sudden death from a heart attack three years ago. Apparently, he had collapsed in the street and died soon afterwards.

As we talked over the next few sessions, Mrs Smith described a vivid experience she had had when, as a 12-year-old evacuee during the Second World War, she vomited with fear while awaiting embarkation at a London bus station. She was 'told off' for this event and remembers being told that no one would accept her 'at the other end' because she had vomit on her coat. This event seemed to me to be acting as a 'trigger' for why she felt so frightened about vomiting now. The experience had somehow become engraved on her memory and any reminder led to distress and a wish to avoid such reminders of this trauma.

I realised that I knew very little about wartime Britain, apart from vague recollections at family gatherings when I was a child. Was this not a time of patriotic cheerful determination? It seemed important and I asked Mrs Smith about her experiences. It emerged that she was moved four times to different billets during the war, one of which she found very traumatic due to major conflicts between her, her brother (with whom she shared some of her billets) and their host family. It later emerged that the father of the family had sexually abused Mrs Smith on several occasions before they were moved by a local billeting officer. Mrs Smith returned home in 1944 in order to prevent further evacuation experience. She experienced persistent nightmares about her wartime experiences, mainly her sexual abuse and her memories of an air raid on Canterbury where she was billeted.

I started my usual treatment of phobias and asked Mrs Smith gradually to expose herself to travel on public transport and to visits by her granddaughter. In order for the fear to go, its meaning in her memory had to alter. Bad or disastrous things would not happen if she was sick; she could avoid being so; it was unlikely that anyone would be sick over her and she would be able to deal with such a situation anyway. After nine sessions of her taking on her fears and detailed discussion of the beliefs and assumptions that she held about them, her 'feelings questionnaire' showed that she no longer felt depressed. Disclosure of her traumatic wartime experiences had begun in the fifth session and some psychological debriefing was carried out, concentrating on her memories of the bombing of Canterbury, which she experienced without injury but after which she had a severe post-traumatic reaction – nightmares, flashbacks to the sound of falling bombs, an altered startle response and periods of tearfulness and of 'feeling low' – both at the time and later after her husband's death.

I thought it would be useful to address these post-traumatic elements of Mrs Smith's difficulties by asking her to keep a diary of her nightmares, and also by looking at her wartime photographs and others taken of various 'civilian' events, particularly the V1 bombing of the shop where she would have been working but was off work the day the bomb fell as she was ill. I was worried that this might merely reactivate painful memories for her, but Mrs Smith appreciated her wartime trauma being taken seriously and discussed some events in detail. I also asked her to imagine her experience of the Canterbury bombing during one session, and we discussed using a relaxation tape and distraction techniques to help cope with her nightmares.

We had met 14 times when we began to discuss the loss of her husband and she found this more difficult, as she felt he had been, 'virtually the only man that I could get on with'. I felt that perhaps my gender was now beginning to get in the way of the therapeutic process and at this point Mrs Smith accepted a referral to a female therapist for some discussion of her abuse and bereavement experiences. I saw her for a review of our work three months later, at which time she had dropped out of therapy, but she felt confident for up to three hours on public transport and had had her granddaughter to stay the weekend before her appointment. By questionnaire and interview, she did not appear depressed. She was experiencing some nightmares about the war but these were now occurring about once a month instead of once a week. She declined further follow-up appointments as she felt that she had got what she wanted, and I agreed that there seemed to be little point in exploring more widely if she felt that to be so and that past trauma was not limiting her present life. As she left, she remarked, 'the war was more important than I thought, but it's gone now'. I have tried to bear that advice in mind ever since.

The Historical Context

Wars have always been with us wherever individuals or groups have been unable to get their own way through other means. The Second World War was the largest such 'disagreement' and few people who might now describe themselves as 'older' were unaffected by it.

A recent popular publication described the effects of the Second World War:

> After fifty years, memories fade, exorcising the horror and stressing the more positive side – yet to many who survived such battles as Stalingrad..., a city's firestorm or who felt the impact of the Holocaust – the nightmares remain. Their stories, locked away for so long, are difficult to tell, but if both the horror and the laughter can be described, those who did not share the experience can start to understand the nature of war and try and avoid its recurrence (Therry, 1994, p.260).

In discussing the psychological effects of the Second World War on a civilian population, two major factors have to be borne in mind. The first is the concept of 'Total War'. This is when the civilian population of a country becomes both the direct and indirect target of an enemy. The second factor is the rise of the refugee. The two world wars brought about the largest movements of the world's civilian population yet seen. Gilbert (1990) indicates that the number of refugees displaced by the major conflicts of the Second World War may have been over 15 million. Most of these people would be displaced civilians and their disposal also formed an important part of a country's 'war effort'. For example, Ponting (1995) notes that the failure of authorities to deal with refugees fleeing the fighting in the Low Countries during the latter part of 1939 probably contributed to the Allies' failure to manoeuvre against the Germans and to subsequent defeat in France.

On 1 September 1939, the largest single movement of the civilian population ever seen in Britain took place. It was known officially as 'E' (Evacuation) Day. It had been meticulously planned by government officials for months in anticipation of the outbreak of war. Fears that hostilities would involve large-scale bombing of cities had been growing in the country since the early 1930s, and the use of poison gas on population centres was also widely expected. Over a million people were moved from Britain's towns and cities to areas of the countryside deemed to be safe from enemy bombers.

As both Wicks (1988) and Inglis (1989) point out, the civilian evacuation of Britain's major cities (mainly London) was not a single event but an ongoing process of ebb and flow between urban and rural areas which continued throughout the war. Figure 13.1 gives an idea of the scale of evacuation of children during the war years and shows clearly how, at any one time, the number of child evacuees varied.

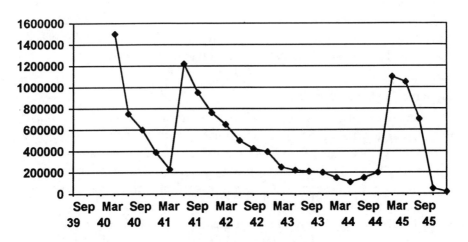

Source: Imperial War Museum, London and Holman (1995).

Figure 13.1 War billeting of child evacuees 1939–1945

The process developed initially from a highly organised, planned evacuation to far more informal evacuations, when the movement of people more closely resembled that of refugees than organised evacuees. Although the arrangements for transporting children and other evacuees were meticulously organised centrally, the billeting process (distributing evacuees to homes) was seen as a 'local matter'. The experiences of evacuees' difficulty in finding a billet and receiving a persistently hostile reception were not unusual. More disturbing is the fact that very little screening took place to ensure the suitability of individuals and families prepared to take children or adult evacuees. Incompatibility at best and neglect and abuse at worst, were possible outcomes. The evacuation is commonly seen as involving British children, but it also included the distribution of thousands of foreign refugee children and adults to billets as well. The evacuation was vastly heterogeneous in its effects on its participants but the occurrence of psychological trauma in this planned, altruistic response to the harsh realities of modern warfare went largely unrecognised. In a contemporary account MacIntosh (1944) observed: 'Many mistakes were made in the initial evacuation scheme, due almost entirely to a lack of psychological insight of those who were responsible for the arrangements. Most of these have been repaired at great cost. There will be no excuse for careless or wanton repetition of these errors' (p.52).

Six years after the war began, its end brought a return to now unfamiliar people and places which was as sudden as the departure had been at the conflict's beginning. Evacuees returned to damaged and altered cities to form families that knew little of each other's war experiences. Some members had had 'a good war' with little exposure to it, easily putting it to one side. Most had experienced some trauma of which others may have been unaware, for this was a time when discussion of war experiences was discouraged both socially and officially. MacIntosh's words proved prophetic in this way.

Literature on Civilian Evacuation

The literature on the psychological effects of wartime experiences on civilians is surprisingly sparse, although it is beginning to grow. Some work has now been done with civilians of more recent wars, such as Vietnam (Karnow, 1987; Van Der Kolk, 1987), as well as with some groups of civilians affected by the Second World War. The most intensively studied of these groups have been survivors of the Holocaust, but I will not examine the specific literature here as my fellow contributors do this in far greater detail. Haas (1995) provides a good summary of most of this work. Suffice it to say that the findings of these studies are alarming in their depiction of the far-reaching consequences of war trauma on this group of civilians and their families. There are few clear estimates of the psychological impact of the Second World War on civilians, probably because, unlike combat veterans, there was no obvious procedure for dealing with psychological casualties. The impact was dissipated among large populations and the heterogeneity of their experiences may have led to less realisation of their plight. In addition, in Britain the maintenance of morale in the civilian population was seen as a task of paramount importance (Calder, 1969) and psychological trauma was usually interpreted as a sign of constitutional weakness rather than as a reaction to extreme life events. Little systematised support was available and demonstrations of psychological distress or failure to cope with trauma were actively suppressed.

Some recent work has hypothesised possible mechanisms for the perpetuation of traumatic wartime experiences into old age. Van Der Kolk and colleagues (Van Der Kolk, 1994, 1996; Van Der Kolk and Van Der Hart, 1991) have suggested a psychobiological model for war trauma in which the experience becomes 'engraved' in the memory by a series of psychophysiological changes which, when activated, cause intrusion of trauma and subsequent avoidance phenomena. The one factor that seems to remain in distantly experienced trauma seems to be altered physiological responses to threat (Van Der Kolk, 1994), and thus such a psychobiological model is an attractive explanation. Interestingly, Hunt and Robbins (1995) report intrusion as a mediating variable between war trauma and its psychological impact in Second World War male combat veterans, whereas Waugh (1994) indicates that avoidance may be the more significant factor in the wartime trauma of women. Davies (1992, 1994) has indicated in a sample of London blitz survivors that some demographic factors such as educational level and location of home (which gives an indication of bombing intensity) mediate the psychological impact of war trauma. In general terms, evacuees seem to have undergone a greater variation in war trauma than blitz survivors.

Early in the war, the Maudsley hospital (London's specialist psychiatric centre) was divided into a hospital receiving military psychiatric casualties in Sussex and the Mill Hill Emergency Hospital in North London, which was primarily intended for psychiatric casualties of London's bombing. A number of anecdotal accounts exist of adults receiving treatment at Mill Hill during the London bombings of 1940 to 1944. Most cases seemed to receive diagnoses of various hysterical reactions and 'damaged nerves' (Russell, 1995). The other main source of anecdotal evidence for civilian war trauma in London comes from the work of Anna Freud and her colleagues at the Hampstead Nursery, which provided substitute care for the children of working, displaced or missing parents. The impressions of Freud and her colleagues are distilled in Freud and Burlingham (1942) and Burlingham and Freud (1944). Severe disruption in psychological functioning among some separated and orphaned children was noted as well as the traumatic effects of various wartime experiences on children.

There are few examples of empirical studies of psychological trauma in British civilians during the Second World War. The Cambridge Evacuation

Survey (Isaacs, 1941) provides the most detailed record of the social and educational effects of the more organised evacuation upon mothers and their children. Isaacs, a psychiatrist, and her colleagues conducted this anecdotal study over a one year period between the end of 1939 and 1940 with some comments on trends in 1941. Their interest was in the increased number of children referred to them, a significant number of whom were evacuees. They noted that parents usually removed their children from billets because these children 'appeared chronically homesick', when there were clashes between natural parents and 'foster' parents or because of the financial burdens of travel and dual provision for natural parents who were often from poor, inner city areas. The researchers also noted that children evacuated to Cambridge had high rates of nocturnal enuresis and disciplinary problems in schools. However, their conclusions were that these children were primarily from two inner London boroughs with high levels of deprivation and it was surmised that the prevalence of such difficulties would be higher there anyway. They also commented that the class and cultural differences between those evacuated and those billeting them could have contributed to the conflicts of class and role which often occurred. This in turn could have contributed to the psychological difficulties of evacuees. Isaacs and her colleagues make a few oblique references to the abuse of adult and child evacuees, but the only reports occur in the reminiscences of those participating in the many experiential accounts of the evacuations. A similar survey by the Institute of Education at the University of London (1947), this time on London children evacuated to Oxford, showed very similar trends and views to the Isaacs' undertaking.

The long-term psychological effects of the evacuations have been studied indirectly as part of investigations into the effects of childhood separations on adults. Tennant, Hurry and Bebbington (1982) studied the effects of four types of childhood separation, including wartime evacuations. There was no positive relationship between adult psychiatric morbidity and wartime evacuation unless the factors of parental illness or death or marital discord between the parents were added. This study was conducted in Australia, however, where the further factor of UK children ('Seavacs') in a different environment was not taken into consideration. There is some considerable literature on the psychological effects of childhood separation in adults (see Rutter and Rutter (1995) for a good summary). Birtnell and Kennard (1984) found that poor psychological adjustment in adulthood was associated with an emotionally distant relationship between mother and child. They felt that poor parent–child relationships were more damaging than a break in the continuity of care. They did not examine the role of 'foster parents' or the environments that children were exposed to during such separations. No systematic studies have yet been completed on the long-term psychological effects of the civilian evacuations.

Finally, a number of anecdotal accounts of personal experiences of the Evacuation have been written over the past ten years (for example, Gardiner, 1991; Green, 1989; Wicks, 1988, 1990). These accounts of the experiences of mainly child evacuees are useful in providing some insights into the daily lives of some civilians during the war, but discussion of the long-term psychological effects of this experience is noticeably absent. Two more detailed and comprehensive accounts of the Evacuation are provided by Inglis (1989) and Holman (1995), where there is more reflection but no data on the possible psychological effects of the Evacuation experience. Ziegler (1995) also gives a detailed account of wartime London. These accounts describe the difficulties faced by families of 'putting their members back together again' after the war, with no external help and gross social denial of the psychological effects of the war. Turner and Rennell (1995) provide detailed anecdotal accounts as well. The lack of available literature suggests that the denial continues to persist for all older civilians to this day. It is further worth noting that however sparse the British literature may be, there appears to be no German literature at all on the subject.

Some Clinical Implications of Civilian War Trauma and Notes on its Treatment

Both combat stress and Post-Traumatic Stress Disorder have become more recognised elements of the impact of warfare on the psyche since the Second World War (Van der Kolk, 1994). There is also a growing, if reluctant, realisation that wartime experiences may have long-term psychological effects on civilian populations as well. Little treatment is available now for the civilian casualties of recent and current wars, so it is not difficult to see how much less existed for those who suffered a long time ago. Yet the events of the Second World War are being writ large again on the minds of the older people who underwent them, as 50 year commemorations of these events are produced by the media. Older people are being bombarded by images of this war again and the popular expectation is one of celebration. This may be true for some, but for others it may be proving a time of great emotional pain as the dust is disturbed on their memories of terrible sights, of long separations or of tragic losses. There can be little doubt that war is generally a bad experience and the civilian war in Britain was no exception to this. In London 'The myth of the blitz', that all civilians pulled together in a common effort, is exposed by writers such as Calder (1991) and Ziegler (1995), who further show that the public view of what happened and the private recollection of those evacuated or bombed may differ markedly. These are the kind of points that must be borne in mind when considering clinical work with this group of older people.

Almost all older people in Britain and most of continental Europe are likely to have had some wartime experiences. These may have been positive but are likely to have included some negative events which they may not talk about. Mrs Smith did not want to tell me about her wartime experiences at first because they hurt; she felt that she was betraying the memory of those who died in the war by 'complaining' and she assumed that I would be upset or disgusted by a frank account of her experiences. Older people need time and space to relate these experiences if they want to. If an older person has been referred to a therapist then an assessment of such experiences is important but should not be intrusive or given too much emphasis. At present, these experiences receive little attention but the opposite position is also an error. The most important element of assessing these experiences is examining how they have impinged on the older person's life since their occurrence.

Some knowledge of the main events of the Second World War by the therapist is essential to provide an accurate assessment of war trauma. It is insulting to the older person for this knowledge to be absent, and with it the therapist can sometimes relate his or her knowledge of the effects of particular wartime events if the older person appears to be presenting a sanitised version of experiences. The therapist has to 'know where to look' in a sensitive and cautious manner and with the consent of the older person. It may take some sensitive interviewing over an extended period to give the individual freedom to discuss the wartime trauma.

Several texts (Calder, 1991; Ziegler, 1995) have indicated that Second World War Britons were told that such discussions would damage morale and were therefore undesirable. However, now may be the best time for older people to be able to discuss their experiences, as public attitudes and understanding towards the war are probably more enlightened.

The behavioural elements of treatment, such as exposure to avoided situations and the accompanying reminiscences, are probably an important part of the healing process. Such interventions by the therapist may allow some relief from the legacy of unhelpful learned behaviour engendered by such experiences. It enables the older person to exercise some measure of control over these experiences, perhaps for the first time. However, time for reflection on the meaning of such experiences also promotes the healing process. This may be the first opportunity for the older person to consider such experiences in the light of their subsequent life and to allow some integration of them into their view of themselves and their world. In the light of recent work, some non-verbal therapeutic intervention such as art or drama therapy may be utilised. Such work may be useful when the recording of the traumatic memories is primarily pictorial, but should always, in the wider context of linguistically based therapy, be aimed at a narrative recollection of these experiences.

The use of groups in war trauma treatment is not straightforward, a point reinforced by Coleman and Mills in Chapter 12. Some individuals may benefit from sharing their wartime experiences with others. For some, especially when their experiences were unusual or incongruent with their view of themselves (for example, running away and 'allowing' their child to be killed by falling masonry), this social support might actually do more harm than good. This is not only important for therapists working with individual older people but also for all professional care-givers in contact with older people. In particular the use of wartime reminiscence in groups is a venture to be cautiously entered into. Some older people may feel very vulnerable in such situations and their experiences may attract censure rather than support from the others in the group. Generally, membership of such groups should be carefully selected, relatives should be talked to about possible adverse events, audio-visual material should be carefully selected, with an emphasis on the general state of affairs rather than specific incidents, and there should be some mechanism by which older people who become distressed are followed up individually or are referred to therapists. War reminiscence for cognitively impaired older people is probably not a good idea on a group basis, as they may have fewer defences to cope with such experiences. Celebrations of anniversary wartime events (for example, in Britain, VE and VJ days which celebrated the end of the war) need to be carefully planned with consent from those participating and are probably better presented as 'a party' rather than as 'a war party'. A supportive social environment, the availability of staff for private, one-to-one contact with older people, and the use of caution in such areas of experience are the important elements of a service that will be able to deal effectively with older people's wartime experiences.

An altered pattern of physiological responses to threat is a significant part of the long-term consequences of war trauma. People with such problems may experience chronic difficulties with 'getting worked up' very easily and may suffer from fears to do with their experiences. The use of various clinical methods to combat this chronic physiological overarousal, such as relaxation therapy or biofeedback, may need to form a part of the treatment process.

Discussing wartime experiences can be very distressing. Older people engaging in this activity need to give informed consent to participate in treatment, following an analysis of the benefits of the treatment to them, as well as its potential drawbacks. This has to be kept in mind by the therapist throughout the treatment process and, as in Mrs Smith's case, the person should feel free to decline further treatment. It is the therapist's responsibility that the process of monitoring the risks and benefits of treatment by discussion with the older person is maintained throughout treatment. It is also the therapist's responsibility to look after themselves. About a year ago my wife told me that I was more short-tempered than usual. Secondary traumatisation is a very real phenomenon and therapists need to recognise this. Emotional support, peer supervision groups and an appropriate number of these cases is important. Full-time work in this area may ultimately be very difficult.

There is no one theoretical framework to the psychological treatment of older people's wartime experiences. However, Robbins' four-stage model of war trauma treatment for war veterans (this volume, Chapter 5) comprising disclosure of traumatic events, identification of dysfunctional cognitions and emotions about them, the use of behaviour change strategies and termination, is also useful for those suffering from civilian war trauma. In addition the use of Knight's model of maturity/specific challenge, which allows for the incorporation of particular experiences in a longitudinal perspective, provides a helpful way of viewing the difficulties suffered by this group of older people (Knight, 1986).

As the title of this chapter suggests, people who have experienced significant war trauma are likely to meet these events again in old age in some way. British evacuees during the Second World War met a huge variety of experiences, both positive and negative. Their ability to meet with these experiences again, and for others to contribute to the means for coping with the darkest of them, is the challenge for both client and professional.

References

Birtnell, J. and Kennard, J. (1984) 'How do the experiences of the early separated and the early bereaved differ and to what extent do such differences affect outcome?' *Social Psychiatry 19*, 4, 163–171.

Burlingham, D. and Freud, A. (1943) *Infants without Families*. London: Pimlico.

Calder, A. (1969) *The People's War: Britain 1939–45*. London: Pimlico Books.

Calder, A. (1991) *The Myth of the Blitz*. London: Pimlico Books.

Davies, S. (1992) Long term psychological effects of the civilian evacuations in World War Two Britain. Unpublished paper presented at PSIGE Conference, Canterbury, UK, July.

Davies, S. (1994) Remembering traumatic wartime experiences in old age: an initial investigation into the relative significance of episodic and semantic autobiographical memory. Unpublished paper. European Colloquium, University of Stirling, May.

Freud, A. and Burlingham, D. (1942) *Children and Wartime*. London: Allen and Unwin.

Gardner, J. (1991) *The People's War*. New York: Selecta Books.

Gilbert, M. (1990) *Second World War*. London: Fontana.

Green, B. (1989) *Britain at War*. Milton Keynes: Coombe Books.

Haas, A. (1995) *The Aftermath: Living with the Holocaust*. Cambridge: Cambridge University Press.

Holman, R. (1995) *The Evacuation: A Very British Revolution*. London: Lion Publishing.

Hunt, N. and Robbins, I. (1995) 'Perceptions of the war 50 years on. What do veterans remember?' *British Journal of Health Psychology 1*, 2, 23–28.

Inglis, R. (1989) *The Children's War; Evacuation 1939–1945*. London: Collins.

Institute of Education, University of London (1947) *London Children in Wartime Oxford: A Survey of Social and Educational Results of the Evacuation*. London: Institute of Education.

Isaacs, S. (ed) (1941) *The Cambridge Evacuation Survey: A Wartime Study in Social Welfare and Education*. Cambridge: Cambridge University Press.

Karnow, S. (1987) *Vietnam: A History*. New York: Penguin Books.

Knight, R. (1986) *Psychotherapy with Older Adults*. California: Thousand Oaks.

MacIntosh, R. (1944) *The War and Mental Health in England*. New York: Commonwealth Fund Publication.

Ponting, C. (1995) *Armageddon: The Second World War*. London: Sinclair-Stevenson.

Russell, S. (1995) The wartime evacuation of the Maudsley Hospitals; 1939–1945. Unpublished paper presented at the Society for the Study of History in Medicine 12th Conference, Wellcome Trust, London, May 1995.

Rutter, M. and Rutter, E. (1995) *Continuity and Change: Development across the Lifespan*. London: Penguin Books.

Tennant, C., Hurry, J. and Bebbington, P. (1982) 'The relation of childhood separation experiences to adult depressive and anxiety states.' *British Journal of Psychiatry 141*, 475–482.

Therry, A. (1994) *The War Years, 1939–1945, Eyewitness Accounts*. London: Marshall Cavendish.

Turner, V. and Rennell, A. (1995) *When Daddy Came Home: How Family Life Changed Forever in 1945*. London: Hutchinson.

Van Der Kolk, B. (1987) *Psychological Trauma*. Washington DC: American Psychiatric Press.

Van Der Kolk, B. and Van Der Hart, O. (1991) 'The intrusive past: the flexibility of memory and the engraving of trauma.' *American Imago 48*, 4, 425–454.

Van Der Kolk, B. (1994) 'The body keeps score: memory and the evolving psychobiology of post traumatic stress.' *Harvard Review of Psychiatry 1*, 253–265.

Van Der Kolk, B. (ed) (1996) *Traumatic Stress*. New York: Guildford Press.

Waugh, M. (1994) Women and War: The long term effects of war trauma on women. Unpublished paper presented at the British Psychological Society, London Conference, December 1994.

Wicks, B. (1988) *No Time to Wave Goodbye*. London: Bloomsbury.

Wicks, B. (1990) *Nell's War*. London: Stoddart.

Ziegler, P. (1995) *London at War; 1939–1945*. London: Sinclair-Stevenson.

Further Reading

Robbins, I. (1994) 'Conceptualisation and treatment of war trauma.' Unpublished paper presented at British Psychological Society, London Conference, December 1994.

PART FOUR

The Journey Continues

Up to this point in the book, the chapters have been about trauma in the past that continues to affect older people in the present. This next chapter has as its starting point disaster and trauma of the present.

Faith Gibson is writing about the particular circumstances of the continuing violence in Northern Ireland – a remorseless, low-level conflict punctuated by larger-scale incidents of bombing or shooting. A resident in Northern Ireland, she writes as a 'participant observer' of the conflict. As she explains, she is not professionally involved in dealing with the consequences of the bombings, shootings and physical assaults. But with her interest in social work practice with older people, she views the present with an eye on its possible future impact. There is no knowing what this might be; silence is a feature of Northern Ireland society, so the extent of pain and trauma is extremely difficult to gauge. But even if this were not the case, accuracy would still be impossible. Not only are we dealing with highly personal experiences in a form of warfare which is not officially recognised as such, but the meaning of the event(s) may change over time, from one life stage to another and perhaps, too, as the political context changes.

To pursue the theme of this book, therefore, many people in Northern Ireland who are not yet old will have to make sense of what has been done to them or what they have done to others. For some, it will be necessary for helpers – both formal and informal – to be with them in this work. In many ways, therefore, the journey to understanding continues.

To assist this continuation, Hunt provides a final chapter which draws together the implications for practice. She shows that there is a body of good practice which applies across settings and professional disciplines, and that the challenges facing workers and carers have a remarkable similarity, irrespective of the training the workers and carers have received. In this sense, therefore, it is the responsibility of us all to be mindful of, and responsive to, the significance of other people's pasts and their influence upon their present lives.

Cherry Rowlings

CHAPTER 14

Political Violence and Coping in Northern Ireland

Faith Gibson

Case History

Some 20 years ago, a 19-year-old Catholic university student coming out of mass at a church in a middle-class area of Belfast was assassinated by a lone gunman of similar age. His mother was subsequently told by the police that the gunman had been paid five pounds to do the job. A deeply grieving family of mother, father and ten-year-old sister was left to come to terms with this random sectarian killing perpetrated by one young man upon another.

For months after the killing, the family home never emptied. People came to express their outrage, comfort the parents and offer consolation in a society which was becoming increasingly polarised and segregated as one atrocity followed another, inflicted by Protestant and Catholic paramilitary terrorists portraying themselves as freedom fighters and protectors of their own communities.

Initially the student's sister appeared to cope. While the parents and other adults overtly grieved she would quietly retire upstairs to her bedroom and immerse herself in her homework for, as the family doctor had remarked, children are not affected by such things and, 'she is alright'. A year later she became acutely ill, complained of severe headaches and, with a soaring temperature and hallucinations, was admitted to hospital with possible meningitis. All tests and investigations proved negative, the illness continued and no physical cause could be identified.

The puzzled physician, in pursuing further general inquiries with the parents about the family situation and relationships, discovered the information about the brother's death. Immediately she went into the little girl and said directly to her: 'That was a terrible thing they did to your brother'. At once the child began to cry. She cried and cried, as did her mother and her father with her, and after several hours, once her crying subsided, all physical symptoms of her illness had disappeared. In the years following, her successful academic career continued without further interruption or illness and now, happily married, she is pursuing a successful career as a physician in palliative medicine.

Her mother's mourning took a different course. She found she had an overwhelming need to transcend her devastating feelings of having failed as a parent to protect a child, albeit an adult child. In her grief, she reached out to others and founded a mutual aid, cross-community group for violently bereaved women. It meets monthly in members' houses, where people come together to talk, have a cup of tea and share their individual and family concerns.

The group, known as the Cross Group, has been sustained with minimum formality over 20 years. Members are drawn from all religious and social backgrounds and come into the group by the founder making contact with them by following up newspaper information about atrocities. She either writes, telephones or calls, briefly mentions the group and leaves a contact card with telephone number. Sometimes many months or even years elapse before a person joins the group, which tries to make no demands and warmly accepts people at whatever stage of the grieving process they are at.

Each summer, members and their families holiday together and in sharing good times as well as bad times they sustain each other: 'We talk about everything but politics and religion. We all know each other's stories. We don't have to tell them.'

Many of the members are widows. Some, but by no means all, are members of the interdenominational religious Correymeela Community of Reconciliation. In the past, for many members, raising their families as single parents absorbed their energies. Many are now in their 60s with their children grown and most away from home. These women face loneliness, not dissimilar from other widows, yet exacerbated by the memories of untimely, unnecessary, violent death. As they age, they need the group more than ever but their changing circumstances, including deteriorating health, transport difficulties and geographic dispersement, threaten their continued participation.

Introduction

This chapter is concerned with examining the effects of the past 25 years of civil disturbance in Northern Ireland (a period euphemistically referred to as the 'Troubles') on older people. It explores some ideas about the possible future responses required by the community and by health and social care professionals as they seek to offer services to people who have suffered past trauma and who may present with emotional problems as they age in the years ahead. The chapter is based on a review of general clinical literature because no research work specific to the impact of this prolonged period of civil unrest on people over 60 has been identified. Discussions with several of the authors cited have been undertaken within the last year and supplemented by a small number of semi-structured interviews with health and social care professionals whose current work is also thought to be relevant. For ease of presentation, they are subsequently referred to as 'respondents'.

Background

Northern Ireland consists of six counties in the north-eastern corner of the island of Ireland. It has a total population of approximately 1.6 million people, of whom some 60 per cent are Protestants and 40 per cent are Catholics. It was established under the Government of Ireland Act (1920) which partitioned it from the rest of the island and confirmed it as part of the United Kingdom of Great Britain and Northern Ireland. It is beyond the scope of this chapter to summarise the protracted history preceding these changes. Yet the origins of the past 25 years of violence can only be understood within the context of the long and complex relationship which has existed over many centuries between mainland Britain and the island of Ireland (Beckett, 1958; Foster, 1989).

Like several other contemporary 20th century societies, Northern Ireland is marked by deeply divisive, recurring conflict to which historic annexation, conquest and colonisation, differences of religion, identity, power, privilege and economic opportunity have all contributed.

This latest period of violence developed in the wake of the international civil rights movement of the late 1960s which triggered a similar upsurge of protest in Ireland. Old sectarian hatreds, entrenched discrimination by a Protestant majority and political marginalisation served to reactivate the Irish Republican Army (IRA), which embarked on a terror campaign designed to achieve the political end of a re-united Ireland. Protestant paramilitary organisations emerged as counter-terrorists and the British army was sent in to prevent the feared slide into civil war. This period recently gave way to the peace process, which began with the ceasefires declared first by Catholic and later by Protestant paramilitary organisations in September and October 1994. So far, all-party political talks to agree a future form of government have not commenced because of a profound lack of trust which underlies disagreements about disarmament or decommissioning of weapons. At the time of going to press (autumn 1996), the early optimism about peace has receded, as sporadic punishment beatings, intimidation and arson attacks have continued and bomb attacks by the IRA have returned to mainland Britain. Hopes of a political settlement acceptable to all the people of Ireland, north and south, and agreed by the governments of Ireland and the United Kingdom have again suffered a severe setback.

Northern Ireland society is deeply polarised. Both before and since partition, extreme nationalists and extreme unionists have sought to use violence to obtain political objectives. For many years, the area has also suffered intractable unemployment, incomes lower than UK averages (except for public sector workers), conflicts of identity, discrimination and sectarianism manifest in marked segregation in housing, education, sport and recreation (Gibson, Michael and Wilson, 1994). A majority of Protestants wish to remain part of the United Kingdom (unionists), while most Catholics, including constitutional nationalists, aspire to a united Ireland. Paramilitarists on both sides have little electoral support. Sinn Fein, the political wing of the IRA, generally gains some 10 per cent of the Catholic nationalist vote in Northern Ireland and about 2 per cent throughout the whole island. The same level of electoral support in Northern Ireland is achieved by the non-sectarian moderate Alliance Party, whose membership is drawn from both Catholics and Protestants. Nevertheless, this is a deeply divided society marked by sectarian suspicion and considerable social and economic deprivation. It is against this background that the following statistics of the last 25 years of the 'Troubles' are set.

Statistics of the 'Troubles'

The official statistics concerned with death, injury and damage to property paint a starkly incomplete picture of the numbers of people affected by violence in the years 1969–94. A breakdown of these statistics of deaths and injuries by age is not readily available. Nor do the statistics record the vast numbers of family members, friends and associates affected, others who have witnessed atrocities and explosions or who have suffered in other ways, directly or indirectly, as a consequence of loss of property, employment or peace of mind. The impact of imprisonment, intimidation, punishment, relocation, enforced exile or emigration is also undocumented. The scale of past and present suffering cannot be fully accounted, nor is it possible to quantify how many 'Troubles'-related problems will emerge in the future for any age group. Given experience in other places, however, and what has been written elsewhere in this book, it seems reasonable to assume that problems requiring skilled attention will emerge as people age.

Between 1969 and 1994 3186 people have been killed. Of these, civilians numbered 2238 and Crown security forces, including police, accounted for 948. A further 16,651 people were injured, of whom 24,333 were civilians and 13,406 members of the security forces.

Between 1969 and 1995 there were 35,087 shooting incidents and 11,181 firearms were recovered. Bomb explosions and defusing numbered 14,886 and armed robberies numbered 9224. A total of 16,651 persons were charged with terrorist offences. Between 1969 and 1992 involvement in claims for criminal damage and personal injury, always complex, protracted processes, totalled 6232 and 11,045, respectively.

These statistics (Royal Ulster Constabulary, 1995) are no real measure of how the population has experienced this prolonged period of violence and at what personal cost a semblance of normal life has been maintained. Nor do they indicate how the experience of people has differed markedly according to where they live, the occupation (if any) they follow and whether or not they or their family have directly experienced violence, the nature, intensity and targets of which have varied over time. Violence has been largely, but not exclusively, concentrated in working-class areas of urban Belfast, Derry City (Londonderry) and rural areas along the meandering border with the Irish Republic. Earlier urban street rioting has largely disappeared. Commercial and business interests and the security forces, especially the police, have been targeted in more recent years. The partiality of impact, which has protected many people, may be one factor accounting to some extent for the prolongation of the strife, political intransigence and the lack of urgency in reaching a settlement.

Research Review

Compared with the thousands of historical and political studies which have been undertaken, there has been relatively little research concerned with the impact of the 'Troubles' on adult mental health. Some studies about the impact on children have been undertaken. A number of early studies by Lyons (1974) concluded that the vast majority of people recovered with outpatient treatment and generally showed, 'a remarkable resilience and tolerance' (p.19). Hadden, Rutherford and Merrett, (1978) reported on 1532 consecutive patients admitted to an accident and emergency department of a Belfast hospital because of bomb explosions. Only 50 per cent displayed 'nervous shock', with women predominating.

A series of reports have described individuals referred for medicolegal psychiatric assessment between 1978 and 1984 (Bell *et al.*, 1988; Curran, 1988; Kee *et al.*, 1987; Loughrey and Curran 1987, Loughrey *et al.*, 1988). This series included passive victims of political violence as well as victims of sexual and common assault. Approximately 5 per cent of these 643 litigants were aged 65 plus. Only 23 per cent of the total were assessed as suffering from Post-Traumatic Stress Disorder (PTSD) as defined by DSM-III. The PTSD group was significantly older and contained more single, unmarried and widowed women, who reported more depression and sexual marital disharmony since the violent incident. Unlike many PTSD studies of combat populations, and unlike, too, the Holocaust survivors described by authors of other chapters in this book, there was a low frequency of restlessness, irritability, explosive outbursts, impulsive behaviour, substance abuse, psychosomatic symptoms, and 'as if' behaviour.

Curran *et al.* (1990) examined at six month and one year intervals 33 litigant survivors of the 1987 no-warning Enniskillen Remembrance Day bomb, when 11 people were killed and some 60 injured. PTSD rates varied between the time of the two assessments, which led them to conclude that PTSD is phasic and, like Hadden *et al.* (1978), that it is not correlated with the seriousness of physical injury sustained. Their findings suggest the possibility that PTSD may occur or reoccur at any time following a traumatic incident, no matter how much time has elapsed. The study of 67 civilian and security forces conjugally bereaved widows by Dillenburger (1992, 1994) identified differences in mental health outcomes, as measured by the General Health Questionnaire, an instrument used in the UK for studying the state of mental and physical health in the general population. Longer-term bereaved widows had lower scores, although all, regardless of lapsed time, reported more evidence of psychiatric disturbance than the general population.

Cairns and Wilson (1993), like Lyons (1974), inferred that the Northern Ireland population has coped very well with violence by means of denial and distancing. They suggested that the abnormal features of living with prolonged violence were reconceptualised as normal by people who learned to manage stress by adopting a personally perceived appraisal of the level of violence which differed from the actual violence.

Loughrey and Curran (1987) suggested stress may depend less on the *perceived experience* of violence and more upon the *perception of the outcomes* of violence conceived in political terms. If this is true, such defences may become less efficacious as the violence recedes, the peace process accelerates and an eventual political accommodation is achieved. Perhaps future functioning, whether it entails coping or breakdown, may be influenced by how people view their past trauma in terms of what was won or lost, not only personally, but in terms of how acceptable they find the eventual political outcomes.

Many children have experienced direct and indirect violence and continue to live in families in which its effects are ongoing. It is not known if the common practice of trying to shield children from adult distress and exclude them from the overt grieving process will have long-term deleterious effects. Until recently most schools tried to ensure neutrality, which excluded attention to violence and its consequences. As one teacher, who now meets in an interprofessional cross-community group working with disturbed children, said: 'We were not allowed to deal with politically induced stress, loss and bereavement. We were not allowed to talk about it'.

The trades unions likewise have been committed to maintaining neutrality in the workplace. In seeking to outlaw sectarianism on the factory floor, as in schools and some families, personal pain may have been driven underground. Such appearance of normality may have been a short-term gain purchased at the price of unresolved longer-term problems. Coping with, and adapting to, communal violence by such means may have benefited the many, but may have placed inestimable strain on traumatised individuals whose needs have remained unaddressed.

Studies of psychiatric hospital admissions, prescriptions for psychotropic drugs, alcohol-related disorders, and suicide and parasuicide rates indicate that throughout the 1970s and 1980s, the Northern Ireland population generally coped well. If peace holds, we may speculate that most people will probably continue to cope as they did in the past. Such global statements, however, may very well obscure the present and emerging problems of specific sub-groups, for example disabled policemen, child witnesses of parental violent death, victims of paramilitary punishment squads or families of the 'disappeared'. If lasting peace with a widely acceptable political settlement is not realised, and violence recurs, repetitive trauma on a wide scale may be anticipated. Whether or not a lasting peace is achieved, professional opinion suggests that an unknown number of people both now and as they age may become emotionally distressed as a consequence of earlier trauma experienced by living in an abnormal society.

There are early indications that the peace process is creating a climate in which some people are beginning to feel more able to address the pain which hitherto they have repressed for the sake of keeping up appearances and surviving in the present. As one social worker put it: 'Once people no longer have to cover up for the sake of the tribe, the stories will begin to be told'.

Hindrances to Recovery

Respondents identified factors which appeared to either assist or delay the development of coping mechanisms and recovery from 'Troubles'-induced stress, as indicated by absence of disabling physical and psychological symptoms, and investment in new interests, activities and relationships.

An unresolved sense of grievance exists for many, and personal grievance is reinforced when whole communities share a sense of outrage and grief. It is felt acutely by some Catholics in relation to the security forces. For example, it was especially apparent in a study of families of the victims of Bloody Sunday (Hayes, Smyth and Hayes, 1994), when 14 unarmed civilians were shot dead by Crown forces while participating in a civil rights march in Derry, that such feelings have incredible endurance in both families and tightly knit geographic localities where everyday reminders abound. Similar examples where place names have become synonymous with group atrocities and there is persistent, unresolved personal and communal pain, include, among many others, Enniskillen, Teebane, Loughanisland, McGurk's Bar, the Shankill Road and Greysteel.

Memories, often selective and focused only on atrocities experienced by one's 'own side', are passed from generation to generation and over time may assume mythological proportions within communities and within families. Children may be brought up in terms of life scripts or life narratives which have been written for them and imposed upon them by others, with unforeseen longer-term consequences (Freeman, 1993). While some people may find strength and support from families and close-knit communities, others feel trapped and escape by distancing themselves, often literally by emigration, thus compounding their own and others' sense of loss.

Being locked into social constructions of grief by precipitate media appearances immediately after involvement in a traumatic incident, when private grief is turned into public property, makes it difficult for people to deal adequately with their loss and to move on. They are trapped in whatever public roles and behaviours they first displayed. Some victims and family members, especially parents of children who were killed or injured in violent incidents, no matter how old the child, seem especially burdened by guilt. There are, however, many examples throughout the past 25 years of people acting either as individuals, families or groups, who have sought to resolve their anguish by investment in constructive peace projects of various kinds, and society has greatly benefited from these numerous cross-community ecumenical activities.

Repeated media exposure, which serves to reinforce past pain and postpone the extinction of grieving behaviours is unhelpful. The deleterious effect of media replays of traumatic events at times of fresh outrages and anniversaries was commented on by some interviewees, although it is recognised that some people are helped by the recognition of anniversaries and pilgrimages. An early visit to the site of an atrocity is commended by some professionals as an essential means of helping survivors and mourners surmount denial (Gibson, 1991).

Fostering Future Coping

Various means of helping people to cope with stress which may emerge in the future are now suggested. It has been difficult to develop a satisfactory classification, as the various types of intervention identified are not mutually exclusive, and some people will find their own spontaneous healing process sufficient for survival without needing or using any specific kind of external help. It is suggested, however, that change and action are required at national and communal levels if families and individuals are to be adequately supported. Both societal and personal change is important. Many people will probably require more than one type of assistance, either simultaneously or at different stages of their journey as their needs alter over the life course.

Nationally, mutual forgiveness, acknowledgement of shared responsibility for past wrongs, repentance and reconciliation founded on emerging trust, need to provide the foundation for a broadly acceptable political settlement which will provide the framework for a lasting peace. Constitutional arrangements, desirably supported by a bill of rights, and institutions of the state, especially those concerned with law and order, must command wide respect.

Public acknowledgement of failures, mistaken judgements and miscarriages of justice, with or without financial compensation, are crucial aspects of the healing process for communities, families and individuals. So far miscarriages of justice have been slow to be rectified, while others await long overdue resolution. For example, Bloody Sunday victims and supporters continue to campaign for a declaration of the innocence of the 28 civilians killed and wounded by the army 22 years ago. Such a declaration is a necessary prerequisite to peace and reconciliation at a community level. Whether it will be sufficient to heal at a personal level remains to be seen. The issue of prisoners requires urgent resolution, as does the return of the bodies of terrorist victims for proper burial. Perhaps we could learn from Chile's truth and reconciliation commission, which is an example of a state seeking to acknowledge publicly the wrongs done in its name (Dorfman, 1994) or from similar moves developed in post-apartheid South Africa.

It appears that so far few older people have sought help for 'Troubles'-related stress, either close in time to traumatic events or since. The reasons for this are unclear and are probably complex. Professionals interviewed were unaware of any specific age-related factors or of examples of delayed development of symptoms. Possibly needs are being cloaked in somatic symptomology, as Robbins earlier (Chapter 5) describes in respect of combat stress. Or perhaps they are attributed to other causes or are going unrecognised and unattended, with people being left to cope with either inappropriate or inadequate support.

Generally recognised means of help, including supportive counselling, may be equally relevant for older people, even if they so far have been underutilised by them. Many different types of formal and informal assistance have been identified. Some people have found healing through their family, friends and faith. Others have profited from mutual support groups such as the Cross Group described earlier, although these are few in number and most appear to cater for women. Not all have overtly therapeutic or supportive purposes. Some are politically motivated, some are closely tied to paramilitary organisations and some tend to address issues rather than the pain of individuals.

As time passes and survivors age, health and social care professional practitioners will need to be sensitive to the possibility that 'Troubles'-related traumas, even if occurring in the distant past, may have reverberations in the present. They should be alert to the need to include relevant questions in medical and social history-taking, and not to continue to collude with the denial and silence which appeared to sustain so many people during the period of overt conflict. Professionals need to be willing to use a wide range of conventional talking therapies and other creative therapeutic approaches and to make appropriate referrals to various sources of help.

There is growing evidence that numerous creative means exist for helping older people address their problematic life experience, whatever its origins and nature. Music, art, dance, drama, creative and autobiographical writing are all relevant. Life history and reminiscence work with either individuals or small groups has proved a fruitful means of assisting some older people who are troubled about aspects of their past, and whose behaviour or distress is troubling to those with whom they live in the present. Coleman and Mills in Chapter 12 emphasise the importance of careful and sensitive use of such work with unhappy older people; it is not appropriate for everyone, but in the right circumstances can help people to rework their problematic pasts and to some extent come to terms with life as it has turned out (Gibson, 1994).

Sensitivity to people's own timing about being able and willing to face their hurt is, however, crucial. Denial and repression may have sustained survival until ageing brings more time for reflection. Earlier personal denial may have been reinforced by norms within local communities or groups which portrayed suffering as noble, heroic and a necessary sacrifice. Contemporary normative hazards of late life, such as loss, bereavement, ill health and manifold threats to independence and coping, may trigger a desire to review one's life, to bear witness and address past pain, however caused and however publicly or historically portrayed. Sometimes it becomes more possible to face the past, 'to tell the story' for the sake of informing grandchildren, whereas children may be too close to the suffering and may have colluded with the silence for the sake of surviving the present. The elapse of time between the trauma and the telling can be considerable.

Respondents cited some examples to support the widely accepted idea that contemporary events can trigger or reactivate past pain. For example, one witness to an atrocity had coped quite well for 15 years until faced with losing his job, when intrusions, dreams and other symptoms of anxiety related to the previous event overtook him. And there is another example of a woman, now middle-aged, who had suffered horrific burns in a hotel explosion and fire, necessitating 172 operations for reconstructive surgery. She managed all right, after initial recovery, until the ceasefire was declared. Then, although now living in England, she telephoned the social worker she had known in the hospital burns unit many years before. In great distress she poured out her reactivated anger which had been triggered as she viewed on television the triumphalism of the Sinn Fein leaders declaring their ceasefire. In the years between she had been denied the opportunity to talk by a well-intentioned, loving husband who had moved the family away from Northern Ireland to give them a fresh start and help put all those things behind them. The parallels with case examples provided throughout the preceding chapters are immediately apparent.

Most professionals in health and social care agencies who were interviewed suggested that a safe place to be heard (when ready) and to have recurring anger, grief, despair and depression attended to is essential. As this book demonstrates, many different approaches to such listening exist, and some people may require medication and/or environmental assistance as well. Recovery has to be recognised as a process, not an event. Dillenburger (1994) suggests it may be possible using a behavioural/cognitive approach to encourage the extinction of grieving behaviour rather than its reinforcement. Others adopt more conventional psychotherapeutic approaches. Whatever intervention is used, relapses are likely and people may need safe listening places, either regularly or intermittently, for many years to come.

Who does the listening is also important in Northern Ireland, as other contributors to this book have found in their respective countries. It does not all need to be done by professionally qualified staff, although selection, training, support and supervision of the listeners may be highly desirable. Mutual aid is sometimes more acceptable. Some victims believe that other victims are the best equipped to help. Some women believe that only other women will appreciate their pain and be able to help them:

> I put a lot of emotions on hold when my husband was shot dead when I was pregnant. I shut down my scream. I did not deal with my loss. There are a lot of broken women – we don't take up weapons and go out and kill others. It is the women who have been broken who have to be part of the healing process. We need mediators – not politicians who speak in clichés. Victims must be able to grieve. (C. McKay, widow of a mistaken identity assassination victim, 1994)

Paramilitarists also need help. The expression of personal remorse, confession and investment in efforts to make amends, either at an individual or community level, is being undertaken by some, especially those who have undergone an experience of religious conversion:

> We started off with the ideology – we had to do it for the 'cause'. Then you come to like what you're doing – you depersonalise the violence. Members of organisations are not people. They become legitimate targets. If you regard a member as a non-person, you can do horrific things. (W. Mitchell, ex paramilitary prisoner, 1994)

In a province where church attendance remains common, there are frequent reports of terrorists, security force members, victims and other survivors finding new hope through religious experience, which often transcends sectarian boundaries and holds the promise of the churches becoming more a part of the solution and less a part of the historic problem.

In this small country, in addition to existing statutory health and social services agencies and the churches, it has been suggested that upwards of some 50 voluntary organisations of varying levels of sophistication exist which offer help of different kinds to victims and survivors. This does not mean that everyone either knows about them or finds them acceptable. There continue to be further suggestions about what is needed. An ad-hoc group of professional and community leaders called the Remember and Change Group has proposed a positive preventative approach to mental health problems, and is presently seeking funding to train and support 500 listeners who would be available throughout Northern Ireland and the border areas to offer a confidential befriending, listening relationship to any person or group who wished to tell their story. These trained volunteers would refer on to professional specialists any person who required more specialised psychotherapeutic or spiritual assistance. Through a gradual development this network of 'listening ears' may ultimately lead to the establishment of some form of conflict resolution commission (Remember and Change Group, 1995). Other initiatives have also been proposed. For example, Smyth (1995) argues for the creation of a network of community-based mediation centres with open referral and easy access in order to make counselling services acceptable to all who may need them.

Questions about who is best equipped to offer help; what kind of help should be offered; what organisations or agencies should be involved; how should they be funded; and for what period of time should they exist, are all relevant questions. Whoever undertakes this demanding work will themselves require to be supported lest they be overwhelmed in the process of offering help.

Conclusion

It is not possible to identify with any rigour who is a victim of the 'Troubles', nor to predict who is likely to suffer in later life from the consequences of having lived in Northern Ireland during the past quarter-century. It can be reasonably assumed that for individual people, unresolved hurt and anger from the past will re-emerge in the future, probably triggered by other threats to mental and physical health, well-being, security and personal relationships which seem to be inevitable accompaniments of growing old. It must also be assumed that civilians, paramilitarists and security forces personnel are all likely to be at risk and some members from all these groups will need help in coming to terms with their past. Political peace will not necessarily bring personal peace or resolution of past pain. How people cope will depend on their inherent and learned coping strengths, the magnitude of the threats with which they are faced and the availability of acceptable and timely assistance when needed.

As Northern Ireland haltingly moves towards establishing a society freed from sectarianism, discrimination, inequality and injustice, and achieves political and administrative institutions which command the allegiance and respect of all its citizens, some individuals will require help with problems whose origins lie in the old order. For them, whether their past experience labels them as victims, survivors, paramilitaries, security personnel, families, friends, witnesses, professional or informal helpers, a variety of assistance will be necessary. It will need to come from many different formal and informal sources.

The brief case history with which this chapter began well illustrates these points. Opportunities to talk about how people feel about what has happened to them seem to be essential. There should be no demand for people to forget what has happened. Each person will have to make his or her own idiosyncratic journey, in their own time, in their own way, towards dealing with their pain, and finding forgiveness, reparation and reconciliation. There will be a continuing need to attend to everyone of whatever age, including older and younger people, in ways which each finds acceptable. There is a place for professional help, volunteer help and mutual aid. Some people will be best helped by an individual approach. Others may find the support of people with similar problems who meet in groups more appropriate to their needs. Some may only be able to accept assistance from people of the same gender, age, religion, culture or political persuasion. Others may be able to cope with difference. What will be required in the future when people age is the same as what they require now – a state committed to peace and justice for all its citizens; caring communities whose members have a sense of responsibility for each other; skilled, sensitive, creative, health and social work professionals; and various appropriate acceptable services, freely and equitably available to all irrespective of age, gender, religion, identity, income and place of residence.

References

Beckett, A. (1958) *A Short History of Ireland.* London: Hutchinson.

Bell, P., Key, M., Loughrey, G., Roddy, R. and Curran, P. (1988) 'Post-traumatic stress disorder in Northern Ireland.' *Acta Psychiatrica Scandinavica 77,* 166–169.

Cairns, E. and Wilson, R. (1993) 'Stress, coping and political violence in Northern Ireland.' In J. Wilson and B. Raphael (eds) *International Handbook of Traumatic Stress Syndromes.* New York: Plenum.

Curran, P. (1988) 'Psychiatric aspects of terrorist violence: Northern Ireland 1969–1987.' *British Journal of Psychiatry 153,* 470–475.

Curran, P., Bell, P., Murray, A., Loughrey, G., Roddy, R. and Rocke, L. (1990) 'Psychological consequences of the Enniskillen bombing.' *British Journal of Psychiatry 156,* 479–482.

Dillenburger, K. (1992) *Violent Bereavement: Widows in Northern Ireland.* Aldershot: Avebury.

Dillenburger, K. (1994) 'Bereavement: a behavioural process.' *The Irish Journal of Psychology 15*, 4, 524–539.

Dorfman, A. (1994) *Death and the Maiden.* Raleigh: Duke University.

Foster, R.F. (ed) (1989) *The Oxford History of Ireland.* Oxford, Oxford University Press.

Freeman, M. (1993) *Rewriting the Self: History, Memory and Narrative.* London: Routledge.

Gibson, F. (1994) *Reminiscence and Recall.* London: Age Concern.

Gibson, F., Michael, G. and Wilson, D. (1994) *Perspectives on Discrimination and Social Work In Northern Ireland.* London: Central Council for Education and Training in Social Work.

Gibson, M. (1991) *Order from Chaos: Responding to Traumatic Events.* Birmingham: Venture Press.

Hadden, W., Rutherford, W. and Merrett, J. (1978) 'The injuries of terrorist bombing: a study of 1,532 consecutive patients.' *British Journal of Surgery 65.* 525.

Hayes, P., Smyth, M. and Hayes, E. (1994) Post-traumatic stress and the families of Bloody Sunday victims in Derry, Northern Ireland. Unpublished personal communication.

Kee, M., Bell, P., Loughrey, G., Roddy, R. and Curran, P. (1987) 'Victims of violence; a demographic and clinical study.' *Medicine, Science and the Law 27*, 4, 241–247.

Loughrey, G. and Curran, P. (1987) 'The psychopathology of civil disorder.' In A. Dawson and G. Besser (eds) *Recent Advances in Medicine.* Edinburgh: Churchill Livingstone.

Loughrey, G., Bell, P., Kee, M., Roddy, R. and Curran, P. (1988) 'Post-traumatic stress disorder and civil violence in Northern Ireland.' *British Journal of Psychiatry 153*, 554–560.

Lyons, H.A. (1974) 'Terrorist bombing and the psychological sequelae.' *Journal of the Irish Medical Association Vol.67*, 1, 15–19.

Remember and Change Group (1995) *Remember and Change Proposal April 1995.* Belfast: Remember and Change Group.

Royal Ulster Constabulary (1995) *Statistical Information.* Belfast: RUC.

Smyth, M. (1995) Proposal to establish an independent body responsible for the provision of support services to those affected by political violence in Northern Ireland in the last 25 years. Unpublished paper submitted to the Forum for Peace and Reconciliation.

Further Reading

Victim Support Northern Ireland (1994) *Victims of Violent Crime: A Working Party Report.* Belfast: Victim Support.

CHAPTER 15

The Implications For Practice

Linda Hunt

> I was much further out than you thought
> And not waving but drowning.

Stevie Smith

The preceding chapters draw on a wide range of professional perspectives to suggest ways of understanding and working to help older people who are still struggling with the impact of their earlier traumatic experiences. The evidence presented in these chapters shows that elderly people often become well motivated to engage in examination of distressing issues and to work for the resolution of long-standing painful difficulties. The work described by many of the authors makes it clear that elderly people who have survived traumatic events, contrary to frequently heard pessimistic comments, can successfully reach resolution of old problems or a significant reduction in symptoms of stress and in difficulties with relationships (see the chapters by Robbins, Bergström-Walan, de Levita, Sutton, Hassan and Fried, for example). The book amply illustrates the capacity of elderly people for personal growth and change, and points unequivocally to the importance of increasing the attention given to the group of people, who may constitute 10 per cent or more of older people in some European countries, who are still struggling with the effects of earlier trauma. The scope for improving the quality of life of this group of older people would seem to be considerable, since Bramsen's (1995) study of a sample of Dutch people showed that only a third of those who had been highly exposed to shocking wartime experience and who still had symptoms of distress associated with that experience were actually in contact with any member of the caring professions at the time of the study. Coleman and Mills (Chapter 12) also point to the lack of attention by staff in residential settings to the possibility that old trauma may be a current problem for some residents. In this concluding chapter, therefore, an attempt is made to draw out common threads from the rich and diverse material presented by the contributors to this book and to map out key features of effective services for older survivors of earlier trauma. The aim is to help professional practitioners in health and social care services to pursue practice and service developments that will encourage recognition of the circumstances of these elderly people and ensure the availability to them of relevant and appropriate help. The chapter looks in particular at initial contact and assessment, at the engagement of clients in a process of trying to come to terms with their earlier experience, at feelings and reactions that are frequently part of the picture, and at the qualities and skills required by practitioners.

Initial Contact and Assessment

The initial assessment by the professionals involved in health and social care of their clients' position and the interpretations they make of the signals clients are giving are critical determinants of the help that is offered. This is a view already well articulated across all the professional groups providing services to the generality of elderly people. Stevie Smith's well-known poem (quoted at the opening of this chapter) serves as a dramatic metaphor for an assessment where the client's position is not accurately located and the signals are misunderstood. The experience and analysis included in the preceding chapters show us that assessment may repeatedly fail to take account of the possibility of earlier trauma being a significant factor in present circumstances (see, for example, Robbins (Chapter 5) and also Davies (Chapter 13) and that signals frequently go unrecognised or are misinterpreted (see Sutton (Chapter 11) and Fried (Chapter 8), for example). A greater ability among all the professional practitioners who work with older people to understand this, and the readiness to respond appropriately to the signals clients are giving, are the first necessary steps towards the development of more helpful services to the significant numbers of older people for whom earlier trauma is still a potent source of distress.

For one reason and another there has remained a kind of 'conspiracy of silence' around the types of experience that have led to traumatisation. In this book, the chapters which focus on people traumatised by persecution and experience of combat and bombing in the Second World War frequently make mention of the expectation within society that survivors would make a fresh start, putting their experience behind them once the war or their imprisonment had ended. A feeling grew up that giving attention to what had happened was not acceptable. Talking about it and its impact was thought to be unhelpful, and in any case, for many survivors, all their emotional and physical energies were required for their efforts to build new lives. As Fried illustrates, avoiding talking became a feature of family life in many instances too. This kind of distancing and avoidance behaviour has also been a feature throughout the last 25 years of strife in Northern Ireland (Gibson, Chapter 14, this volume; Healey, in press) and it continues to be a factor which inhibits help-seeking 50 years after the end of the Second World War and liberation.

Bergström-Walan (Chapter 3) and Sutton show that avoidance of discussion is also a feature in situations where older people have been struggling to survive traumatising sexual abuse and other family violence experienced as a child or younger adult. Indeed the constraints against talking may be even stronger in these situations. The change towards a more open approach in society, which Bergström-Walan notes, is taking place only very slowly. The slow pace of this change is further illustrated by more recent events, such as the disaster at Hillsborough Stadium in 1989. The indications are that the survivors of these types of disaster do not readily talk about their experience either (Hodgkinson and Stewart, 1991). It seems that there are some senses in which it 'suits' survivors, those around them and society in general to avoid talking about and hearing accounts of traumatising experiences and the distressing impact they have had. Talking and listening means opening oneself to feelings and to thinking about frightening events over which those involved had no effective control and which challenge the normal view of human relationships and the social, moral and technical worlds we have constructed. This is a distressing situation for survivors and for all those who listen to their stories, so it is avoided.

Clearly, without some readiness by clients to talk and by the helping professions to listen, assessment will be incomplete and the capacity to notice and understand spoken and unspoken signals will be limited. Equally important to note at this point is the evidence of the therapeutic benefits of talking through the story (see Robbins and Crocq (Chapter 4), for example) and giving testimony (see Hassan (Chapter 9) and Fried, for example). When the right kind of supports are in place, talking really does help. Bramsen's (1995) study also shows that avoiding talking and avoiding situations which might act as reminders of shocking experiences are associated with a higher level of continuing problems, while talking is associated with fewer current problems connected to experience of war that took place 50 or more years ago.

What, then, are the factors which work to maintain avoidance behaviour? They seem to fall into two groups: those which relate particularly to the older people themselves and those stemming from the helping professions.

The Position of the Older People

> I had killed a man, and remembered his shocked, angry eyes. There was nothing I could say to him now. I began to have hallucinations and breaks in the brain. I lay there knowing neither time nor place. Some of our

men found me, I don't know who they were, and they drove me back speechless to Tarazona.

Was this then what I'd come for, and all my journey had meant – to smudge out the life of an unknown man in a blur of panic which in no way could affect victory or defeat?

This is how the writer Laurie Lee (1991, p.161) described one element of his own traumatic experience of the Spanish Civil War over 50 years after the events. This was a war to which he had determinedly trekked on foot over the Pyrenees in mid-winter, with the conviction that he would be able to help a just cause. He returned to England in a shocked and distressed state and, although he published other books about his travels in Spain, he seems to have been able to write an account of his wartime experience only when more than half a century had passed. The words he used suggest he was still struggling to make sense of his experience at the time of writing.

As the contributors to the preceding chapters have made clear, traumatic experiences overturn morality, creating situations in which the unacceptable and abnormal are treated as acceptable and normal. In these circumstances, people are faced with a chaotic, frightening world in which trust and confidence are undermined. The horrors and fears that they have experienced may seem literally 'unspeakable'. As they truly know that anything can happen, survivors may be left with a deep sense of insecurity about the nature of the world and with a high level of anxiety about the potential for further traumatic events occurring. The effort of holding themselves together in these circumstances will be very great and may be complemented by a fear that they will personally disintegrate if they speak about what has happened. This effort and the fear of disintegration are even greater for those who are beginning to suffer from dementia, as Hassan and Miesen and Jones (Chapter 10) have illustrated in different ways. Just as alarming and inhibiting is the fear experienced by some elderly survivors that their stories and their current experience are so frightening and horrifyingly powerful that they will harm anyone to whom they are told. This appears to be a factor for former combatants (see Robbins), for survivors of the Holocaust (see Brainin and Teicher (Chapter 6); Hassan) and for those who have suffered family violence (see Sutton). In these grim situations silence may well seem a safer option than talking.

Characteristically, traumatic events are unexpected, with those who experience them having no possibility of controlling what happens and, as those who have experienced the horrors of the implementation of Nazi policies have graphically testified, survival is often a matter of chance. As people move through the later stages of life, increasing frailty and awareness of death serve as reminders of the pain of the unexpected and the distress of loss of control and autonomy. The contributors to this volume are clear that it is through this process that old, unresolved difficulties stemming from earlier traumas are often triggered (see de Levita (Chapter 7), for example). The wish to retain autonomy and control in these circumstances will be great, and in northern Europe, where independence and the ability to deal with one's own problems (especially if these are psychological or social) without recourse to outside help are strongly valued, cultural norms may serve to reinforce avoidance of discussion of what is troublesome.

Since survivors are themselves often still trying to make some sense of their experience and the impact it is having on their lives many years after the traumatic events, it is not surprising that they seem often to doubt that they will be understood if they try to talk about what has happened and is happening. Their own current experience may include frightening and strange occurrences (see, for example, Schreuder (Chapter 2)), which they fear may be regarded as bizarre indicators of mental illness or dementia. This fear may well be realistic, as several contributors (for example, Sutton and Schreuder) indicate that diagnoses of mental confusion and dementia are mistakenly applied to some older people whose symptoms actually stem from their continuing struggle with earlier trauma. Uncertainty as to whether others can be trusted with their stories is then another reason for reluctance to talk.

Hassan, and Brainin and Teicher give emphasis to the bizarre experience of power and authority that Holocaust survivors have suffered, and convincingly argue that professional helpers will be perceived as authority figures, thus compounding the difficulty in trusting them. It is not hard to understand that anger and fear may be the dominant feelings expressed towards authority by those who have experienced its misuse. People who were persecuted in Europe and the Far East during the Second World War may have especially strong cause for such feelings, but those who have suffered sexual abuse and other violence from parents or people of standing in their community (such as churchmen or youth leaders) are also likely to have difficulty in trusting the authority of professionals and to have low expectations of the effectiveness of the treatment and support that might be available.

Attitudes and behaviour in our society tend to convey the message to older people that they are not 'useful', thus reinforcing in their minds the idea that they are unimportant and even unworthy. Older people will so often tell us, 'I don't want to be a nuisance'. Several contributors to this volume have described the feelings of guilt and lack of worth associated with survival of traumatic experience, and this powerful sense of guilt is included among the criteria defining Post-Traumatic Stress Disorder (PTSD). Bergström-Walan shows that those who have had traumatic sexual experience are burdened by guilt and may also have been taught forcefully by the perpetrators of abuse to fear punishment if they ever tell their story. The feelings of guilt and the messages from younger people combine together to suggest to older survivors that they have no right to raise their problems and that those professionals who might be able to help should be giving their time to more worthy people who are, perhaps, also in greater need.

These factors inhibit elderly survivors both in seeking any help and in sharing their experience. If professional practitioners in health and social care are successfully to overcome the difficulties inherent in making initial contact and enabling the older person to focus on distressing issues, a high level of sensitivity and openness is required of them. This is particularly the case for the great majority of professional practitioners who work in settings which do not specialise in trauma and its impact, and to which older people usually come for other reasons. It is general practitioners, residential and field social workers, psychiatrists, psychologists and nurses working in geriatric services, rather than agencies specialising in work with the survivors of trauma, who will usually be in a position to recognise the signals, engage in discussion that enables a sound assessment to be made and make it possible for a helping process to begin. Non-specialist practitioners play a critical role, therefore, in reaching out to older people struggling to survive earlier trauma and making it possible for them to talk. From the contributions to this volume it is possible to identify a number of aspects of practice that will help them to fulfil this role. These are drawn out in the remaining sections of this chapter.

The Position of Professional Practitioners

The preceeding chapters describe the positive and supportive atmosphere that is essential for survivors to be enabled to make initial contact. If practitioners are to establish this atmosphere, they have to be able to demonstrate a real and sympathetic understanding of the social and political circumstances of the years in which the traumas occurred and awareness of the impact of those circumstances on everyday life then and now. This is a point emphasised by contributors to all of the three earlier sections of this book. Historical knowledge of the period is required, as is a readiness to learn from the accounts of older people who have lived through it. The fact of being old enough to have personal knowledge of some of the relevant social and political circumstances or of having had experience relevant to the circumstances in which trauma has occurred can be a positive help to practitioners in enabling clients to talk, as Bergström-Walan and Robbins show. However, Davies and Sutton provide illustrations of how a willingness to learn, sensitive observation and active listening can enable younger practitioners with less relevant experience to provide the help people need.

In any case, it is only in very exceptional circumstances that practitioners will have experience comparable with that of their clients. Hassan makes this point very clearly in relation to Holocaust survivors, but it is also true for other types of trauma. It is fundamentally important, therefore, that from the beginning practitioners are open to learning from their clients and ready to take in the facts and feelings about each individual's experience. This means being ready to give some time to listening, thus making sure the older person does not feel pressured or rushed. It will be much easier for practitioners to allocate time for listening when their managers and senior colleagues recognise its importance and are ready to help to structure working arrangements to allow for it. Chapter 12, by Coleman and Mills, points out the importance of this in residential settings, where the demands of providing physical care can so easily squeeze out listening and talking time. Sutton provides one example of how time for attentive listening and support can be secured even in such a pressured environment.

Attentive listening is also required to help ensure that each individual's experience and distress are the focus of attention and to avoid making inappropriate generalisations. Schreuder goes further and says that the practitioner needs to be a 'passionate' listener. It is interesting that emphasis is given to the listening activity in three chapters whose authors specialise in working with survivors of trauma (Schreuder, Brainin and Teicher, and Fried), and it may be a factor of particular relevance to practitioners who are regularly exposed to horrifying and distressing accounts of traumatic experience. Such practitioners may sometimes wish to protect themselves from hearing what is being said. However, non-specialists need to give special attention to listening too; it is all too easy in a busy working day to make a quick, but superficial or careless, assessment.

Attentive listening is sometimes a painful activity, as many chapters of this book illustrate. First, there is the distressing nature of the account the client is giving; both client and practitioner will find it upsetting and, as Robbins says, the practitioner may feel overwhelmed by the horror and pain described. Second, as Brainin and Teicher in particular make plain, in the face of the information being given by the client, a practitioner is likely to be confronted with the limits of her/his own personal and professional knowledge and skills. Holding on to a constructive helping role is difficult but critical in these circumstances. Whatever type of traumatic experience is the focus of attention, there are difficulties for practitioners in remaining appropriately centred on the client's needs. At the initial stages of contact and assessment, remaining 'other centred' is especially important and practitioners need to be very aware of the potential for retreat to defensive behaviour that is directed to their own protection, rather than to providing help to their clients.

Sutton, Robbins, and Brainin and Teicher all point to the possibility that practitioners may respond with negative and angry feelings to the stress induced by the information clients have given or the problem behaviour they present, because of the difficulty the practitioners are experiencing with working out what it may be helpful to do and say in the circumstances. Hassan also suggests that practitioners may defensively create distance between themselves and the survivors by labelling the behaviour of survivors 'pathological' rather than acknowledging it to be understandable. All such 'counter-transference' will get in the way of assessment and of establishing a supportive atmosphere in which clients can be helped. Awareness of the possibility of such negative, defensive behaviour interfering with attentive listening should always be in the minds of practitioners. The most effective way of preventing it from intruding in the assessment process seems to be to ensure the availability of professional supervision/consultancy; this important resource is relevant throughout contact with a client and will be discussed in more detail in a later section of this chapter.

Practitioners are all familiar with the injunction to 'work at the client's pace'. However, the principle takes on a special importance in work with older people still struggling to live with the consequences of trauma. As has been emphasised, part of the horror of being caught up in traumatic events is that the person concerned cannot impose any control over what is happening. Schreuder and others point out that this is a continuing aspect of the experience for people coping with intrusive flashbacks.

The sense of not being in control over remembering will be exacerbated among older people for whom dementia begins to interfere with functioning and who, therefore, are even less in charge of which memories are brought to mind and when (Miesen and Jones, Hassan). If clients are to feel confident enough to confide in practitioners and to establish the basis for continuing to work on the difficulties associated with their earlier trauma, it is critical that they feel they have control over how far they go and that they know with what purpose they are asked to engage in assessment. Any support, treatment or counselling programme proposed as a result of the assessment is likely to be effective only if it is understood and agreed by the client. Clarity on the part of the practitioner and a readiness to be direct while giving space to the client to check and question are essential at this stage and throughout contact; it requires an active approach, not simply a supportive or reassuring manner.

Continuing Contact

Brainin and Teicher are clear that presently available theory does not provide a wholly adequate basis for practice, and several authors emphasise that the practice frameworks they are developing have to be regarded as tentative at this stage (see, for example, Robbins, Davies, and Sutton). Brainin and Teicher and Crocq emphasise that the classical approach to psychotherapy is inadequate and that therapists need to take an active approach which sets limits and is able

Continuing Contact

Brainin and Teicher are clear that presently available theory does not provide a wholly adequate basis for practice, and several authors emphasise that the practice frameworks they are developing have to be regarded as tentative at this stage (see, for example, Robbins, Davies, and Sutton). Brainin and Teicher and Crocq emphasise that the classical approach to psychotherapy is inadequate and that therapists need to take an active approach which sets limits and is able to be confronting as well as protective and supportive. Schreuder, Bergström-Walan, Fried and Sutton, among others, give illustrations of the value of including creative, spiritual and non-verbal activity as well as different forms of psychotherapy and counselling in the programme that is offered. Fried and Hassan suggest that social interaction is an essential component of the services offered to Holocaust survivors. The chapters by Coleman and Mills and Davies note that reminiscence and life review have developed popularity among staff in many services for elderly people, and they give a timely warning that unthinking or wholesale application carried out without awareness of the meaning of past events or of what horrifying memories and feelings can be triggered has the potential to damage rather than help. It is clear, too, that social and cultural factors will influence the acceptability of different kinds of help. Hassan illustrates this from one perspective in relation to survivors who are members of the Jewish community in London, and Gibson describes how important some of these factors will be in any attempt to help the Northern Ireland community to come to terms with the traumatic events of the last 25 years.

What emerges from these chapters is that while further research and development are needed to create more effective models of practice, there is now enough knowledge and experience to make possible some generalisations and to formulate some hypotheses about what interventions help. It is clear, too, that older survivors do not all present in the same way or with the same constellation of difficulties, and consequently there is no one preferred method of working. A range of approaches is required, together with a high level of flexibility on the part of practitioners. Once again the point to be taken is that practitioners need to be open and sensitive to what clients are conveying and be ready to experiment with different approaches in the light of what they are learning. This requires conscious and disciplined effort on the part of practitioners. That effort should be focused on making use of knowledge and theory that is already available, but equally on identifying what they are doing, how they are doing it and whether it is helpful.

The content of these last two paragraphs might very well be found in a general text about working with older people, or indeed about working with other groups, such as people with mental health problems. The fact that much of the content and the argument for a consciously thought through and here is very difficult both to achieve and to maintain, and that consequently our ability to evaluate practice and to develop its effectiveness is seriously inhibited. One of the most effective ways of promoting better practice seems to be to make available high quality supervision/consultancy.

Supervision of Practice

Several of the most experienced contributors to this text are among the most emphatic that the availability of regular supervision is essential to ensuring competence in practice with older people needing help with the consequences of earlier trauma (Robbins and Hassan, for example). Supervision can be used to assist practice in a number of ways.

The first and fundamental task in supervision is to assist practitioners in dealing with the stress and distress they are likely to experience as a result of hearing a client's story or observing and responding to the feelings and behaviour of their clients. The contributors to Section 3 vividly demonstrate the levels of stress and the powerful nature of the feelings practitioners experience in everyday practice in everyday settings, such as residential and day care or the geriatric and psychogeriatric departments of our hospitals. It is equally clear, however, that practitioners working in settings specialising in services to people who have experienced trauma are also facing particular stresses. The necessity of support and assistance to enable all practitioners to work appropriately with clients still struggling with their experience of trauma seems irrefutable. Without it, practitioners really can become overwhelmed, unable to remain open to their clients' needs, preoccupied with their own feelings and, consequently, liable to develop negative, uncaring attitudes. In residential settings, and perhaps in some medical settings, practitioners can become preoccupied with physical care, arguing that this is the priority and leaves them no scope for any other focus during the time they are with their clients/patients. The everyday pressures of practice are considerable and it is well known that preoccupations like these develop and are used as a defence against anxiety. Menzies' seminal paper (1967) points the way towards recognising this process and working to counteract it. Regular, structured supervision and consultation are the means most likely to help counteract these understandable, but unhelpful, responses and can also serve to support the capacity of practitioners to develop their skills and knowledge to the benefit of their clients.

As has already been pointed out, practitioners will sometimes find their knowledge and skills inadequate to the situation. This is an alarming position in which they may become demoralised and angry by turns and will experience great difficulty in maintaining the appropriate consistent, thought out approach to their clients. Within the supportive framework provided in regular supervision and consultation, feelings can be explored more freely, goals can be established and methods of achieving them worked out. Supervision also provides the opportunity for identifying areas where a practitioner's knowledge or skill might be improved. All these activities help practitioners to structure the helping process and to make sure that realistic approaches to the work are maintained, that methods of practice are monitored and their usefulness assessed. It is through the supervision process that practitioners will develop and hone their skills. Supervision is not only an activity for beginners, but also for experienced and knowledgeable practitioners. Distress and defensiveness are not confined to young, inexperienced and junior staff; nor is the responsibility to develop greater skill in direct practice.

If supervision is to achieve its purpose, it has to be planned and regular. It requires time and attention and, if practice is to develop really well, time also has to be allocated to reading, recording, relevant training and the evaluation of practice. It is critical that managers and senior practitioners acknowledge the importance of supervision and its related activities. It will be very difficult indeed to establish and maintain them all as integral elements of working with older people without the help and encouragement of senior staff.

Methods of Practice

The contributors to this volume have described a number of methods that can help older people who, in various circumstances, are still struggling with the consequences of earlier traumatic experience. What is clear is that while it may be necessary to use a variety of methods and to be open to try new ways of working, it is equally necessary to have a rationale and a structure for practice. Anything does not go and lack of clarity should not be permitted to masquerade as an 'eclectic approach'.

The first essential is to ensure that continuing contact consistently works towards the building of trust, confidence and security in clients. All of these are elements that are undermined by traumatic events, and for many survivors subsequent experience has failed adequately to repair the damage done. All of the preceding chapters provide illustrations of the painstaking work required to make repair possible. Fried and Hassan describe the value of peer support and peer activities for setting a solid foundation of confidence and security; others (for example, Bergström-Walan) use the development of a relationship in counselling or psychotherapy; Coleman and Mills, and Miesen and Jones point to the possibility that the way in which physical care is provided in residential settings can help to rebuild trust and self-confidence.

Clients need to feel accepted and supported. Here, again, interaction with a group of peers can be very helpful and the inclusion of members of their family in some elements of counselling or therapy will be important for some clients. This may be especially important for clients whose family have been unaware of their struggle and distress or whose relationships have become strained or distorted. Recognition of, and assistance with, practical difficulties, such as housing and finance, are other ways of demonstrating concern and support and will sometimes be critical to the building of sufficient confidence to address painful feelings or difficult behaviour (see Brainin and Teicher, and Hassan, for example). Support by itself will not resolve all the difficulties clients are experiencing, however. It is particularly important to keep in mind that, if clients are to achieve a comfortable adjustment and reduction of remaining difficulties, they have to face up to talking about their experience of trauma and the way it continues to affect their lives.

Robbins, Crocq and Davies all describe ways in which they structure their time with clients to enable the story to be told; each of them recognises the value of structure for maintaining focus and for clarifying and delimiting goals. Sutton similarly introduces structure for these purposes, while retaining flexibility to give a very disturbed client unpressured scope to address what is distressing. Hassan and Fried also emphasise the importance of going through the story in counselling; Bergström-Walan shows in her case example how the planned use of indirect approaches can facilitate the use of counselling to explore what happened and to come to terms with, and move on from, earlier trauma; de Levita and Brainin and Teicher use a psychoanalytic framework to confront the trauma and connect it with present circumstances; Schreuder uses a combination of group and individual psychotherapy for the same purpose. The recounting and restructuring of their traumatic experiences in a realistic form are essential to many clients who may never have been listened to before and a necessary part of the process of 'moving on' in psychological and social terms. Hassan and Fried also argue that for Holocaust survivors it is helpful to go further and to find ways of 'giving testimony' about what has happened. They give a number of examples of ways in which this might be done, giving emphasis to the life-affirming value of testimony that is used to help educate others and so prevent the development of similarly dangerous political situations in the future.

Common to the approaches to confronting and resolving the painful issues is a thought out model of practice and recognition of the importance of the negotiation with clients of agreed goals. Emphasis is also given to the importance of setting realistic and, therefore, limited goals. Not only is this helpful to clients, it will help practitioners to avoid being drawn into trying to solve all problems in order to appease their own guilt or to fulfil a wish to make reparation.

Many of the practice examples quoted by contributors testify to the courage and strength of clients who have confronted what has happened to them and in the process have made a painful journey through frightening terrain to a calmer place in which they can live more comfortably at the end of their lives. There are other clients, no less courageous, for whom a different route is required. That route enables them to find ways of containing rather than resolving their difficulties, so that they can avoid the worst of the stress and pain that has been disrupting their journeys through life. Brainin and Teicher, Fried, de Levita, Davies and Schreuder all make mention of the fact that there are some survivors for whom resolution is not possible and for whom the burden of stress, anxiety and guilt are so great or so regularly visited upon them by continuing re-enactments that help has to be directed to enabling them to strengthen their defences against these intrusions. When this can be achieved they gain some respite from the burdens they have been carrying and which may have been becoming even heavier in later life, when earlier feelings of triumph over adversity and hope for the future are challenged by their own frailty and awareness of the world's continuing problems (de Levita). Elie Wiesel, who survived incarceration in Auschwitz and whose life's work has been to bear witness (he was awarded the Nobel Peace Prize in 1986), offered a disturbing illustration of this last point in a recent interview (Phillips, 1996). He is quoted as saying:

> When I read what is happening in the world I feel humankind hasn't listened much. If anyone had told me in 1945 I would have to fight anti-Semitism I wouldn't have believed it. I was convinced anti-Semitism died in Auschwitz but now I realise only the victims perished. Racism is contagious. In 1945 it had only one name; now it has many names: fundamentalism, super nationalism, xenophobia.

The ability to distinguish those survivors for whom containment is the way forward from those who will benefit from (re)-examination of their experience is critical, as Schreuder and Hassan make clear in rather different ways. Robbins offers some help with defining the indicators that suggest confrontation and exploration will be helpful, and Schreuder's analysis helps to clarify the factors which make containment the preferred option and to explain what makes these factors relevant. These two chapters begin to show how practitioners can contribute to the development of methods of practice and to the evaluation of practice. The quality of future services is crucially dependent on this kind of contribution by practitioners, which is only possible with a careful, consciously thought out and monitored approach to helping. As Robbins also points out, this kind of approach is required if the organisations that provide services are to be enabled to adapt to take better account of the needs of the older people who are still burdened by their earlier traumatic experiences.

Following assessment it is clearly essential to match the method of practice with the goals established. Just as essential, clients should be as clear as possible what continuing contact involves and what can be expected from it. As Davies and others point out, clients need to know what they are letting themselves in for and what they can expect to gain. When clients are affected by dementia, as Miesen and Jones have described, it becomes necessary to understand where they are in the progress of that condition and to formulate goals and methods which are consistent with their stage in its development.

Ending Contact

For some of the survivors described by Hassan and by Fried, continued contact with each other remains important. Hassan also suggests that, because of the difficulties that are inherent for professionals who have no experience of the Holocaust, it is important that survivors are directly involved in developing services. Both she and Fried point to the therapeutic value to survivors of helping others. Gibson suggests that continuing involvement in self-help organisations may also be of importance to some people in Northern Ireland. In these situations, the helping process blurs with friendship and social activity and, as Hassan points out, professional practitioners have to think very carefully about the nature of boundaries and of relationships and try to monitor the risks they are taking and the means of maintaining a constructive approach. In other situations, a clear end to the contact agreed between the practitioner and the client will be more helpful. A follow-up letter or phone call, perhaps three to six months after the contact ends, will make it easier for clients to make known any need for further help.

Service Provision in the Future

It is argued in this chapter that greater skill and participation in the provision of help to older people affected by earlier trauma is needed among the practitioners providing everyday services (for example, in residential and day care and in hospital and general practice) to older people. Their ability to identify problems stemming from traumatic experience and their readiness to support and encourage the efforts of their clients to deal with those problems will be a central factor in the development of improved services in the future.

It is clear that specialist practitioners have an equally important part to play. They have the best opportunities to build up detailed experience and skill and to monitor and test methods of practice. They are likely to have referred to them the older people most seriously affected by the continuance of symptoms of PTSD. They will be at the forefront of developments. By disseminating their knowledge through publications, providing supervision and consultancy to less experienced and non-specialist practitioners, and by contributing to professional education and training, they will make special contributions to the development of good quality services in both specialist and general settings. Education and training are the principal means by which the importance of the continuing impact of earlier trauma on the lives of older people is understood and incorporated into the mainstream of practice and service development and, as such, merit a high priority.

Together generalists and specialists can show service-providing organisations the importance of being sensitive to the possibility that earlier trauma is a major current factor affecting the quality of the lives of a significant number of older people in many European countries. The indicators are that many of the older people who are still suffering from the impact of their traumatic experiences can be helped to achieve a better integration of memories of their bad experiences and significant relief of their symptoms and distress, and consequently to move more happily and more peacefully through the later part of their lives.

Working to achieve this seems an altogether justified activity. The older people on whom this book has focused have lived through horrifying experiences and have often suffered the physically and/or the psychologically incapacitating consequences for the greater part of their lives. In the present climate of cost-cutting, the focus on those most in need and realistic goal-setting, it is important to make two further points. First, it really is essential to give time and high levels of skill to making assessments of the nature and extent of need among older people referred for help. Second, effective practice that enables older people to resolve their difficulties or to make a more comfortable adjustment to the burdens they are bearing as a result of earlier trauma will be of considerable benefit both to informal carers and to public and private organisations providing services for older people.

References

Bramsen, I. (1995) *The Long Term Psychological Adjustment of World War II Survivors in the Netherlands.* Delft: Eburon Press.

Healey, A. (in press) Systemic therapy in a culture of conflict: developing a therapeutic conversation. London: Central Council for Education and Training in Social Work.

Hodgkinson, P.E. and Stewart, M. (1991) *Coping with Catastrophe.* London: Routledge.

Lee, L. (1991) *A Moment of War.* London: Viking.

Menzies, I. (1967) The functioning of social systems as a defence against anxiety. London, Tavistock Pamphlet No. 3. Tavistock Institute of Human Relations.

Phillips, M. (1996) 'Bearing witness.' *The Observer,* 9 June.

Sassoon, S. (1947) *Collected Poems.* London: Faber and Faber.

The Contributors

Maj-Briht Bergström-Walan, PhD was born in Stockholm, Sweden in 1924. She is a registered midwife and psychologist, psychotherapist and sexologist. In 1970 she founded the Swedish Institute for Sexual Research and has been its Director since that date. An expert in sexual education, she lecturers in sexology at universities in Europe, the USA, Canada and Australia. She is the author of books on sexual education, education for childbirth and sexology, and is currently researching on sexuality and elderly people.

Elisabeth Brainin, MD is a psychologist and training analyst. She is Director of a Child Guidance Clinic in Vienna and co-editor of *Kinderanalyse*. She has a particular interest in the phenomenon of anti-Semitism and on the application of psychoanalytic theory to the experience of imprisonment in concentration camps, and has written (with Samy Teicher) on this subject.

Peter Coleman is Professor of Psychogerontology at the University of Southampton and holds a joint appointment between the Departments of Geriatric Medicine and Psychology. A psychologist by background, he has a particular interest in the study of identity processes across the life span, and is well known for his research on the varied functions of reminiscence in later life. He has collaborated with clinical geriatric and psychogeriatric teams on the development of services for patients with dementia and depression.

Louis Crocq is Consultant Social Psychiatrist to the Secretary General of National Defence and Professor at the Rene Descartes University, Paris. He has extensive experience in the treatment of victims of military trauma and civilian disasters, and throughout his career has used a variety of treatment methods.

Stephen Davies completed his training in clinical psychology in South Africa at a turbulent time in its apartheid history when he witnessed the psychological impact of trauma. He began working with older people in Britain seven years ago and soon became aware of the hidden influence of the Second World War on this group. This area of work developed during his time as a Lecturer in Psychology at the Institute of Psychiatry in London, where he carried out clinical and research work with the civilian survivors of wartime London. His interests have continued into his present post as Head of Clinical Psychology Services for Older People with Essex and Herts Community National Health Service Trust, where he is currently interested in the mechanisms that perpetuate the psychological consequences of trauma and the impact of childhood attachment experiences on older people.

Hedi Fried was born in 1924 in Sighet, Romania, and was transported from Hungary to Auschwitz in 1944, and later to labour camps around Neuengamme. She was liberated from Bergen-Belsen on 15 April 1945, and in July of that year was taken by Red Cross Buses to Stockholm, where she has lived ever since. She studied at Stockholm University, (MA 1980) and became a licensed psychologist in 1992. She runs Café 84, a social and rehabilitation centre for survivors, child survivors and second generation survivors. She lectures about the Holocaust and its consequences to schoolchildren, universities and other bodies in Sweden. She has written an autobiographical book *Fragments of a Life*, which has been translated into Russian, German and Hebrew. A semi-documentary, *Back to Life*, has just been published in Sweden.

Faith Gibson is a Professor of Social Work at the University of Ulster at Jordanstown in Northern Ireland, where she teaches professional social work students and undertakes research in social gerontology and social work. Her major research interests concern the therapeutic use of reminiscence in small groups and life history writing, developing methods for introducing older learners to information technology, and the development of community-based social services for older people, especially those with dementia who live in rural areas.

Judith Hassan is a social worker who, since she qualified in 1977, has specialised in working with survivors of the Nazi Holocaust. She is the Director of Shalvata (Jewish Care), a London therapy centre for adults with emotional difficulties and she chairs the management committee of the new Centre for Holocaust Survivors in the adjoining building. She has written, lectured and broadcast widely, and internationally she has recently advised on the setting up of Holocaust Centres in Eastern Europe.

Gemma M.M. Jones, PhD is a neuropsychologist, and presently an honorary Academic Research Fellow with St Mary's Hospital Medical School, London, Section of Old Age Psychiatry. She also holds degrees in cell biology and nursing, and has lectured in Canada and Europe on care-giving in dementia. Her latest work, *Care Giving in Dementia*, is co-edited with Bere Miesen.

David de Levita is a psychoanalyst who is based in Amsterdam. He combines his professional practice with research and teaching, and is a Visiting Professor at the University of Nijmegen.

Bere M.L. Miesen, PhD is a clinical psychogerontologist, educated at the University of Nijmegen and working at the Psychogeriatric Centre 'Marienhaven' in Warmond (near Leiden) in the Netherlands. Since 1970 he has worked with elderly people with dementia, their families and professional care-givers. He is involved in clinical work, counselling, education and research. He works from the perspective of life span psychology, gerontology and attachment theory in the field of psychogeriatrics (including dementia), which means often meeting/helping people experiencing current trauma and, in some cases, the reactivation of past trauma.

Marie A. Mills, PhD, CSS is a residential care specialist with some 20 years' experience in residential social work. She is also a Visiting Fellow in the Department of Social Work Studies at the University of Southampton, England. Her interests include narrative psychology, life history/reminiscence work and psychotherapeutic interventions for people with dementia.

Ian Robbins, PhD is Consultant Clinical Psychologist and Head of Adult Clinical Psychology Services, North Devon Health Care Trust, England. Before qualifying as a psychologist he was a charge nurse, working in acute psychiatry in Britain and a nurse/relief worker in Uganda and Somalia. He became interested in Post-Traumatic Stress Disorder when working in the Queen Elizabeth Military Hospital and has recently completed research on the long-term impact of war trauma on elderly veterans.

J.N. Schreuder, MD is a psychiatrist and psychoanalyst. He is the Director of the Centrum '45 Foundation, the Dutch National Centre for the treatment of victims of organised violence, and Assistant Professor at the Department of Psychiatry at the University of Leiden. During the last twenty years in private practice and in hospital he has offered psychotherapy to severely traumatised people such as war victims, veterans and sexually abused people. Currently he is participating in several studies on the long-term effects of organised violence.

Laura Sutton is a clinical psychologist at the Western Community Hospital in Southampton. She specialises in working with older people and has a particular interest in the psychology of memory, depression and dementia in old age.

Samy Teicher, Dipl-Psych is a psychoanalyst, a child and group analyst and a psychotherapist in a Drug Addiction Clinic. He practises in Vienna. He has written on psychoanalysis and anti-Semitism, often collaborating with Elisabeth Brainin.

Editors

Linda Hunt is a qualified and experienced social worker with particular experience of work in psychiatric services and with people with alcohol problems. She was a lecturer in social work at Manchester University before joining the Scottish Office, where she was Assistant Chief Inspector in the Social Work Services Inspectorate. She has published books and articles and has edited collections of papers.

Mary Marshall has worked with older people for more than 25 years as a social worker, researcher and lecturer. She is now Director of the Dementia

Services Development Centre at the University of Stirling. She has edited and written several books, and contributed to numerous books and journals in the subject area of old age and dementia.

Cherry Rowlings is Professor of Social Work at the University of Stirling, where she teaches social work on qualifying and post-qualifying programmes. She has a particular interest in social work with older people, and has researched and published in this area. Her book *Social Work with Elderly People* (1981, translated into Dutch, 1982) has made a significant contribution to the development of practice with older people in the community.

Subject Index

Author Index